Winning the Tax Wars

Series on International Taxation

VOLUME 62

Series Editors

Prof. Ruth Mason, University of Virginia School of Law
Prof. Dr Ekkehart Reimer, University of Heidelberg

Introduction & Contents

The Series on International Taxation deals with a wide variety of topics in the global tax arena. The authors include many of the field's leading experts as well as talented newcomers. Their expert views and incisive commentary have proven highly useful to practitioners and academics alike.

Objective

The volumes published in this series are aimed at offering high-quality analytical information and practical solutions to international tax practitioners.

Readership

Practitioners, academics and policy makers in international tax law.

Frequency of Publication

2-3 new volumes published each year.

The titles published in this series are listed at the end of this volume.

Winning the Tax Wars

Tax Competition and Cooperation

Edited by

Brigitte Alepin
Blanca Moreno-Dodson
Louise Otis

Wolters Kluwer

Published by:
Kluwer Law International B.V.
PO Box 316
2400 AH Alphen aan den Rijn
The Netherlands
Website: lrus.wolterskluwer.com

Sold and distributed in North, Central and South America by:
Wolters Kluwer Legal & Regulatory U.S.
7201 McKinney Circle
Frederick, MD 21704
United States of America
Email: customer.service@wolterskluwer.com

Sold and distributed in all other countries by:
Air Business Subscriptions
Rockwood House
Haywards Heath
West Sussex
RH16 3DH
United Kingdom
Email: international-customerservice@wolterskluwer.com

Printed on acid-free paper.

ISBN 978-90-411-9460-2

e-Book: ISBN 978-90-411-9461-9
web-PDF: ISBN 978-90-411-9463-3

© 2018 Brigitte Alepin, Blanca Moreno-Dodson & Louise Otis

All rights reserved. No part of this publication may be reproduced, stored in a retrieval system, or transmitted in any form or by any means, electronic, mechanical, photocopying, recording, or otherwise, without written permission from the publisher.

Permission to use this content must be obtained from the copyright owner. More information can be found at: lrus.wolterskluwer.com/policies/permissions-reprints-and-licensing

Printed and bound by CPI Group (UK) Ltd, Croydon, CR0 4YY

Editors

Brigitte Alepin is a Canadian businesswoman, a Harvard trained tax specialist and tax policy advisor and a professor in taxation at the Ecole des Sciences de la Gestion of the Université du Québec à Montréal. She has led several major researches and projects for governments, Fortune 500 corporations and NGOs, in various fields including environmental taxation, international taxation, oil and gas taxation and health care. She has both public and private-sector experience that allows her to offer a rare multidimensional perspective of tax policies and public finances. She acts as a special advisor to politicians and political parties and she also acts as an expert witness on various committees of the House of Commons and the Canadian Senate. Brigitte Alepin is known for her books *Ces riches qui ne paient pas d'impôt* (English: *The Rich Who Do Not Pay Taxes*) and *La crise fiscale qui vient* (English: *The Coming Fiscal Crisis*). This book inspired the award-winning film *The Price We Pay*, directed by Harold Crooks and co-written by Harold Crooks and Brigitte Alepin.

Blanca Moreno-Dodson is the Manager of the Center for European Integration, the World Bank, Marseille, France. She is an experienced development economist with more than twenty-four years of World Bank service, including operational work worldwide, with deeper regional expertise in Africa and Latin America. She is accomplished in macroeconomics and fiscal policy for developing countries, with a focus on growth, inequality, and poverty reduction. She is skilled in public expenditure analysis, fiscal sustainability, public finance, tax policy reforms, and transfer pricing. Previously, she worked as a junior economist at the European Union (European Commission and European Parliament). She has published three World Bank books: *Reducing Poverty on a Global Scale*, 2005; *Public Finance for Poverty Reduction*, 2007; and *Is Fiscal Policy the Answer? A Developing Country Perspective*, 2012, as well as numerous papers on macroeconomics, public expenditures, tax policy and growth, and other development issues, at the *National Tax Association Journal*, *Banca d'Italia Fiscal Policy Annual Volume*, *Hacienda Pública Española Journal*, *Bulletin of Economic Research*, and the *World Bank Working Papers* series. She has been a guest lecturer at the Duke University Tax Executive Program and John Hopkins University, and a frequent speaker on a variety of international Development Conferences and Workshops. Blanca obtained her Ph.D. in International Economics and Finance from the Aix-Marseille II (*Université de la Méditerranée*) in France and her Masters in Economics from the *Autónoma* University of Madrid, Spain. She is fluent in Spanish, French, English, and Portuguese.

Louise Otis works as a civil and commercial mediator and arbitrator at the Canadian and international levels. She is also Adjunct Professor at McGill University's Faculty of Law. She is a distinguished fellow of the International Academy of Mediators (IAM). She is the President of the Administrative Tribunal of the Organisation for Economic Co-operation and Development (OECD). She is also the President of the Appeal Court at the International Organization of La Francophonie (IOF). She is a member of the Administrative Tribunal of the European Organisation for the Exploitation of Meteorological Satellites (EUMETSAT). She is a retired Justice of the Quebec Court of Appeal where she spearheaded the introduction of judicial mediation. She participated in over 3,000 judgments in civil, commercial, and criminal law. She has conducted over 700 mediation sessions in commercial and civil law. Louise Otis regularly participates in international governance and justice reform missions with the United Nations (UN), International Monetary Fund (IMF), World Bank (WB), and the International Finance Corporation (IFC) member of the World Bank Group (WB). Louise Otis was appointed by the United Nations Secretary-General to a five-member Panel of independent international experts in charge of redesigning the United Nations system of administration of Justice. She has created a system of transitional justice for countries affected by armed conflicts and/or environmental disasters.

Contributors

Allison Christians is the H. Heward Stikeman Chair in the Law of Taxation at the McGill University Faculty of Law, Canada, where she teaches and writes on national, comparative, and international tax law and policy. She focuses especially on the relationship between taxation and economic development; the role of government and non-government institutions and actors in the creation of tax policy norms; and the intersection of taxation and human rights. She has written numerous scholarly articles, essays, and book chapters, as well as editorials, columns, and articles in professional journals addressing a broad array of topics and has been named one of the "Global Tax 50" most influential individuals in international taxation. Her recent research focuses on evolving international norms of tax cooperation and competition; the relationship between tax and trade; and evolving conceptions of rights in taxation. Professor Christians also engages on topics of tax law and policy via social media with her Tax, Society, and Culture blog and on twitter @profchristians.

Vanessa Houlder has worked as a journalist on the *Financial Times* since 1988 writing about companies, the property industry, technology, management, environment, economics, and taxation. During the past decade, she has written extensively about tax policy, in the U.K. and internationally. Awards include the LexisNexis tax writer of the year and prizes for investigative journalism from the Overseas Press Club of America and the Society of American Business Editors and Writers. In 2016 she was named as one of the "Global Tax 50", a list of influential people in taxation chosen by the editorial team of the *International Tax Review*.

Adam Koniuszewski, FCPA, FCA, CFA, is a Fellow of Geneva Center for Security Policy (GCSP), a Fellow of the Quebec Order of Chartered Accountants, Associate Fellow of the World Academy of Art and Science (WAAS), and a Chartered Financial Analyst. After an international business career in finance, strategy, and public affairs, Adam Koniuszewski turned his focus to diplomatic, sustainability, and security matters by joining President Mikhail Gorbachev as Executive Director of Green Cross International in 2008. At the Geneva Center for Security Policy, Mr. Koniuszewski pursues various governance and capacity-building projects to advance the strategic goals of the center and provide expertise, education and dialogue, policy analysis, and forward-thinking solutions to improve the global security landscape. He is also involved in creating educational initiatives for youth and business. He launched The Bridge Foundation initiative in 2009 to raise awareness about global challenges and promote a circular economy. The Foundation engages youth and opinion leaders on global issues through its "Education is a Window to the World" program active in Switzerland, Poland, and Canada. On the invitation of former French Environment Minister Corinne Lepage, Mr. Koniuszewski helped draft a "Declaration of the Rights and Obligations of Humanity" and organized the launch of a campaign for its endorsement in Geneva with the support of 40 million scouts. The Declaration was presented at the 2015 Paris Climate Conference and the UN General Assembly. Mr. Koniuszewski continues to promote the Declaration for its adoption by the UN. Mr. Koniuszewski is a regular contributor to the media and a sought-after speaker on international fora on topics ranging from business and sustainability to climate change, international cooperation, and global governance. An expert on excise and carbon taxation, Mr. Koniuszewski has been advising TaxCOOP, an international non-partisan initiative launched in Canada on international tax competition and challenges of the taxation system.

Lyne Latulippe is a tax professor at the Université de Sherbrooke (École de Gestion) and a Principal Researcher at the Research Chair in Taxation and Public Finance. She holds a Bachelor's degree in Law and a Master's Degree in Taxation. After spending 10 years in private practice, she completed her Ph.D. in Political Science at Concordia University. Her research focuses on various aspects of taxation, including tax fairness, tax planning, and the development and implementation of national and international tax policy, international tax governance and actors involved. She participated in numerous conferences and is a member of the TaxCOOP team since 2015.

Patricio V. Marquez, from Ecuador, is a World Bank Lead Public Health Specialist, who coordinates the Global Tobacco Control Program and the Global Mental Health initiative at the World Bank Group. He has worked in more than 70 countries across different regions in the world. Over 2015-2017 he was a member of the Global Work Group of the Advisory Committee to the Director (ACD) of US CDC, providing recommendations and counsel to the ACD on global public health issues. He served as Public Health Focal Point at the Health, Nutrition and Population Global Practice of the World Bank over June 2014-June 2015, co-led the WBG team that designed the Ebola Emergency Response Program for West Africa and prepared the USD 390 million Ebola Emergency Response Project for Guinea, Liberia and Sierra Leone. He was deployed to WHO Geneva to help coordinate the WB and WHO interface on the Global Response to Ebola over the September-December 2014 period. He also co-led with WHO the Thematic Working Group on Health, Nutrition and Water and Sanitation for the preparation of the UN/WBG/EU/AfDB multisector Ebola Recovery Assessment Report over January-March 2015. In 2013-2014, he served as Human Development Sector Leader for Ghana, Liberia and Sierra Leone, as well as for Malawi, Zambia and

Zimbabwe, based in Accra, Ghana. He has also worked in Angola, Botswana, Equatorial Guinea, and Namibia. Before that, he served as Health Cluster Leader for the countries in Southern Africa in 2011-2012. During 2004-2011, he worked in the Europe and Central Asia (ECA) region, particularly in the Russian Federation, Georgia, Azerbaijan, and the Central Asian Republics, managing implementation support for WBG-funded health system reform and disease-specific projects. Over 1988-2003, he managed health systems development and science and technology projects funded by the WBG in Argentina, Brazil, Chile, Colombia, Dominican Republic, Ecuador, Mexico, Paraguay, and Venezuela, and led the preparation and start-up implementation of Multi-Country HIV/AIDS Program in the Caribbean Region that covered nine countries and CARICOM. He was part of the teams that prepared the USD 1.3 billion Global Avian Influenza Preparedness and Control Framework Program in 2006, and the USD 1.2 billion Global Food Response Facility in 2008 – both covered more than 70 countries across the world. He has authored reports on global mental health, tobacco taxation, as well as on non-communicable diseases and road traffic injuries in Sub-Saharan Africa, road safety in ECA, the demographic and health crisis in Russia, health system challenges in Russia, blood transfusion systems and the spread of HIV in Central Asia, HIV/AIDS in the Caribbean, non-communicable diseases and health systems in Chile, and health system assessments in several LAC countries. He also co-authored a report on non-communicable diseases (NCDs) in China, and a policy note on NCDs and road traffic injuries in Cambodia, and in 2016/2017 he was part of a team that prepared a global report on the economics of antimicrobial resistance (AMR). He pursued his university studies at the George Washington University and Johns Hopkins University Bloomberg School of Public Health, and done executive program training at Harvard University on program appraisal and management, and medical care organization, financing and regulation, and at London School of Hygiene and Tropical Medicine on health economics and financing.

Richard Murphy has been Professor of Practice in International Political Economy at City, University of London since September 2015. He is a U.K. chartered accountant with extensive experience of tax in both practice and commerce. In 2002 he was one of the founders of the Tax Justice Network. He created the concept of country-by-country reporting, now being brought into use with OECD backing in more than 100 countries as a risk-assessment tool to help tackle tax abuse by multinational corporations. In 2009 he defined the term "secrecy jurisdiction," now widely used to describe a tax haven. He has researched on and written extensively about tax gaps. His books include *The Joy of Tax*, 2015, *Random House* and *Tax Havens: The True Story of Globalisation*, 2010, Cornell (with Ronen Palan and Christian Chavagneux). He blogs frequently at Tax Research UK with more than 2.4 million reads likely in 2017.

Erika Siu is a Tax and Development professional. Currently, she is serving as Project Deputy Director for the Bloomberg Initiative to Reduce Tobacco Use project at the Health Policy Center at the University of Illinois at Chicago. Formerly, she directed the Independent Commission for the Reform of International Corporate Taxation (ICRICT). Prior to that, Erika was a Researcher for the International Centre for Tax and

Contributors

Development in the Institute for Development Studies at the University of Sussex and Tax Policy Advisor for the United Nations Development Programme, Office for South-South Cooperation. Erika is a graduate of New York University Law School's Graduate Tax Program and a member of the New York and New Jersey Bar.

Eric M. Zolt is the Michael H. Schill Distinguished Professor of Law at the UCLA School of Law. He specializes in individual, corporate, and international tax law. Working with the International Monetary Fund, the World Bank, US AID and the US Treasury Department, Eric has served as a consultant on tax policy matters in over 30 countries. Before coming to UCLA, he was a partner in the Chicago law firm of Kirkland & Ellis. Eric served in the US Department of Treasury, first as Deputy Tax Legislative Counsel and then as founder and director of Treasury's Tax Advisory Program in Eastern Europe and the Former Soviet Union. Eric also served as the Director of the International Tax Program at Harvard Law School. He is a co-founder of the African Tax Institute, a training and research institute for government tax officials in Africa.

Summary of Contents

Editors	v
Contributors	vii
Preface	xix
Introduction	1

CHAPTER 1
The Evolution of Tax Competition: Vito Tanzi's Contribution and Perspective
Blanca Moreno-Dodson — 3

CHAPTER 2
Abandoning Tax Competition: A Historical Overview and a Way Forward in Achieving the 2030 Agenda
Erika Siu — 15

CHAPTER 3
Tax Competition: An Unleveled Playing Field for Developing Countries – Tax Cooperation to the Rescue
Brigitte Alepin — 31

CHAPTER 4
Taxing Multinationals in a Globalized World
Lyne Latulippe — 47

CHAPTER 5
Offshore Tax Investigations, Tax Whistleblowing, and Global Tax Compliance
Louise Otis & Brigitte Alepin — 59

Summary of Contents

CHAPTER 6
Tax Competition or Tax Cooperation
Vanessa Houlder — 75

CHAPTER 7
Experts Debate: What Is Better for Low-Income Countries, Tax Competition, or Tax Cooperation?
Allison Christians — 93

CHAPTER 8
Wealth Taxes in Developing Countries
Blanca Moreno-Dodson, Richard Murphy & Eric M. Zolt — 107

CHAPTER 9
Taxing to Promote Public Goods: Carbon Pricing
Adam Koniuszewski — 121

CHAPTER 10
Expanding the Global Tax Base: Taxing to Promote Public Goods – Tobacco Taxes
Patricio V. Marquez — 143

Table of Contents

Editors	v
Contributors	vii
Preface	xix
Introduction	1

CHAPTER 1
The Evolution of Tax Competition: Vito Tanzi's Contribution and Perspective
Blanca Moreno-Dodson   3

§1.01	Introduction		3
§1.02	Vito Tanzi and the Genealogy of Tax Competition		4
	[A]	Early Critique	4
	[B]	The Challenges of Tax Competition	4
	[C]	Globalization and the Emergence of "Fiscal Termites"	6
	[D]	The Need for a New Global Architecture	7
§1.03	"Winning the Tax Wars" as Assessed by Vito Tanzi		9
	[A]	Confronting an Ideological Question	9
	[B]	New Options for Tax Avoidance	10
	[C]	Strategies to Limit Abuses	10
	[D]	A Key Challenge: Defining the Base for Corporate Taxation	11
	[E]	Wealth Taxes: Opportunities and Limits	12
	[F]	Taxation to Promote Public Goods	12
§1.04	Conclusion		13

Table of Contents

CHAPTER 2
Abandoning Tax Competition: A Historical Overview and a Way Forward in Achieving the 2030 Agenda
Erika Siu 15
§2.01 Introduction 15
§2.02 Efforts by IOs to Curb Tax Competition 17
    [A] A New Approach to Tax Competition 22
    [B] A Normative Framework for Tax Cooperation 24
§2.03 Conclusion 27
References 28

CHAPTER 3
Tax Competition: An Unleveled Playing Field for Developing Countries – Tax Cooperation to the Rescue
Brigitte Alepin 31
§3.01 Background 31
§3.02 Conceptual Grounding 31
§3.03 Tax Competition Is Real and Important 32
    [A] Policies to Address Tax Competition 33
    [B] Summing Up 35
§3.04 The Ability of the Global Tax System to Address Current Challenges 35
§3.05 Consequences of Archaic Tax Rules and Double Non-taxation 37
§3.06 Leadership from International Organizations 38
    [A] Transfer Pricing Guidelines 39
    [B] Automatic Exchange of Information 40
    [C] Stringent Disclosure Requirements 41
§3.07 Tax Competition and the Need for Better Fiscal Cooperation in a Globalized World 41
§3.08 Achievements and Persistent Challenges: Prospects for Tax Cooperation Among Developing Countries 43
References 45

CHAPTER 4
Taxing Multinationals in a Globalized World
Lyne Latulippe 47
§4.01 Corporate Taxation and Globalization 48
§4.02 Paradigm, Principles and Challenges 50
    [A] Issues with the Unit of Taxation and the Tax Base 51
    [B] Enforcement Issues 51
    [C] Cooperation and Competition 52
    [D] Public Pressures and Transparency 53
§4.03 The Way Forward 53
§4.04 Concluding Remarks 56
References 57

CHAPTER 5
Offshore Tax Investigations, Tax Whistleblowing, and Global Tax Compliance
Louise Otis & Brigitte Alepin 59
§5.01 Introduction 59
§5.02 Offshore Tax Investigations and Tax Whistleblowing 60
    [A] Definitions and Importance 60
        [1] Offshore Tax Investigations 60
        [2] Tax Whistleblowing 61
    [B] Responses from Governments and International Organizations 62
    [C] Guidance in Decision-Making 65
§5.03 Global Tax Compliance 66
    [A] Definition 66
    [B] The Present Compliance System for International Taxpayers 69
    [C] Global Tax Compliance for the Twenty-First Century 71
§5.04 Conclusion 74
References 74

CHAPTER 6
Tax Competition or Tax Cooperation
Vanessa Houlder 75
§6.01 Introduction 75
§6.02 Tax Competition 76
    [A] Definition 76
    [B] Importance and History 76
    [C] Responses of Governments 79
§6.03 Tax Cooperation 81
    [A] Definition 81
    [B] International and Regional Initiatives 81
        [1] International Initiatives 81
        [2] Regional Initiatives 83
            [a] The European Union 83
            [b] West Africa 84
            [c] East Africa 85
            [d] Southern Africa 85
            [e] Southeast Asia 86
        [3] Responses of Governments 86
        [4] Responses of Non-governmental Organizations and Academics 87
§6.04 Conclusion 90
References 90

Table of Contents

CHAPTER 7
Experts Debate: What Is Better for Low-Income Countries, Tax Competition, or Tax Cooperation?
Allison Christians — 93
§7.01 Introduction — 94
§7.02 First Resolution — 94
　[A] Response to First Resolution by Alison Holder — 95
　[B] Response to First Resolution by Veronique de Rugy — 96
§7.03 Second Resolution — 97
　[A] Response to Second Resolution by Alison Holder — 98
　[B] Response to Second Resolution by Veronique de Rugy — 99
§7.04 Third Resolution — 100
　[A] Response to Third Resolution by Veronique de Rugy — 100
　[B] Response to Third Resolution by Alison Holder — 101
§7.05 Closing Remarks — 103
　[A] Final Remarks by Veronique de Rugy — 103
　[B] Final Remarks by Alison Holder — 103
§7.06 Judges' Conclusion — 104

CHAPTER 8
Wealth Taxes in Developing Countries
Blanca Moreno-Dodson, Richard Murphy & Eric M. Zolt — 107
§8.01 Introduction — 107
§8.02 Why Are Wealth Taxes Desirable? — 108
　[A] Equity Justifications — 108
　[B] Efficiency Justifications — 109
　[C] Political Economy Benefits — 110
　[D] Administrative Gains — 110
§8.03 Wealth Taxes — 110
　[A] Types of Wealth Taxes — 110
　[B] Role in Tax System — 112
　[C] Design Issues in Adopting a Wealth Tax — 113
§8.04 Challenges in Adopting Wealth Taxes — 113
　[A] Political Challenges in Taxing Wealth — 113
　[B] Lack of Popular Support for Wealth Taxes — 114
　[C] Administrative Challenges — 116
§8.05 The Changing Environment for Wealth Taxes — 117
§8.06 Conclusion — 117
References — 118

CHAPTER 9
Taxing to Promote Public Goods: Carbon Pricing
Adam Koniuszewski — 121
§9.01 Introduction — 121
§9.02 The Case for Carbon Pricing — 123

	[A]	Closing the Emissions Gap	124
	[B]	Closing the Low-Carbon Investment Gap	125
	[C]	Closing the Climate and Sustainable-Development Financing Gap	125
§9.03		The Paris Climate Agreement and Carbon Pricing Momentum	127
§9.04		Lessons Learned from Existing Carbon Pricing Initiatives	133
§9.05		Framework Convention for Carbon Control (FCCC)	138
References			140

CHAPTER 10
Expanding the Global Tax Base: Taxing to Promote Public Goods – Tobacco Taxes
Patricio V. Marquez — 143

§10.01	Background and Objectives	143
§10.02	Making the Public-Health Case for Tobacco Taxation	144
§10.03	A Framework for Discussion	147
§10.04	Conclusions	174
References		176

Preface

The title of this book, "Winning the Tax Wars," is very evocative. It refers both to the war against tax unfairness and to the victory of quality of life in our societies.

Throughout the chapters, we learn that this sophisticated war will be waged through negotiations between states, the firm persuasion of global financial elites, inter-state collaboration and the conclusion of multilateral agreements and treaties. As for the expected victory, it would be that of a growing global awareness regarding three fundamental issues – tax competition, tax avoidance and tax evasion – which reduce the power of sovereign states and limit their spheres of public action in key sectors such as the environment, education and health.

The globalization of trade, the digitization of the economy, tax competition between sovereign states, the erosion of the tax base and the transfers of profits have all revealed the weaknesses of a traditional tax system that has reached its limits. For more than a decade, under the impetus of large international organizations such as the OECD and the UN, numerous states and groups of states have met and tried to join their efforts in creating a new international tax system designed to counter tax avoidance and evasion. The inter-state exchange of information on tax planning schemes and strategies constitutes the core measure of this tax collaboration. In this regard, Tax Inspectors Without Borders (TIWB) is an essential initiative for international tax transparency.

In addition, we cannot underestimate the importance of tax whistleblowers, which have courageously brought to light the deviant behavior of the ultra-wealthy and their advisers and disclosed to the global public the names of those for whom greed trumps the collective interest. It is high time to adopt robust measures to protect whistleblowers against retaliation in order to legitimize their action.

Above all, destructive tax competition is a topic of rising concern, particularly for developing countries that experienced tax wars during the recent years. Many tax systems are moving to a territorial tax system which makes it even more necessary to understand the transnational implications of national tax policies, as well as the reactions of local governments.

Preface

In the end, the goal is to revive the notions of common good and general public interest, which now transcend national borders and are attached to the international community of men and women. We must increase the level of transparency and accountability of private and public economic actors and restore the citizens' trust in the fairness of our global governance systems.

The Honourable Louise Otis

Introduction

Tax wars have been scattered throughout history since the constitution of modern states. These wars originated in the inequitable redistribution of wealth and the polarization of the common good. The French Revolution (1789) and the American Revolution (1774) are eloquent manifestations of it. History reveals that the taxpayers' passivity should not be taken for granted in the face of tax injustice. Two centuries after the French Revolution, the unequal distribution of wealth is no longer confined to a nation but now covers all the countries of the world. Over the last few decades, the concentration of wealth and property in the hands of a few has been facilitated by tax evasion, tax avoidance and above all by tax competition. Countries, which have lost their fiscal sovereignty over international taxpayers, are ready for all matters of concessions to retain the rich. Gradually, the States weaken themselves to the benefit of the large corporations and the privileged citizens of this world.

The global tax agenda is neglecting the impacts of tax competition and the tax wars it can create for developed and developing countries, and the objective of this book is to present the impacts of tax competition and the possible solutions that can be explored.

This book brings together outstanding contributions of various authors and is structured as follows. Early chapters clarify fundamental historical and conceptual issues. Chapter 1 reflects the insights of one of the architects of the contemporary field of international tax policy, Vito Tanzi. The chapter reviews Tanzi's contributions as one of the first observers to describe tax competition, beginning in the 1970s. In Chapter 2, Erika Siu further analyzes the historical development of the tax competition concept, in order ultimately to question the continued validity of the concept and to propose an alternative way forward that, she argues, is more conducive to sustainable development. Chapter 3, by Brigitte Alepin, opens by drawing on the insights of Michael Keen to deepen the conceptual inquiry around tax competition. Alepin then builds on these foundations, in particular, to consider the role of international organizations in mediating tax competition or cooperation. The chapter presents possible solutions to global tax cooperation challenges while identifying topics for fresh analytical work.

Chapters 4-6 then focus on more specific, and in some cases politically volatile, issues. In Chapter 4, Lyne Latulippe summarizes conference debates around taxing multinational corporations. She documents failures and challenges of the current system to tax these corporations, in conjunction with an analysis of the dominant international tax paradigm and its possible evolution – or replacement. Chapter 5, by Louise Otis and Brigitte Alepin, details interlinkages between offshore tax investigations, tax whistleblowing and global tax compliance. The chapter analyzes the present system and offers proposals towards a global tax compliance for the twenty-first century and proposes innovative thoughts such as international tax court and the necessity to analyze the constitutions of countries and the "fair share" article they often include to better understand the global tax situation and the possible tools the fervent of tax justice could rely on. In Chapter 6, Vanessa Houlder focuses primarily on the issue of tax cooperation, moving beyond conceptual questions to dissect the political realities. She analyzes, for example, the unfolding of the G20-led initiative to tackle base erosion and profit shifting, as well as a number of current regional initiatives aiming to strengthen cooperation.

Chapter 7 then shifts gears and format. In it, Allison Christians presents an edited transcript and analysis of a public debate that was a distinctive feature of the conference TaxCOOP2016 livestreamed to a global audience of over 10,000 viewers, the debate opposed two speakers – Alison Holder of ActionAid and Veronique de Rugy of the Mercatus Center at George Mason University – on a series of resolutions concerning the impact of tax competition on developing countries.

The final three chapters of this book enlarge our vision of the "tax wars" theme. They look at specific opportunities to use tax policy to promote public goods and expand revenue, particularly in developing countries. In Chapter 8, Eric Zolt, Richard Murphy and Blanca Moreno-Dodson explore wealth taxes in developing countries. They review why wealth taxes might be desirable on equity and efficiency grounds, as well as the political and economic obstacles these taxes face. They argue that recent economic, political and technological changes may increase the desirability and administrative feasibility of wealth taxation. Chapter 9, by Adam Koniuszewski, makes the case for effective carbon pricing as a key element in comprehensive global, regional and national climate strategies. The chapter argues that carbon pricing can help fill gaps in current efforts to address climate threats and achieve the Sustainable Development Goals. While acknowledging political and other obstacles, Koniuszewski argues that carbon pricing now has growing momentum in its favor. Finally, in Chapter 10, Patricio Marquez provides a detailed record of the conference's special session on tobacco taxation. The chapter argues that tobacco taxation constitutes a unique policy lever to improve population health while increasing government revenue. Perhaps most importantly, the chapter presents the details of a series of country experiences and results, in some cases analyzed by key protagonists themselves.

This book has been inspired by the conference TaxCOOP2016 convened at the World Bank Headquarters in Washington, DC. The conference took place in a distinctive political context which is being highlighted in this book.

CHAPTER 1
The Evolution of Tax Competition: Vito Tanzi's Contribution and Perspective

Blanca Moreno-Dodson

§1.01 INTRODUCTION

This chapter lays down conceptual foundations and opens lines of inquiry for the discussions to follow in the remainder of the book. The chapter draws on the analytic insights of one of the architects of the contemporary field of international tax policy: Vito Tanzi. In the course of his distinguished career, Tanzi may have contributed more than any other single individual to our understanding of the phenomenon of tax competition, including its origins, implications, and possible solutions.

The first section traces the broad outlines of Tanzi's evolving analysis of tax competition. It reflects on the historical development of both tax competition itself and Tanzi's critical perspectives and proposals. The trajectory extends from Tanzi's first descriptions of tax competition, as far back as the 1970s, via a series of historical stages, in the course of which Tanzi helped create the conceptual vocabulary through which these issues continue to be understood.

The second section highlights the contemporary thinking on tax competition. On May 23-24, 2016, the Global Tax Team at the World Bank organized a conference on a theme of great importance and growing actuality, a theme that is on the minds of policymakers in both rich and poor countries: "tax competition," which has more recently manifested as "tax wars." Vito Tanzi was tasked to deliver a presentation and above all to make the final synthesis of the conference based on the presentations provided by the speakers and the discussions.

A brief word on Tanzi's career: Vito Tanzi holds an exceptional position in the study and practice of public finance and taxation. For several decades, he has contributed to building the field, while occupying a series of influential positions in scholarship and public life. After some 10 years as a leading academic researcher,

Tanzi was named as Head of the Tax Policy Division at the IMF. He would go on to serve for two decades as Director of the Fiscal Affairs Department of that same institution. Tanzi has also worked at high levels in government, notably as Undersecretary for Economy and Finance in the Italian government from 2001 to 2003. His analysis of tax policy issues, including tax competition, reflects this range of experience in academic research, the practice of government, and leadership in multilateral organizations.

§1.02 VITO TANZI AND THE GENEALOGY OF TAX COMPETITION

[A] Early Critique

As early as the 1970s, Tanzi was among the very first observers to caution against the risks of tax competition, at a time when economies had started to experience deepening integration, capital was becoming increasingly mobile, restrictions on the international flow of goods and services were loosening, and the multi-country economic activities of corporations had started to expand. In 1986, the United States (U.S.) introduced a "fundamental tax reform" that rapidly led to significant reactions by other countries (Tanzi 1987). This development could be considered an early example of tax competition. These patterns were accompanied by growing mobility of high-net-worth individuals (HNWI) from countries with high tax rates to those with low tax rates.

While globalization and the associated developments may have been favorable to economic progress, they also generated economic risks and social costs that would become increasingly evident in later years. With striking prescience, Tanzi warned that one of the fundamental risks associated with globalization was its impact on tax competition and the architecture of tax systems.

[B] The Challenges of Tax Competition

Subsequently, in numerous publications spanning four decades, Tanzi has argued that globalization's implications for countries' fiscal architecture have not been adequately understood. As a result, governments have not given this issue the attention it deserves.

In recent years, nonetheless, there has been an increasing interest in the study of tax competition, and more political discussion on what to do about it. There is now more compelling evidence that a nation's potential tax base is no longer strictly limited by its jurisdiction, nor to its own economy, and that tax policies may have cross-country spillovers. It is now possible for some countries, especially smaller ones, to "export" part of their tax burden and to import some tax bases from other economies (Tanzi 2016). Individual countries can attract tax bases from other countries in the form of taxable financial capital, profits, consumers, wealthy foreigners, and even foreign pensioners.

The incentives that are created to attract business activities and financial capital from other countries have led to falling statutory tax rates across countries on taxes on personal income and corporate profits, and consequently to the loss of revenue for many countries, contributing to their macroeconomic difficulties. Though lower tax rates on incomes in a country can attract foreign capital, Tanzi has noted that other factors may be equally important for particular countries and can neutralize or reinforce the flow of economic activities and resources. These other factors include the overall investment climate, the predictability of the tax system, compliance and administrative costs, as well as the countries' fiscal deficits and public debts that may create uncertainty.

Tax competition threatens governments' ability to provide the public goods that their citizens demand. Available estimates of these revenue losses, for groups of countries, have indicated that they can be very large. Strong emerging evidence indicates that tax competition has indeed contributed to eroding the tax bases of many countries. This process has forced some countries to reform their tax structures in ways not always considered desirable from an efficiency or an equity angle. In many cases, the tax reforms have made the tax systems far less equitable, thus contributing to the growth of inequality and the rise of populism experienced by many countries in recent years (Tanzi 2014).

Even though falling tax rates monopolize much of the attention, Tanzi has argued that tax competition also distorts tax systems (and the role of the state) in less visible ways. These subtle distortions may actually have a greater impact on countries' economies and the welfare of citizens in the long run. The impact on the overall *tax architecture* of economies is crucial. Tax competition is not limited to the rates at which the bases are taxed. It also incorporates variations in the types of taxes used, in the tax distinction of different types of taxable incomes and assets, in the mobility of tax bases, and in systems' sensitivity to risks of evasion and avoidance. Tax competition forces countries' governments to choose tax structures less desirable than those that would have been chosen in the absence of tax competition.

Tanzi has identified various aspects that need to be closely examined, when assessing the full impact of tax competition. His analysis distinguishes between the impact of tax competition on small countries and tax havens, which often benefit from tax competition, and the impact on larger countries and developing countries, which often lose out. Small and tax-haven countries can more easily attract financial capital and taxpayers from larger countries by lowering tax rates, at times close to zero. However, these jurisdictions are often not the hosts of real investment, which prefers larger countries. Tax havens, broadly defined, serve mainly as conduits for various operations of multinational corporations and HNWIs that allow them to reduce their tax burdens.

Countries that lose tax base, in the form of outflowing financial capital, lose far more in tax revenue than that is gained by the small countries that formally attract the base. When tax competition occurs between larger countries and is also followed by flows of capital and by a subsequent reallocation in *real* investment, from countries with high tax rates to those with low rates, it often leads to the misallocation of *real* resources and to a fall in the rate of return on the world's capital. In Tanzi's analysis, this misallocation of real capital emerges as one of the more undesirable consequences of tax competition, besides the direct, unwanted changes in tax systems.

[C] Globalization and the Emergence of "Fiscal Termites"

As mentioned above, Tanzi warned early on that globalization and subsequent changes in the economic landscape had, and would continue to have, considerable consequences for countries' tax systems. Among the most consequential developments have been: the opening of economies and the extraordinary growth of international trade; the extensive growth in cross-border capital movements; the enormous rise and growth in the multinational real activities of corporations; and the increasing importance of intellectual property in countries' trade and economic activities. The risks for taxation associated with these developments have been compounded by the strong incentives that nation-states have had to try to attract economic activity and benefits by increasing tax bases that they can exploit.

In the 1990s, Tanzi cautioned about the dangers that what he called "fiscal termites" could pose for tax systems. As he put it: "While the fiscal houses are still standing and look solid, it is easy to visualize various 'fiscal termites' that are busily gnawing at their foundations." According to Tanzi, these termites are part of the evolving "ecosystem" of globalization and the free movement of factors of production. Tanzi identified several such "fiscal termites" that result from the interplay of globalization, tax competition, and new technologies. In recent years the number of fiscal termites has increased. Major examples include:

- **Offshore financial centers and tax havens** – The number of these tax havens has increased over the years, and the tax planners that advise on how to exploit them have become more numerous and more clever, in exploiting and in manipulating tax evading opportunities for the greatest advantages of their clients. Increasingly more imaginative tax-avoidance schemes have been created by tax planners and by the (not always transparent) tax rules introduced by small countries and by tax havens. Taxpayers have exploited these opportunities to shift taxable profits where they would be less taxed, resulting in the erosion of tax bases. Wealthy individuals and multinational corporations have made increasing use of the available strategies to reduce their tax burdens.
- **Electronic commerce and electronic money** – E-commerce and the fast-growing use of economically valuable intellectual capital and non-tangible products, both within and between countries, have created new transactions that present tax administrations with major problems. These transactions leave fewer traces than did traditional transactions that were mostly domestic and that involved tangible products. The new transactions are more difficult to identify, to value, and to tax. In addition, electronic money is now the most dominant form of payment, increasingly using distributed ledger systems and cryptocurrencies. In the absence of a central record of transactions, many new transactions pose growing risks for taxes, including sales and income taxes.
- **Transfer pricing** – With the rise of large multinational corporations, operating from different countries and using inputs for their final products coming from different parts of the same enterprises but located in different countries, it has

become difficult to assign correct market values to the inputs used in one country by the multinational corporations but coming from other countries. Since these transactions occur within parts of single legal entities and cross-national borders, they cannot be and are not valued by the market. It is thus difficult to assign correct prices to the costs of these inputs. The potential for abusing "transfer prices" to erode tax bases and shift profits from high- to low-tax jurisdictions is great and has grown significantly over the years, as multi-country production has increased. The OECD has recommended "arms-length rules" for determining those prices, but abuses have continued. The use of virtual inputs has made this problem even more acute.

– **Other termites** – The growth of new financial instruments and institutions, including derivatives and hedge funds, has made the identification and evaluation of tax subjects, transactions, and jurisdictions difficult. Concerns about capital flight have reduced governments' willingness to tax financial capital and the incomes of the ultra-wealthy at rates similar to those on dependent labor (Tanzi 2014). As a result, the effective taxation of the ultra-wealthy and their financial capital is an arduous task for tax authorities. The difficulties are compounded by the growth of foreign economic activities on the part of individuals and firms. Secret or confidential agreements between some countries' authorities and some corporations have made the situation even more complex.

These developments impose risks. However, Tanzi's diagnosis has identified opportunities for progress. Tanzi has noted that reinforced collaboration among tax administrations could ease their shared challenges. Progress in information technology, combined with greater willingness to collaborate and to exchange information among countries, could make governments more efficient and tax administrations less costly. But all or most governments would have to be ready to collaborate in a dispassionate and honest way. It is an open question whether this collaboration will be forthcoming.

[D] **The Need for a New Global Architecture**

Tanzi has long called for an ambitious international cooperative scheme to facilitate tax collection (e.g., Tanzi 1988). He has advocated for the creation of a World Tax Organization (Tanzi 1995, 1999) or a World Tax Authority (Tanzi 2016) to address the challenges that countries face from tax competition. An institution fully charged by international agreement to pursue this objective would have some realistic chance of making a difference. He has emphasized the opportunities that exist for international coordination among fiscal authorities, to counter the "race to the bottom" in taxation.

Two considerations are critical in the drive towards establishing these frameworks among countries.

The first is the need for broad and full political support for the success of such international cooperation. Given that the gains and losses from tax competition are not equally distributed across countries, it would be politically difficult to build full support and consensus among all or most nation-states. The decision by countries to commit to such schemes would depend on the trade-off between the advantages that are perceived to come from an independent strategic action (from tax competition) and those perceived to come from full cooperative action. This different perception of costs and benefits from cooperation possibly underlies the absence of such an international institution to date, despite relative successes achieved in other areas, as for example in trade from the World Trade Organization and in the fight against epidemics from the World Health Organization. Tanzi argues that real, actionable progress has been limited so far, in spite of valiant efforts by the Organisation for Economic Co-operation and Development (OECD). In his view, the rise in discourse and debate within some regional and international institutions has not yet translated into workable frameworks, though momentum has been gathering.

The second consideration is technical. That is, what would be the purpose and mandate of such a world institution if it were created? Its role could range from the modest task of providing surveillance and advice to the highly ambitious charge of setting tax rules; establishing administrative regulations and procedures (for instance, on the exchange of information among countries); and enacting other specific rules for tax behavior on the part of member countries. In his writings and talks, Tanzi has provided some indications on the expected functions of such an institution. They might include:

- Exercising surveillance on countries tax systems and examining the implications of countries specific tax rules and tax reforms for other countries.
- Providing a global forum where all countries' tax policies and tax reforms that are expected to have significant cross-country implications would be debated.
- To follow and document tax developments around the world, to identify trends, to anticipate problems and to collect and report relevant tax statistics.
- Resolving disputes between countries, arising from tax competition.
- Communicating information on best practices and encouraging their use.
- Developing and disseminating codes of conduct for tax administrations, and perhaps also for corporations and individuals that operate globally.

The success of these schemes would rely on the extent of commitment by each country to abide by multinational agreements. In addition, it would rely on the extent of information exchange about taxpayers, international capital movements, and agreements between tax administrations and taxpayers. Recent efforts that promote automatic information exchange would promote more transparency and would enhance taxing capacity of countries, by providing information about the income and the wealth of individuals and corporations that operate either within a specific country or globally. Automatic information exchange should reduce the possibility of tax arbitrage as well as of strategies to either evade or avoid paying taxes. They should provide a high level of transparency onto the values and the movements of capital, wealth, and the profits that they generate.

Recent efforts in automatic information exchange, particularly those promoted by the OECD are aimed at bringing actionable progress. For example, the OECD's

Chapter 1: The Evolution of Tax Competition   §1.03[A]

Common Reporting Standard (CRS) could be a good start towards an internationally coordinated scheme to exchange and to disclose information, on the earnings of individuals and corporations. A related U.S. scheme – the U.S. Foreign Account Tax Compliance (FATCA) – requires that countries report to U.S. authorities the bank accounts of U.S. citizens that are held in foreign countries. Such efforts provide some underpinning for subsequent automatic information exchange schemes on a global scale, but in Tanzi's view they do not go far enough.

§1.03 "WINNING THE TAX WARS" AS ASSESSED BY VITO TANZI

Debates on the issue of tax competition have intensified over the years, as governments have been increasingly deprived of needed tax revenue. Such revenue losses have been experienced by both advanced countries, some of which have accumulated large public debts, and poor countries, which urgently need to provide essential services to their populations.

The World Bank Conference held in 2016 under the initiative of the Canadian Organization called "TaxCOOP" gave rise to broad exchange of views demonstrating the willingness to search for mechanisms to address tax competition.

[A] Confronting an Ideological Question

As the rapporteur, Tanzi pointed out that the conference addressed an important *ideological* question: Is "tax competition" necessarily a bad thing? This is clearly a fundamental issue, and the answer is not obvious, given that there are experts and politicians who believe that:

(a) Governments are inevitably inefficient in the use of public resources. Therefore, they should not have easy access to them.
(b) Governments tend to be "Leviathan monsters." They are never satisfied with the revenue that they receive.
(c) Because of the above, governments tend to impose excessive tax burdens and tax rates on economic activities. These have a negative impact on economic efficiency and personal effort. As a consequence, they reduce countries' economic growth.
(d) Because it forces governments to keep tax rates low, and because it reduces tax revenue, tax competition could be seen as a desirable influence on governments. It might even promote efficiency, prosperity, and economic growth.

At the conference, the two sides of this question were presented and defended in a formal public debate by two able and articulate exponents. After their presentations, the conference participants were asked to express support for either of the two sides. There was overwhelming support for the view that tax competition is damaging overall, because it deprives governments of badly needed revenue, and because it makes it more difficult for them to provide services and public goods that citizens need. In addition, some forms of tax competition (not only on rates but also on the tax base or particular privileges) further contribute to the complexity and lack of transparency of taxation globally and deepen the divide between developed and developing countries. For developing countries, these pressures will make it more difficult to meet the Sustainable Development Goals.

[B] New Options for Tax Avoidance

In his synthesis report, Tanzi observed that several experts' presentations focused on the new possibilities for tax avoidance that tax competition has created, especially for multinational corporations and HNWIs. Tax competition has made it possible to shift profits from high- to low-tax countries, and to move tax bases out of high-tax countries. It has also facilitated the concealment of incomes from the national authorities that should tax them.

Small countries and jurisdictions defined as tax havens especially tend to benefit from these maneuvers. It was reported that secret, or non-transparent, agreements have been made between some corporations and country tax officials. This has allowed or facilitated tax-avoiding actions. As a result, some of the largest companies in the world have, at times, paid little in taxes to the countries where they have an official residence. These actions have resulted in large revenue losses for some countries, including developing countries.

Indirectly, these actions have had an undesirable effect on the distribution of income and wealth in many countries. Tax avoidance or tax evasion has benefited HNWIs more than normal workers. Ample evidence indicates that income and wealth distributions have become much less even in many countries and worldwide in recent decades.

Several speakers addressed the need to exchange tax-related information among countries and evoked the role that certain large banks have played in facilitating tax evasion for some individuals. Estimates suggest that a large share of global wealth has been deposited in these banks, some of it held anonymously.

[C] Strategies to Limit Abuses

Tanzi noted examples of policy actions taken by some individual countries. Senator Carl Levin of the U.S. detailed what the American government has done in recent years to track American citizens attempting to use secret foreign bank accounts to escape U.S. taxes. Specific U.S. government actions have included changing legislation and imposing high penalties on some foreign banks. Others report on the role of investigative work in unmasking tax-avoidance schemes, the role that whistleblowers played and could play, as this requires some globally agreed definitions and standards.

Recent actions undertaken by G20 member governments and international organizations to increase the exchange of tax information among countries, reduce tax avoidance, and establish better international rules are equally noted. The OECD's work to promote information exchange and coordination among the growing number of countries that have committed to collaborate in reducing "base erosion and profit shifting" must also be acknowledged.

Tanzi observed divergent views and considerable debate among participants on whether enough countries would adopt these measures to make a significant difference globally. It was recognized that tax competition is a game in which some countries have gained and are therefore motivated to exploit the existing possibilities as long as they can get away with it. The complexity of existing tax rules and the globalization of economic activities and financial markets have together created numerous tax-avoidance opportunities for taxpayers, and many possibilities for certain countries to profit. Moreover, a growing industry of able and well-informed tax advisers assists those who seek to reduce their tax liabilities with aggressive tax planning.

Tanzi also pointed out that, recently, some countries, including very large ones, have announced their intentions to lower their tax rates and otherwise alter their tax systems to "become more internationally competitive." These actions do not bode well for current efforts to resolve the tax wars.

There was extensive discussion on what to do about multinational enterprises that operate in many countries with different rules and tax rates. For these enterprises, profit shifting and tax-base exporting or base reductions are often easy. Some advocate *country-by-country reporting* to address this problem. However, Tanzi cautioned, given the complexity of corporate taxation, other participants expressed doubts about whether such measures can yield significant changes in taxpayer behavior and outcomes. Some policymakers, Tanzi recalled, continue to insist that taxation is an exclusively national prerogative and should not be constrained by other countries or by international rules.

[D] A Key Challenge: Defining the Base for Corporate Taxation

Tanzi draws attention to a key practical problem: the tax systems of different countries continue to include substantial differences in their definitions of taxable bases. Tax systems are complex, and linguistic differences inevitably add to the difficulties encountered in determining tax abuses from information that may be exchanged among governments. Exchange of information is clearly an important goal to pursue, but it would be naive to believe that, in itself, it will solve all problems. Full transparency that is symmetric to all sides may remain a dream, Tanzi warns, and "second-best" solutions may offer more promising results.

It would be ideal if agreements (bilateral or multilateral) among countries could be reached regarding the *definition of the base* for corporate taxation, and if all countries followed similar definitions. This would require, for example, reducing and/or eliminating the use of tax incentives by countries. Such agreements could be based on the best technical concepts of "what should be taxable" and would limit tax competition to the more transparent differences in tax rates, differences that are easier to understand. However, governments continue to show considerable enthusiasm for granting tax incentives and for the use of various loopholes. Many will likely find justifications to continue using these approaches.

[E] Wealth Taxes: Opportunities and Limits

The income distributions of many countries have become increasingly unequal in recent decades, and wealth is distributed even more unequally than income. Therefore, it is argued, it would be desirable to use wealth taxation to raise revenue and bring more equity to income distributions. Technological developments have increased the information that governments can now obtain the wealth owned by rich individuals. Registries of assets and their owners can be created and can help. Therefore, wealth taxes could be used to make the distribution of income more even, as some economists have argued in recent years. Such taxes could complement the use of income taxes and raise additional tax revenue for countries that need it.

Tanzi notes the contradicting views of others towards wealth tax. Globalization has created ample opportunities for individuals to spread their wealth globally. The official ownership of wealth can also be spread to other individuals, using the identity of those willing to lend their names. Much wealth is now held in forms that are difficult to identify and/or in the form of intellectual property that is difficult to value. For many assets, their value changes frequently or is known in only an approximate way, as in the case of real estate.

The experience of most countries indicates that some forms of wealth can be taxed. Nevertheless, it is not likely that wealth will play a major role in providing tax revenue in a globalized world. In Tanzi's view, a realistic conclusion is that income and consumption are likely to continue to be the main tax bases for years to come.

[F] Taxation to Promote Public Goods

Considerable global attention is being paid to the taxation of tobacco products, even though, Tanzi noted, this form of taxation does not play a major role in international tax wars as generally understood.

In recent decades, increasing evidence has shown that smoking is the main source of death from preventable diseases worldwide, and that the effects of smoking significantly lower the life expectancy. It has also been demonstrated that tobacco taxes are the most effective tool to curb tobacco consumption, while the demand elasticity of tobacco products is much higher in poor individuals and poor countries, which makes the tax progressive over the medium term.

Empirical evidence shows that tobacco taxes do in fact reduce smoking, especially for young smokers. Therefore, they also reduce health costs and contribute to higher life expectancy. In addition, they can generate substantial tax revenue, potentially expanding the fiscal space needed to finance public services that benefit lower-income groups.

Tanzi points out that the use of tobacco taxes also includes some aspects of tax competition in the strict sense. If two jurisdictions are close to one another, and one of them taxes tobacco products significantly less than the other, consumers will seek to avoid the higher taxes by purchasing tobacco products where they are cheaper. Therefore, some coordination of tobacco taxation is desirable to reduce tax competition between jurisdictions, especially at regional levels.

Finally, Tanzi highlights the discussion of energy taxation and some interesting reports on the use of carbon pricing, another area where, he suggests, coordination is desirable but difficult. However, as part of the Climate Change National Determined Commitments (NDCs), most countries are in the process of designing a carbon tax that may trigger a reduction in CO_2 emissions worldwide. Despite difficulties in determining the level of such a tax rate, there is more consensus than ever that it must be designed proportionally to the carbon content emitted and levied in a coordinated manner.

§1.04 CONCLUSION

This chapter has provided initial conceptual framing and historical context for the theme of tax competition. It has sketched some of the important motifs that will be explored in detail in subsequent chapters of this book. Our guiding thread has been the work of Vito Tanzi, one of the shapers of the field of international tax policy.

In the 1970s and 1980s, Tanzi was among the first observers to describe the phenomenon of global tax competition and to alert governments and the international community to its likely consequences. Tanzi's analysis and proposals have evolved over four decades, tracking the evolution of the globalized economy and the practice of tax competition itself. This chapter has evoked, in a summary fashion, some of the main stages in the development of Tanzi's critical perspectives, while awaiting the more exhaustive analysis that Tanzi's intellectual itinerary deserves.

Tanzi's work represents a bridge between the origins of the modern phenomenon of tax competition and the contemporary situation analyzed by the experts who participated in the "Winning the Tax Wars" conference. Tanzi's comments on the highlights of the meeting, summarized in the second half of this chapter, suggest entry points to the array of topics that readers will find debated in the remainder of this book.

CHAPTER 2
Abandoning Tax Competition: A Historical Overview and a Way Forward in Achieving the 2030 Agenda

Erika Siu

Although numerous studies have demonstrated the ineffectiveness of tax incentives in spurring long-term sustainable growth, they are often accepted as inevitable, given the ever-present and mysterious forces of "tax competition." This chapter analyzes the historical development of the tax competition concept and the efforts of international organizations (IOs) to ameliorate the negative effects of tax competition. The continuing validity of the tax competition concept is questioned, and an alternative way forward for achieving sustainable development is advanced. The chapter sets out three foundational principles of transparency, accountability, and universality to guide the development of this new agenda for international tax cooperation. It proposes future research to institutionalize these principles within the IOs currently working on tax capacity building and international tax norm-setting.

§2.01 INTRODUCTION

Although the traditional goal of taxation is revenue raising, sometimes, governments use tax rules to incentivize or disincentivize certain activities. In the realm of the corporate income tax, incentives and other preferential regimes are used in particular to encourage investment. These incentives generally take three different forms. First, they may affect the tax base, i.e., how taxable profits are calculated, by establishing for example: investment allowances, what income is exempt, what costs/expenses are deductible, and so forth. Second, incentives may provide targeted exemptions, for example, tax holidays or tax exemptions for activities taking place in special economic zones. Alternatively, countries may reduce nominal corporate income tax rates. Tax competition in this chapter refers more specifically to the lowering of rates and the use of such incentives to attract foreign direct investment (FDI) by multinational enterprises (MNEs) and to promote certain business activities by domestic and foreign enterprises.

For the past two decades, studies have shown tax incentives to be "ineffective, inefficient, and associated with abuse and corruption" (International Monetary Fund (IMF) 2015). Systematically, surveys have noted that tax incentives are not a major factor in the location choice of businesses (James 2014), while other analyses indicate "some evidence that lower corporate income tax rates and longer tax holidays are effective in attracting FDI, but not in boosting gross private fixed capital formation or growth" (Klemm et al. 2009). Despite such evidence, tax incentives in the form of tax holidays were offered in over 80% of low income, Sub-Saharan African countries in 2005 (Keen and Mansour 2010).

Developing countries, in particular, continue to hemorrhage millions of dollars annually through the granting of tax incentives that often come up short in providing commensurate economic development. ActionAid estimates developing countries' average losses from corporate tax incentives at USD 138 billion annually for the period 2005-2012. This is USD 10 billion more than the total aid distributed by the OECD countries in 2012 (ActionAid 2013).

In all tax systems, there is a tension between the use of tax measures to stimulate desired activities, such as investment, and ensuring fairness and equality among taxpayers. Fairness and equality also suggests the desirability of tax neutrality, and a system with a broad tax base and lower tax rates, rather than one with many specific preferences and special allowances and a higher nominal rate. A country's tax regime often reflects a compromise between its economic, social, and environmental development priorities. Thus, tax incentives, which are often additions to an existing regime, should be carefully designed. In particular, countries should aim to ensure fiscal discipline through budgetary procedures, such as requiring preferences to be given through regular legislative procedures with public debate. Incentives should be treated as "tax expenditures," be costed and regularly reviewed, and should be subject to sunset clauses that limit them to a defined number of years. In addition, and most importantly, transparency of incentives should be ensured (IMF/OECD/UN/World Bank 2015). Although these suggestions are put forward for low-income countries (LICs), they are generally desirable and should also be followed by high-income countries.

The more specific issue of tax competition worldwide concerns the interactions between national tax systems and the ways in which one country's taxes can affect other countries. These effects are referred to in economic terms as "externalities" or "spillovers" (IMF 2014, p. 12). Spillovers in international corporate tax are a particular concern because of the importance of investment by MNEs, especially for developing countries. Also, depending on the mobility of the assets involved, MNEs can choose between possible investment locations and may take tax into account when doing so. In practice, MNEs face a number of constraints in making location decisions, and tax may not be a decisive or even significant factor (UNIDO 2011). Nevertheless, its influence affects government decisions and leads to the offering of tax incentives to attract FDI (IMF 2015). The problem is exacerbated when countries establish laws that create an unlevel playing field. Examples include the provision of services for non-residents, encompassing, for instance, the formation of shell companies which are exempt from reporting requirements, banking facilities with strong secrecy protections, and exemption of foreign-source income.

A lack of coordination on international tax rules also contributes to tax competition. Until now, the international tax system, mainly composed of bilateral tax and investment treaties, has provided partial coordination to prevent double taxation. But this lack of comprehensive coordination has paved the way for a great deal of tax arbitrage by MNEs, ultimately leading to double non-taxation. This began with the classic tax havens, which offered low or even zero tax rates, often for companies owned by nonresidents or not engaged in the domestic economy, such as "international business corporations." Some countries have even provided confidential tax rulings for specific MNEs, as revealed in the Luxembourg Leaks. At the same time, others have provided protections of secrecy, either directly through obscuring the identity of the person owning the assets, or indirectly through the provision of business entities that the benefiting owner can hide behind. Both forms of secrecy block enforcement of other countries' laws. Thus, depending on the type of business the country wants to attract, preferential tax regimes and treaty networks may work hand-in-hand with secrecy laws to enable not only tax avoidance but also tax evasion. Mechanisms might include secret bank accounts or providing permanent storage for stolen or hidden assets – such as gold, diamonds, wine, artwork, or similar goods – in "free ports." Activities might also include the "laundering" of money to fund terrorism or of proceeds derived from corruption, illicit trade of drugs, tobacco, alcohol, and human trafficking. The Panama Papers have exposed the global reach of these networks, enabled by a chain of intermediaries, such as banks and law and accounting firms (Stiglitz and Pieth 2016). Although countries may derive a short-term benefit from these policies, such as incorporation fees, and business for its legal and accounting industry, they tend to benefit a small class of elites, while damaging other sectors of the economy and population. For example, these policies may contribute to high real estate prices and create unfair competition for local companies that must comply with the tax laws but do not engage in international actors' profit-shifting schemes. Moreover, any potential domestic benefits that accrue are greatly outweighed by the damage done to the tax base of other countries, not to mention the enabling of criminal and terrorist activities globally.

§2.02 EFFORTS BY IOs TO CURB TAX COMPETITION

Individual efforts. A number of measures have been introduced in different contexts by the various international tax organizations to improve tax coordination and restrict tax competition. (The relevant IOs include the IMF, the Organisation for Economic Co-operation and Development (OECD), the United Nations (UN), and the World Bank Group (WBG)). What follows is a discussion of this work. This is not intended to be an exhaustive account, as the IMF and WBG in particular have advised LICs for decades on tax policymaking and the use of tax incentives through their technical assistance work. At the political norm-setting level, however, the OECD has historically taken a leading role, and we begin with a discussion of this involvement.

Concerns about harmful tax practices led to action first through the G7 leaders in 1996-1997, resulting in the OECD report on *Harmful Tax Competition* (1998). This report stimulated: (i) an attempt to define "harmful tax practices" and apply these standards through a Forum on Harmful Tax Practices (FHTP) and (ii) an effort to improve exchange of tax-related information undertaken through a Global Forum on Transparency and Exchange of Information (Global Forum). The *Harmful Tax Competition* report outlined a work agenda to identify preferential regimes among OECD countries. It also created a "blacklist" of tax havens including both OECD and non-OECD countries. In addition, the report established criteria for preferential regimes, which were potentially harmful, and the FHTP carried the recommendations of the report forward.

By 2000, the FHTP had identified 47 potentially harmful regimes within OECD countries as well as 35 tax haven jurisdictions (most of which were small islands and/or small island developing states). However, six years later, 46 of the 47 potentially harmful regimes were taken off of the list, and the Global Forum was created to engage with non-OECD countries to deal with the "tax haven" classification. An *Agreement on Exchange of Information in Tax Matters* was developed in 2002 as the gatekeeping device for admission of non-OECD countries into the Forum (later renamed the Global Forum on Transparency and Exchange of Information for Tax Purposes). After some restructuring, the FHTP mandate was restricted to deal only with "preferential tax regimes and [with] defensive measures in respect of such regimes."

A new initiative following the 2008 financial crisis was the G20/OECD project on Base Erosion and Profit Shifting (BEPS), launched in 2013. This aimed at a comprehensive reform of international tax rules to ensure that MNEs could be taxed "where economic activities occur and value is created," as opposed to double non-taxation. The BEPS project also included a revision of the definitions of harmful tax practices, and a re-launch of the FHTP. The FHTP work was resumed to clarify the requirement of "substantial activity," particularly in the context of preferential tax regimes for income from intellectual property (IP), so-called patent boxes. While there was no agreement to prohibit patent boxes, or even to agree on a minimum rate, the FHTP agreed to a "nexus" principle – taxpayers may only benefit from tax incentives to the extent of qualifying "research and development" expenditures made in the tax jurisdiction. It was also agreed that the only IP assets that could qualify for benefits are patents or assets that are similar and functionally equivalent to patents.

During the BEPS process, a review was conducted of 43 preferential regimes of OECD and G20 countries. Sixteen were IP regimes and were all found wholly or partially inconsistent with the nexus criterion. Later in 2017, after a review of over 164 preferential tax regimes, including several newly introduced patent box regimes, the OECD reported that all except one of the 16 original regimes were abolished or amended to conform with the nexus criteria (OECD 2017). Many observers have

Chapter 2: Abandoning Tax Competition §2.02

criticized this BEPS reform outcome on patent boxes as legitimizing and even intensifying tax competition.

Such an outcome is logical, given that it has always been made clear that the work of the OECD on harmful tax competition set out to create a wall between "helpful" and "harmful" tax competition. The report of the FHTP states that the forum is "not intended to promote the harmonization of income taxes or tax structures generally within or outside the OECD, nor is it about dictating to any country what should be the appropriate level of tax rates." The forum is concerned only with "reducing the distortionary influence of taxation on the location of mobile financial and service activities," in order to encourage "free and fair tax competition," a "level playing field," and "expansion of global economic growth" (OECD 2015, 11).

The decision of the G20 in February 2016 to establish an Inclusive Framework means that the BEPS reform measures can now be extended worldwide (OECD 2016). BEPS Associate status in the OECD's Committee on Fiscal Affairs is being offered to all interested countries that will commit to both the BEPS standards and BEPS implementation monitoring. Moreover, jurisdictions which opt not to commit, but which are regarded as relevant for ensuring a level playing field in tackling BEPS issues globally, will be subject to review, including by the FHTP.

For decades, through its technical assistance programs, the IMF has advised countries on the use of tax incentives, although much of this advice has not been made public. In recent years, the IMF Fiscal Affairs Department has issued research focused on the international spillover effects of tax regimes and the disproportionate effect of tax avoidance on developing countries (IMF 2014). The paper argues that tax incentives "may to a large extent be a spillover reaction to policies pursued in other countries: a clear instance of tax competition" (2014, 7).

The World Bank has supported tax policy reforms, including reducing tax incentives, in developing countries through lending, advisory services, and technical assistance. In particular, support has been given to regional unions (WAEMU, East Africa) to help them meet fiscal targets set up by the members. At the same time, many countries have provided uncoordinated tax incentives, resulting in tax base erosion and unfair competition within their regional markets.

The Capacity Building Unit within the Financing for Development Office of the United Nations Department of Economic and Social Affairs directs its capacity building initiatives toward developing countries, especially the least developed. Recently, the Capacity Building Unit worked to develop the *United Nations Handbook on Selected Issues in Protecting the Tax Base of Developing Countries* and is now working to develop more practical guidance in this regard.

Joining Forces. As part of the G20/OECD BEPS project, the G20 Development Working Group requested that IOs formulate a "developing country toolkit" on tax incentives for LICs. The goal was to "level the playing field" on tax competition. Given the broad adoption and largely unsuccessful use of tax incentives by LICs, the IOs are providing many developing countries, including LICs, with extensive technical assistance, evaluation tools, and advice on how best to evaluate the effectiveness and efficiency of these instruments. On the issue of tax incentives, these institutions produced a report to the G20 Development Working Group, entitled *Options for Low income Countries' Effective and Efficient Use of Tax Incentives for Investment*. A background paper accompanied the report describing five analytical tools for assessing tax incentives. The advice includes the following recommendations:

- Use cost-based allowances (depreciation and credits) more aggressively than profit-based incentives, such as tax holidays and income exemptions, because the former yields more investment.
- Avoid tax incentives for sectors producing for domestic markets or extractive industries, as they have little effect.
- While tax incentives targeted to export-oriented sectors and mobile capital are generally effective, trade policy consistency under WTO rules and tax competition concerns should be considered.

At the same time, the report notes that there is a broader political economy issue in the use of these tools. On page 28, the report states:

[P]oliticians may find it attractive to introduce new tax incentives to reveal their proactive stance in addressing weak economic performance, or to favor particular regions. The fiscal costs of granting those incentives, moreover, are usually not transparent and only arise as forgone revenue in the future. Tax incentives also create vested interests among businesses and within government, making them difficult to repeal, even if they are ineffective. Indeed, economic elites are sometimes able to influence the governance and design of tax incentives and shape public opinion where it suits their objectives.

In response, the IOs have begun to suggest more governance reforms at the domestic level. Their advice includes the following recommendations:

- The granting of tax incentives should be transparent to the public, usually through tax expenditure reporting.
- Tax incentives should be approved through a legislative process and not on a discretionary basis.
- All tax incentives should be located in one place in the law.
- Tax incentives should be reviewed annually to evaluate their effectiveness.
- Approval processes for tax incentives should be consolidated under one ministry and administered by the Tax Administration.

While the IOs offer advice on the calibration of tax incentives, the report also notes that a helpful way to address this aspect of tax competition is regional and international coordination, with two caveats on the scope of coordination: (1) coordination on some tax incentives may result in greater competition on others; (2) regional coordination may increase tax competition with "outsiders." Examples of tax coordination include the Code of Conduct for business taxation in the European Union, as well as the state-aid rules, which limit tax subsidies to areas with "abnormally low" living standards and are regulated by the Commission.

However, in LICs, the report finds that the political will to cooperate and effective supranational enforcement mechanisms are often absent. In this regard, it suggests interim steps, such as common reporting of tax incentives and information sharing.

The report notes modest successes in regional cooperation among regional economic communities such as the East African Community and the Southern African Development Community. At the international level, the report notes that there are international tax rules, such as territorial systems and weakly controlled foreign corporation rules, which have the consequence of increasing tax competition among LICs. More broadly speaking, to the extent that the reforms of the G20/OECD BEPS project disable loopholes that allow profit shifting and base erosion, tax incentives may become more appealing.

In early 2016, the IOs announced the formation of a *Platform for Collaboration on Tax*, largely to formalize their increasing collaboration on tax issues. This collaboration received initial impetus from the G20's 2011 request to produce a report identifying the key tax challenges facing developing countries (IMF et al. 2011). It is envisioned that the IOs will work together to produce the eight toolkits and reports for the G20 in order "to translate the complexity of BEPS outcomes (in relation, for instance, to transfer pricing), into user-friendly guidance for low capacity countries" and to "address international tax issues not included in the BEPS project (such as indirect transfers of assets)" (IMF 2016, 2). Discussions in the G20/OECD inclusive framework will feed into the outputs of the Platform and "possibly" vice versa (IMF 2016, 2).

The Platform is not expected to serve as a norm-setting body, but to provide more of a research and capacity-building function in relation to the current international tax agenda. This approach is consistent with prior individual IO mandates (particularly of the IMF and WB), directed at technical assistance in the area of tax reforms (policy and administration). However, the Platform is expected to help facilitate the roadmap for taxation to contribute to the achievement of the Sustainable Development Goals (SDGs), and will particularly support developing countries' efforts in this context.

In some areas, however, efforts of the IOs have run counter to the aim of reducing tax competition. In addition to the above-mentioned "patent box" authorization within the OECD FHTP, we can cite certain underlying assumptions and potential impacts of the WBG's annual flagship report, *Doing Business*.

For the past 13 years, *Doing Business* has been "one of the world's most influential policy publications" (World Bank 2016, iv). The report bases its analysis on 10 areas of business regulation imposed on medium-sized "domestic" businesses in each of the 189 countries from which the WBG collects data in partnership with PricewaterhouseCoopers (World Bank 2016, 144). The findings are used to formulate an overall score and ranking based on the ease of conducting commercial activities within each jurisdiction. "Making it Easier to Pay Taxes" is one of the indicators, and within this indicator, total (effective) tax rates is one measure, which it describes as a "cost to business" (21). The report goes on to cite improvements in this measure in the form of reduced headline tax rates (e.g., 44), reductions to the base, for example through accelerated depreciation (e.g., 37), as well as elimination of tax rates as a percentage of the base and replacement with flat fees (which favors regressivity) (e.g., 15). Moreover, because the effective tax rate is derived, not by nominal rates, but instead by total tax payable divided by commercial profit, the measure includes other types of tax incentives which may reduce tax rates, shrink the tax base, or even eliminate taxation of profits completely for a given taxpayer (147).

In order to reduce a bias in the scoring toward low- and no-tax jurisdictions, an effective tax rate threshold is set "at the lower end of the distribution of tax rates levied on medium-sized enterprises in the manufacturing sector," below which countries receive the same score as other countries at the threshold (145). Additionally, in computing the overall score, increase in the total tax rate for countries with below-average total tax rates are computed differently than all other measures, so as to have a smaller impact on the total score (166). On the other hand, the opposite is true for countries with rates that are very high relative to the average (166).

This adjustment appears to operate as a "curb" on the race to the bottom. However, one wonders if such numerical adjustments amount to a "race to the middle," while the "middle" keeps moving lower and lower so that, in the end, we are left with the same result. Nominal corporate income tax rates have already decreased by 19 percentage points in the last 30 years. The fact that total tax rates are even used as a measure fuels the race to the bottom (Ocampo and Fitzgerald 2016). Other measures in the "Making it Easier to Pay Taxes" indicator, such as time and compliance costs, for example, and whether tax administrations allow electronic filing, would be sufficient to reflect the nature of the indicator.

The International Finance Corporation (IFC), a member of the WBG, specializes in private-sector investments in developing countries, with a USD 15.3 billion syndicated loan portfolio (IFC 2015, 36). Within the B Loan Structure, all IFC financing is exempt from withholding tax, so that borrowers are not required to pay withholding tax to their governments on debt service payments. Such loans have undoubtedly provided access to capital for many entrepreneurs and have fueled economic development. However, policymaking in tax matters should also take into account governments' interest in providing adequate infrastructure and social investments to enable sustainable development, as well as the fulfillment of human rights.

[A] A New Approach to Tax Competition

In order to make real headway in mobilizing domestic tax revenues, a new approach is needed. The remainder of this chapter aims to formulate a normative framework on tax competition that incorporates the sustainable development dimension and suggests three principles as a way forward.

Beginning with an image may be useful. Have you ever been in a public space – on the street, for example – and suddenly been caught in a rush of pedestrians walking briskly or even running? Without knowing why, without explanation, you may find yourself running, too. Maybe there's an important reason to run, but maybe it's all a joke. In the same way, we can ask: Is the notion of "tax competition" or "tax wars" a viable concept or just rhetoric designed to make us believe we need to run ever faster? A good starting question in the race to the bottom might be: "Why are we running?"

In approaching tax competition, I would posit that this question is a necessary one and the answers fall somewhere along three orientations: atheist, agnostic, and believer.

The atheist argument goes like this: The underlying justification for tax competition is a fallacy based on the inaccurate notion that systems like governments "compete" in the same way as private firms. There is no "market" for tax rates or other incentives, because States do not function like markets. In fact, States step in where markets fail. Elected officials make laws in the public interest and, while they seek to encourage inward investment, tax policies are set based on national revenue collection and spending targets that reflect the choices of a nation's citizens, whereas markets fail to reflect those preferences. Moreover, the theory of systems competition is often justified by Tiebout's notion that taxpayers "vote with their feet" by moving to jurisdictions with goods that suit their preferences (Tiebout 1956). But Tiebout's model does not account for negative externalities or spillovers between jurisdictions, which leads to underprovision of public goods: in other words, market failures. This is where the State should step in – if it weren't already chasing its tail in the "race to the bottom" (Sinn 1997; Dietsch and Rixen 2014).

The tax competition atheist would argue that, regardless of the behavioral outcomes of States, the whole "tax competition" discourse is a hoax to "divide and conquer" weaker, smaller countries, especially developing ones and prevent them from realizing and making investments in their own social and economic capital. A better policy would seek to promote national priorities by making investments in physical, legal, and educational infrastructure that have the double benefit of supplying citizen's preferences and attracting business.

On the other side of the coin, the traditional believer's argument goes like this: Tax competition is a force for efficiency because it places a constraint on big government collection and spending (government's so-called Leviathan tendencies), and requires a more efficient allocation of resources (Brennan and Buchanan 1980; Edwards and Keen 1996). This means that jurisdictions compete for desired goods such as capital, labor, and other business activities by providing attractive policies, and the citizen-taxpayers' location choices determine which political structures survive (Tiebout 1960, Weingast 1995).

In place of these two extremes, however, a synthesis view is proposed, based on the theory that governments are neither always "intrinsically untrustworthy revenue maximizers" nor "benevolent maximizers of their citizen's welfare," but are, instead, a little of both (Edwards and Keen 1996, 115). Therefore, tax competition and coordination may in some cases be helpful, while they are not helpful in others. The economic literature provides models in which either coordination or competition may be helpful, both from the traditional international tax coordination approach and from a game-theoretic framework (*see* a survey in Sörensen 1990). But these models are built on assumptions difficult to replicate in reality, leaving policymakers left with the basic question of where to draw the line.

Thus, I prefer to take the agnostic route on tax competition, because it seems that we have been going in circles for easily three decades. Meanwhile, the attempts to control the negative effects of tax competition have engendered minimal political commitment and established almost no normative underpinning except for a few catch phrases here and there.

If we are really intent on realizing the 2030 Agenda for Sustainable Development, the streams of international tax cooperation and financing for development must merge. And this cooperation should go beyond the mere capacity building. Although many of the challenges States face in mobilizing domestic tax revenues begin domestically, financial and tax policies of one country inevitably affect the revenue mobilization prospects of neighboring countries. In other words, domestic resource mobilization is inextricably linked to a globalized economy and an international tax and financial system.

So I suggest we stop talking about tax wars. Let us begin a new conversation, focusing on a framework to deliver financing for quality public services, assist governments in fulfilling their human rights obligations to citizens, and enable sustainable development. Why not start a conversation focused on tax cooperation to mobilize financing for development and get to the work of establishing a consensus on a normative framework?

[B] A Normative Framework for Tax Cooperation

I suggest we begin with three principles for tax cooperation: (1) Transparency; (2) Accountability; and (3) Universality.

Transparency. Transparency is a central pillar of international cooperation, good governance, and efficient markets. Under legal principles of contract theory, as well as the economic literature, information asymmetries lead to undesirable outcomes (Akerlof 1970), and resulting legal conflicts should be resolved according to the understanding of parties who lack relevant information (Restatement (Second) of Contracts § 201). Transparency (and implied relevancy, accessibility, timeliness, and accuracy) of information is necessary to prevent failures in markets and governance, and this transparency should extend to the end users of markets and governments: citizens and consumers.

In the realm of tax incentives, governments should ensure, through public hearings and intergovernmental forums, that information about preferential arrangements is well known to other governments, as well as its own citizens, before those arrangements are carried out. Additionally, tax expenditure reports should be published annually, along with monitoring and evaluation reports on tax-incentive effectiveness (ICRICT 2016).

Transparency also requires that business entities file country-by-country reports to tax administrations on the revenues, expenses, taxes paid and due, and labor and assets employed in each jurisdiction. These reports should also be accessible to the public to ensure that tax administrations carry out their responsibility to administer and enforce tax laws adopted by parliaments. Finally, governments and citizens should know who owns corporations and other business entities, such as trusts and private foundations.

In the wake of the Luxembourg and Swiss Leaks, as well as the Panama Papers scandals, global calls for greater transparency have gained political momentum, beginning with the G8 in 2013 and continuing through the 2016 push by the U.K. and the European Union to adopt public, national registries of beneficial owners. In September 2017, 49 jurisdictions began exchanging information on financial accounts under the Common Reporting Standard and another 53 jurisdictions are expected to begin exchanges in 2018. These exchanges, however, come with the promise of confidentiality. The G20/OECD reforms also call for country-by-country reporting of tax information to tax administrations; these exchanges are expected to begin in June 2018 with 55 jurisdictions having already adopted reporting requirements of ultimate parent entities. Similar to the information on financial accounts, this reporting will only be available to tax administrations and not the public. Moreover, many corporations fall below the high threshold of reporting (annual consolidate group revenues of EUR 750 million).

In the midst of this push, calls for taxpayer confidentiality have gone up from corporate taxpayers and from more than a few governments. They claim that confidentiality of tax information helps both governments and corporate taxpayers by limiting the ability of the corporation's "stakeholders and agents to engage in benchmarking and reverse engineering, behaviors that would likely cause some tax directors to pursue more aggressive tax planning and reporting" (Blank 2014, 37). Others have argued that if the identity of natural persons who owned reported assets were revealed, such persons could be endangered by potential kidnappers or subject to malfeasant governments, which might expropriate their wealth.

Many of the arguments in favor of confidentiality are founded on the assumption of an unaccountable State: either because of actual malfeasance or the inability to enforce the rule of law, even if provided with the necessary information. However, an important aspect of transparency is that it enables accountability on all sides. If the government and citizens have access to basic tax information, they are in a better position to hold each other accountable: Taxpayers will be held accountable to pay the appropriate amount of tax, since they may be pressured not only by the government but also by their fellow taxpayers. Government will also be held accountable by citizens to administer and enforce its tax power according to the law. Finally, parliaments will be held accountable by citizens to change tax laws when necessary.

Moreover, given the globalized nature of much of today's economic activity, effective transparency cannot be restricted to the domestic sphere but must be delivered at international scale. Given the diversity in the way income is defined and taxable income is determined among countries, harmonization of tax bases, including removal of tax incentives that exempt income or provide generous allowances, may be necessary in order to exchange "apples to apples" information. However, even if harmonization of the tax base is required, countries retain the sovereignty to set rates according to their fiscal objectives. This is the route taken by the Common Consolidated Corporate Tax Base (CCCTB), which has been under negotiation among the Member States of the European Union since its first release in 2011, and again in 2015. Such work is slow going, both technically and especially politically – but highly necessary for governments to keep pace with a globalized economy.

There is also the question of the repository for such information if exchange takes place beyond bilateral partner agreements. At present, there is no international body to administer fully multilateral tax information exchanges, although the OECD has poised itself for such a task by building the Common Transmission System, a technology infrastructure that facilitates exchanges among signatories of its Multilateral Convention on Mutual Administrative Assistance in Tax Matters (MCAATM).

Accountability. States must be answerable to their citizens at the domestic level, as well as to international repercussions of national policies. For its own citizens, governments should require justification of each tax incentive, stating the precise economic activity that is being induced as well as estimation of the social benefits expected to exceed the cost of foregone revenues. Governments should also monitor and evaluate the effectiveness of tax incentives on a regular basis and eliminate those which are not effective.

In the international tax realm, States should abide by the "Do No Harm" principle by inducing real economic activity through other non-tax incentives and not merely undercutting the tax base of other countries. Practically speaking, governments should conduct spillover analyses of in-place tax incentives to avoid beggar-thy-neighbor tax competition and modify or eliminate incentives that merely undercut other countries' tax bases. States should also avoid the inclusion of provisions in investor protection treaties, resource extraction agreements, or other non-tax agreements that weaken or circumvent tax law. Additionally, States should refrain from advocacy, through diplomatic or other means, for their multinational corporations involved in a tax dispute with other countries.

At the same time, fiscal sovereignty implies that each country exercises its right to decide how to define its tax base and what deductions from the base are acceptable in meeting national economic, social, and environmental development objectives. Moreover, unilateral action still has a vital role in curbing tax avoidance by strengthening the negotiating position of the State, including with regard to multinational corporate taxpayers whose economic position is often stronger and whose interests are often protected by the government of residence.

Moreover, the two concepts of sovereignty and accountability do not have to be viewed as mutually exclusive. As Dietsch and Rixen argue, strong international tax cooperation could in fact "protect national fiscal self-determination by imposing certain limits on the fiscal choices of nation states" (2014, 171). Dietsch and Rixen propose a two-part limitation on all aspects of a State's tax regime, and those policies that fail both tests should be prohibited (165). The first restraint is outcome based. It provides that, "A tax policy is legitimate if it does not produce a collectively suboptimal outcome. A collectively suboptimal outcome is here defined as one where the aggregate extent of fiscal self-determination of states is reduced" (162). The second restraint is intention based. It requires that governments conduct an analysis of the proposed policy change along the following lines: "Suppose the benefits of a tax policy change in terms of attracting tax base from abroad did not exist. Would the country still pursue the policy under this hypothetical scenario? If yes, the policy is evidently not motivated by strategic considerations and therefore is legitimate" (164). They argue that imposing this two-part test on tax rules would force States to bear the full cost of their tax structures while not moving to complete harmonization (172).

In the end, accountability at both the domestic and international levels must be invoked and maintained by citizens. Without pressure from the ground up, parliaments have a tendency to go astray. The importance of a vibrant civil society that engages the research and advocacy community as well as the media cannot be overstated in this regard. Indeed, provision of quality education services strengthens the ability of citizens to hold their governments accountable, and this is largely made possible through tax revenues. This vital link should not be ignored.

Universality. Finally, the principle of universality is a key pillar for effective international tax cooperation. Universality does not demand uniformity; instead, it is an acknowledgment of the global shared agenda for sustainable development. Universality recognizes the interconnectedness of all countries in the need for raising revenues to fund sustainable development. Lack of opportunity, lack of safety, and lack of provision for basic human needs have dire spillover effects for bordering countries. Therefore, the challenge of achieving sustainable development should be internally owned and driven, but cannot be an exclusive responsibility.

Secondly, universality acknowledges the effects that one country's tax system and international tax norms have on all countries. Beggar-thy-neighbor tax regimes and secrecy provisions of one country erode the tax base of other countries and cannot be justified by lack of capacity or economic development objectives. Instead, they fuel a race to the bottom and provide hiding places for funds linked to crime and terrorism on a global scale. Moreover, international tax norms that benefit some countries over others, for example source countries versus residence countries, are not sustainable in the long term but instead spur more radical attempts to mobilize revenues, and overall create uncertainty for multinational commerce.

Finally, universality accepts the imperative for equal decision-making power in regard to global tax governance. Global representation on tax matters implicates fundamental issues of fairness and integrity of the global social contract. All countries, and all countries' citizens, are impacted by the current corporate taxation system, and all should have a say in promoting fair, effective, and sustainable tax solutions. An intergovernmental body with institutional legitimacy would be required to effectively respond to globalization with coherent global standards on tax. Although the developed nations (notably the U.S. and the U.K.) have argued that including everyone in the discussion would result in politicization of the tax system (and thus grave inefficiencies), this view ignores that tax is inherently political, as it involves issues of equity, justice, and the common good. Indeed, it was a key driver of the creation of democratic parliaments.

§2.03 CONCLUSION

This chapter has argued that establishing a normative framework for international tax cooperation is the first step in finding our way out of the thickets of tax competition. Regardless of one's views on tax competition, it is time to concentrate on the task of finding common ground on ways to work together to achieve the 2030 Agenda for Sustainable Development. This chapter has proposed three foundational principles for this effort: transparency, accountability, and universality. Further work could explore how to institutionalize these principles within the current IOs, the Platform for Collaboration on Tax, and possibly through new institutional settings.

REFERENCES

ActionAid. 2013. *Give Us a Break: How Big Companies Are Getting Tax-Free Deals.*
Adler, J.H. 2012. "Interstate Competition and the Race to the Top." *Harvard J. Law & Pub. Pol.* 35: 89-99.
Akerlof, G.A. 1970. "Uncertainty and the Market Mechanism." *The Q. J. Econ.* 84: 488-500.
Blank, J. 2014. "Reconsidering Corporate Tax Privacy." *N.Y.U. J. L. & Bus.* 11: 31-121.
Brennan, G., and J.M. Buchanan. 1980. *The Power to Tax: Analytical Foundations of a Fiscal Constitution.*
Dietsch, P., and T. Rixen. 2014. "Tax Competition and Global Background Justice." *J. Pol. Philosophy* 22: 150-170.
Independent Commission for the Reform of International Corporate Taxation. 2016. *Four Ways to Tackle International Tax Competition.*
International Finance Corporation. 2015. *Annual Report: Opportunity, Growth, Capital, Impact.*
International Monetary Fund. 2014. "Spillovers in International Corporate Taxation." IMF Policy Paper. Washington, DC: IMF.
International Monetary Fund; OECD; United Nations; World Bank. 2011. *Supporting the Development of More Effective Tax Systems – A Report to the G-20 Development Working Group.*
James, S. 2014. "Tax and Non-Tax Incentives and Investments: Evidence and Policy Implications." Washington, DC: World Bank.
Keen, M., and J. Edwards. 1996. "Tax Competition and Leviathan." *Eur. Econ. Rev.* 40: 113-134.
Keen, M., J. Edwards, and M. Mansour. 2010. "Revenue Mobilization in Sub-Saharan Africa: Challenges from Globalization II – Corporate Taxation." *Dev. Policy Rev.* 28: 573-596.
Klemm, A., and S. van Parys. 2012. "Empirical Evidence on the Effects of Tax Incentives." *Int'l Tax & Pub. Fin.* 19: 393.
Ocampo, J.A., and E.V. Fitzgerald. 2016. "*Doing Business* Should Stop Promoting Tax Competition." Project Syndicate. November 23, 2016.
OECD (Organization for Economic Co-Operation and Development). 1998. *Harmful Tax Competition: An Emerging Global Issue.* Paris: OECD.
OECD (Organization for Economic Co-Operation and Development). 2017. *Harmful Tax Practices – 2017 Progress Report on Preferential Regimes, Inclusive Framework on BEPS: Action 5.* Paris: OECD.
Sinn H.W. 1997. "The Selection Principle and Market Failure in Systems Competition." *J. Pub. Econ.* 66: 247-274.
Sörensen, P.B. 1990. "Issues in the Theory of International Tax Coordination." Bank of Finland Discussion Paper.

Stiglitz, J.E., and M. Pieth. 2016. *Overcoming the Shadow Economy.*
Tiebout, C.M. 1956. "A Theory of Local Expenditures." *J. Pol. Econ.* 64: 416-424.
UNIDO. 2011. *Africa Investor Report: Towards Evidence-Based Investment Promotion Strategies.*
Weingast, B.R. 1995. "The Economic Role of Political Institutions: Market-Preserving Federalism and Economic Development." 11: 1-31.
———. 2001. *Towards Global Tax Co-operation: Progress in Identifying and Eliminating Harmful Tax Practices.* Paris: OECD.
———. 2006. *The OECD's Project on Harmful Tax Practices: 2006 Update on Progress in Member Countries.* Paris: OECD.
———. 2015. *Countering Harmful Tax Practices More Effectively, Taking into Account Transparency and Substance.* Action 5 – 2015 Final Report, OECD/G20 Base Erosion and Profit Shifting Project. Paris: OECD.
———. 2015. *Options for Low Income Countries' Effective and Efficient Use of Tax Incentives for Investment: A Report to the G-20 Development Working Group by the IMF, OECD, UN and World Bank.*
———. 2016. *Concept Note for the Platform for Collaboration on Tax.*
———. 2016. *Secretary-General's Report to G20 Finance Ministers and Central Bank Governors.* Paris: OECD.

CHAPTER 3
Tax Competition: An Unleveled Playing Field for Developing Countries – Tax Cooperation to the Rescue

*Brigitte Alepin**

§3.01 BACKGROUND

This chapter brings multiple perspectives and instruments to bear on the issue of tax competition and the prospects for advancing tax cooperation as an alternative. In the first part of the chapter, we establish a conceptual grounding for the discussion. In the second part of the chapter, we build on these insights to explore a series of questions around: (1) the ability of the global tax system to address current challenges; (2) the imperative for greater fiscal collaboration; and (3) the prospects for actually achieving greater tax collaboration among developing countries, and what this effort will require. The chapter aims in particular at capturing the ideas and discussions generated by the representatives of international organizations who spoke at the conference.

§3.02 CONCEPTUAL GROUNDING

The notion that mobility of the international tax base prompts arbitrage by the taxpayer, which in turn sets in motion competitive tax cuts by national governments, leading to a race to the bottom, is not new. But there has been increased interest in this idea among policy makers and academics in the past two or three decades, in the wake of increased integration and globalization precipitating greater mobility of capital (Picciotto 1992). The extent to which increased mobility of capital and the desire to

---

* In collaboration with *Alexander Ezenagu*, Doctoral Candidate in International Tax Law at McGill University.

attract such capital has contributed to global tax competition has become a central concern for policy makers in both developed and developing economies. Michael Keen has been among the few pioneers in the discipline who have provided theoretical frameworks to think about global tax competition, the challenges it poses, and good practices. In a 2004 paper entitled "Is Tax Competition Harming Developing Countries More Than Developed?,"

Keen directs attention to how international tax competition is affecting developing and emerging economies in particular. Before that, discourse on tax competition was largely restricted to developed economies (Michael Keen and Alejandro Simone, 2015).

Keen notes that while tax reform in the wake of tax competition has reduced statutory tax rates in both developed and developing economies, in developing economies the tax base has not expanded enough to offset the revenue loss from the decline in statutory tax rates. In a 2015 paper, Keen et al., suggest that spillover effects – "the impact on a country's policy choices of tax changes abroad: tax competition" – are a greater concern for developing countries than for advanced countries (Ernesto Crivelli, Ruud de Mooji and Michael Keen 2015). This highlights the need to understand the challenges faced by developing countries in the current competition for tax bases.

In the following pages, we address both the positive and the normative aspects relating to: the reality and consequences of tax competition, the challenges countries face in addressing tax competition's effects, and the way forward.

§3.03 TAX COMPETITION IS REAL AND IMPORTANT

Keen (2008) defines tax competition as: "strategic tax-setting in a non-cooperative game between jurisdictions – whether countries or states or provinces – ... with each setting some parameters of its tax system in relation to the taxes set by others." It is often a reaction that sets off further episodes of tax changes across countries, as each seeks to improve its attractiveness for both real investment and as a jurisdiction into which to shift paper profits.

The first task in understanding the challenges of tax competition is recognizing the reality and scale of the associated losses. In spite of variations in approach, there is now clear evidence that tax competition permeates the global business and fiscal architecture and that costs are particularly significant for developing countries. Keen reports that tax competition coupled with the ease of global capital mobility has led to decline in statutory tax rates in both developed and developing countries, as shown in Figure 3.1.

Chapter 3: Tax Competition §3.03[A]

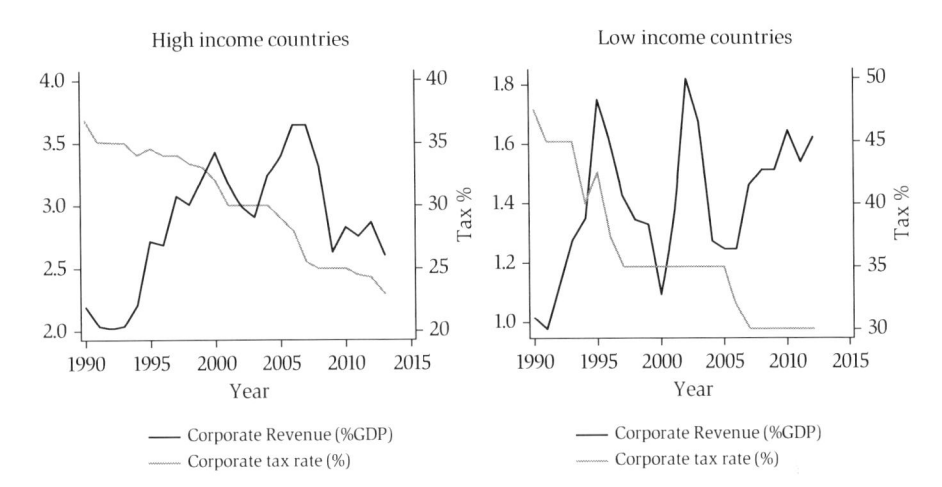

Figure 3.1   Developments in Corporate Tax Rates and Revenues

High income countries / Low income countries
— Corporate Revenue (%GDP)
------ Corporate tax rate (%)

There is a strong evidence that this is a result of strategic interactions between countries. One estimate suggests that the OECD countries react by changing their statutory rate of corporate income tax by about 0.7 percentage points for every 1 percentage point change in the statutory rate in the rest of the world.

Keen notes that this responsiveness to other jurisdictions' tax changes is even higher in developing economies. There, the trend is more discouraging, in that not only statutory tax rates but also corporate tax revenue as a percentage of GDP are declining. This contrasts with the trend in developed economies, which have seen an increase in the corporate tax base – likely at least in large part due to an increased share of profits in national income – that has more than offset the direct revenue loss from reductions in statutory rates. In addition to the erratic changes in corporate revenue in developing countries, the decline in revenue due to tax competition has been severe. In poorer economies, moreover, where alternatives to the corporate income tax as sources of revenue are meager, VATs are often under stress, personal income taxation weak, and tariffs needing to be further reduced rather than increased. While tax competition thus poses a significant challenge for all countries, the stakes are especially high for developing economies.

[A]   **Policies to Address Tax Competition**

The fundamental concern with international tax competition is that, when each country simply pursues its own national interest, this will drive effective tax rates so low that there would be a collective benefit to all from raising them. Some, it should be noted, see this downward pressure on rates and revenue as a good thing, serving to constrain governments inherently inclined, in pursuing their own rather than wider national interests, to raise too much revenue – and this remains an issue of contention.

33

The question arises, in any event: If there are indeed a range of alternative tax combinations that could leave all countries better off than in the event of a non-cooperative outcome, why have they not adopted such strategies?

One reason is that, even if there is a collective, global loss from tax competition, some countries – which theory suggests will in many cases be small countries – may be winners. This makes it challenging to solicit political support and commitment across all countries involved. In principle (and perhaps requiring side payments to countries that would otherwise lose from coordination), countries could negotiate a coordinated and cooperative scheme which would ensure that all countries gain from the arrangement. With that in mind, exactly what kinds of forms of international tax coordination are appropriate, and might actually work?

Keen highlights that harmonization – in the sense of complete uniformity of tax systems and rates – is certainly not necessary for mutual gain from such coordination. Harmonization would likely imply considerable inefficiency (and evidently raise political hackles), given the extent to which countries differ in the circumstances and attitudes to taxation and public spending. Keen provides a few alternative recommendations for further discussion and debate in the effort to provide tools for designing coordinated courses of action:

- *Minimum Tax Rates* – One possibility is for countries to agree on some minimum tax rate that none will go below. The attraction of minimum rates is that all countries may gain due to the restriction on the race to the bottom: high-tax countries gain because this makes them less vulnerable to low-tax competition, letting them set higher rates; and even countries required to raise their tax rate benefit because the higher rate that others set limits the revenue loss they would otherwise suffer in raising their rate. There are already some examples of minimum rates, including the West African Economic and Monetary Union's (WAEMU) exercise of a minimum corporate tax rate of 25% and the agreement on minimum excise duties within both the EU and the WAEMU independently.
- *Preferential/Multiple Tax Regimes* – Countries may resort to multiple tax rules for different types of activities, typically setting lower taxes for highly mobile activities, which has the advantage of lessening competition on the most mobile of tax bases. This observation – which runs counter to the notion that special regimes are inherently harmful – needs to be tempered, however, with recognition of the governance problems and other distortions that can arise when departing from the standard principle of applying a common tax treatment to all sectors. Much more thought needs to be given to the notion of "harmful tax practices," so as to understand better precisely what the characteristics are that determine whether or not the spillover effect of some particular tax measure damages others.
- *Regional Coordination* – In the absence of an international agency to coordinate and enforce such contracts on a large scale, existing sub-regional frameworks could be used to coordinate tax policies. However, coordination at the regional bloc may expose the entire region to adverse tax competition from

countries outside the bloc or those who choose to remain outside the coordination. Such adverse tax competition may portend more losses than benefits for the region.

[B] Summing Up

When discussing tax competition, three questions are important: Is it happening? Is it a significant problem? And, if so, what are the challenges in addressing it and the potential policy responses?

There seems little doubt that international tax competition as a result of strategic interactions between countries is resulting in tax structures that are inefficient from a global perspective, with an equilibrium marked by inappropriately low tax rates on capital. The consequences of this are especially stark for developing countries.

Though we have learned much about international tax competition, there are still uncertainties – for example as to which types of tax practices are harmful and which not. There is also need to understand more fully the precise risks that developing countries face – which seem more urgent even than those in advanced economies – and how risks can be addressed.

The central policy suggestion is the need for further coordination and cooperation across countries in addressing the problems associated with tax competition – which is much easier said (as it has been many times) than done. Recent advances in the exchange of taxpayer-specific information between countries and in the OECD-G20 project on Base Erosion and Profit Shifting (BEPS) have shifted the policy discourse on the need for coordination. But it remains to be seen how far these developments will lead.

The remainder of this chapter will build on the conceptual foundations and lines of policy inquiry proposed by Keen. A key objective of our discussion will be to shed light on topics where more analytical work is needed to understand how improved design and enforcement of tax policy, as well as better tax cooperation, can support developing countries. This chapter also presents possible solutions to global tax cooperation challenges. It reflects the views of several expert representatives of international organizations working on taxation. These experts explore the effects of tax competition on the ability of developing countries to enforce a legitimate contract between governments and taxpayers. They also present perspectives on how global tax rules could be improved in order to keep pace with a rapidly changing global business environment, without further aggravating income disparities between developing and advanced countries.

§3.04 THE ABILITY OF THE GLOBAL TAX SYSTEM TO ADDRESS CURRENT CHALLENGES

After the end of World War I, international trade, which was gaining attention in the nineteenth century and had led to trade, shipping, and aviation agreements, expanded as countries were committed to rebuilding their economies and territories after the damage caused by war. These expansionary plans and the attendant cross-border trade meant that states were further determined to secure and increase their revenue streams. Furthermore, multinational companies, which had become the main vehicles of trade, were wary of double taxation of their income, potentially arising from trade engagements with more than one country: their home state and the host state. These concerns brought countries together and, in the end, they agreed on the prevention of double taxation, enshrining the commitment in international tax treaties. All stakeholders agreed that taxation and the risk of double taxation presented hindrances to economic relations between countries.

The League of Nations, which took over the work of the International Chamber of Commerce in this area, commenced efforts in 1923 in response to the mandate to provide a global standard for income allocation arising from cross-border trade and services. The League of Nations opted for the primacy of residence taxation over source taxation in the allocation of taxing rights. This choice meant that residual income was allocated to residence countries, while source countries were left to collect withholding taxes on certain categories of income and where permanent establishment was established in the state. In addition, the experts recommended that companies are always treated as separate entities rather than integrated entities for the purpose of taxation. The result was that companies treated transactions with affiliated companies as if the latter were independent, while being expected to negotiate on market terms–arm's length pricing.

An additional consequence of this approach was the creation of a platform for multinational companies that earns a substantial portion of their income in low- or no-tax jurisdictions, through base erosion and profit shifting. The argument quickly moved from double taxation to double non-taxation. It became obvious to the international community that companies manipulated international transactions, for example through transfer prices, to pay low or no tax in the jurisdictions from which they operated, while shifting profits to low-tax jurisdictions, thus eroding the tax base in countries with high tax rates. The tax rules designed for manufacturers, with physical presence and products, became unsuitable for the current international tax system and international trade. Such manipulations tend to obscure the fact that international trade and collaboration have been key to rapid economic development globally, especially since the Second World War. While there are challenges with the distribution of benefits from cross-border trade among countries, closer economic ties between countries are part of the answer, not the problem. A concerted effort to bring everyone together to address the issues of tax competition is needed to achieve a fair global tax system.

§3.05 CONSEQUENCES OF ARCHAIC TAX RULES AND DOUBLE NON-TAXATION

The current OECD tax model dates back to the League of Nations and, in today's global trade and investment climate, it presents opportunities for rent-seeking, taking advantage of different tax regimes worldwide. The model also provides substantial advantages to multinational enterprises (MNEs) over non-MNEs. The former can shift profits among their subsidiaries, thereby raising vertical equity issues. An unintended consequence may be to put national tax jurisdictions under economic stress, as governments may have to bridge the revenue gap by taxing middle- or low-income earners more heavily than they would otherwise.

The growing mobility of capital and further integration of world economies constitute important challenges for global governance (Peter Dietsch 2015). As recalled by Victoria Perry, "International transactions creating tax challenges are very different today than a hundred years ago, where trans-border issues mainly related to the exchange of physical goods, contrary to today's e-commerce, where financial transactions, and intellectual property rights transfer, for example, occur on a day-to-day basis."

The current international tax system presents a dysfunctional reality, leading to global tax wars among governments[1] and between taxpayers and tax administrations.[2] The system has also spurred direct tax competition among developing countries.[3]

Manuel Montes, in adopting the definition espoused by Tax Justice Network, defines tax competition as: "Jurisdictions' offering facilities that enable people or entities to escape or undermine the laws of other jurisdictions, through secrecy facilities and facilities that disguise the beneficial ownership jurisdictions." Montes identifies three different areas of tax competition: tax competition among developed countries; tax competition between developed and developing countries; and tax competition among developing countries themselves.

Developing countries are particularly vulnerable to tax competition, as corporate taxes tend to account for a larger share of their tax revenue than in developed economies. Recent studies seem to support this fact. A 2011 joint report by the IMF, OECD, UN, and World Bank, under the auspices of the G-20, claimed that, "Many resource-rich countries still struggle to design and implement fiscal regimes that are not only transparent but also capable of securing a reasonable share...." The report further noted that, regarding developing countries, "Profit-shifting by multinationals is an increasing concern; strengthening capacity and legislative frameworks is important, which will require a greater engagement between LDCs, developed countries, and business" (IMF et al. 2011). Tax Justice Network (2013) reported that, "Even when

---

1. *See* for example the Apple dispute over tax revenues between the U.S. and the EU.
2. As the many cases of transfer mispricing audited by tax authorities worldwide indicate.
3. By offering tax advantages to companies that want to invest in their territories, governments in developing countries are competing among themselves for investments that would be made anyway.

natural resource revenues are excluded, corporate income taxes account for some 15 percent of all tax revenues" for developing countries.

The UN Conference on Trade and Development (UNCTAD), in a 2015 publication, claims that developing countries lose USD 100 billion per year due to tax avoidance by multinational companies and as much as USD 300 billion in total lost development finance (*see* Tax Justice Network 2015). Between 1970 and 2010, capital flight through tax evasion and tax avoidance schemes stood at USD 814 billion, exceeding the official development aid of USD 659 billion and foreign direct investment of USD 306 billion for the same period (Boyce and Ndikumana 2012).

Using tax-planning schemes such as "*double Irish, Dutch sandwich,*" companies are able to move the bulk of their revenues to low- or no-tax jurisdictions, such as Ireland, Luxembourg, and Bermuda.

According to Oxfam America (2014), the United States (U.S.) alone lost an estimated USD 90 billion in 2008 to the practice of shifting profits overseas. This represented about 30% of the country's corporate income tax revenues or three times the federal budget for foreign aid.

As concrete examples of MNE tax avoidance in the United Kingdom (U.K.), in 2009, Barclay's Bank declared global profits of GBP 4.6 billion, but paid only GBP 113 million in corporate tax, an effective rate of 2.4%. Similarly, Google was accused of paying just GBP 10 million in U.K. corporate tax, despite having generated GBP 11.5 billion between 2006 and 2011. Starbucks, for its part, though posting sales of GBP 400 million in 2012, paid no corporate tax. Amazon paid GBP 11.9 million in corporate tax in 2014, even though it made GBP 5.3 billion in sales in the U.K.

Another recent example would be the European Court of Justice (ECJ) decision in the case involving Apple and the Irish government, where the ECJ ruled that Apple owed the Irish government EUR 13 billion in tax non-remittance attributable to Ireland's state aid program.

Thus, we are faced with a global issue: finding the balance between the fiscal sovereignty of states and the need to achieve a fair allocation of income, where taxes are paid in jurisdictions according to where income and value-added are generated. Tax policy remains largely a sovereignty issue and governs the economic and political relations with other countries. This discussion is important for developing countries which, with their smaller, stretched economies, are hit the hardest by tax avoidance. This further hampers development, increases inequality, and contributes to poor provision of public services.

§3.06 LEADERSHIP FROM INTERNATIONAL ORGANIZATIONS

Curbing tax evasion and tax avoidance globally depends on cooperation among countries' tax authorities.[4] This cooperation is partly facilitated by the international organizations that provide assistance to states in strengthening their tax systems. These organizations create guidelines, tools, and technical assistance programs to help

---

4. http://www.un.org/press/en/2015/gaef3438.doc.htm.

their members with the design of a tax system capable of financing the necessary level of public spending in an efficient and equitable way, taking into account the international context (Tanzi and Zee 2000). In addition, international organizations serve as a platform to foster global change by interacting with developed countries and influencing their decisions affecting global trade and investments, and particularly their transactions with lower-income countries.

In developing countries, the challenges of tax policy design are more difficult than in advanced economies (Tanzi and Zee 2000). These challenges include: raising enough revenue to finance essential expenditures; promoting equitable income distribution; and minimizing distortions to economic activity without deviating from international norms. For countries that are becoming more integrated in the international economy, the adequate design of the tax system is fundamental.

International organizations are addressing base erosion and profit shifting in both residence and source countries through regimes such as anti-avoidance principles, controlled foreign corporations (CFC) rules, transfer pricing guidelines, exchange of information agreements, and stringent disclosure requirements. Recent actions include the design of transfer-pricing guidelines and providing support to implement exchange-of-information agreements and disclosure requirements.

However, several tax experts argue that global tax policy should move from the current separate-entity and transfer-pricing methodology of income allocation to a unitary taxation and formulary-apportionment methodology of income taxation (similar to the U.S. experience).

[A] Transfer Pricing Guidelines

The OECD's Transfer Pricing Guidelines for Multinational Enterprises and Tax Administrations (the "OECD Guidelines"), which were first issued in 1979 and most recently revised in 2017, provide guidance for application of the arm's length principle. The guidelines detail a nine-step process for conducting an arm's length analysis, which includes implementation of a comparability study using one of five comparability methods (three so-called traditional transactions methods and two transactional-profit methods) to determine what an arm's length price would be. The steps culminate in a comparability adjustment, and a determination of an arm's length price. These guidelines have been adopted by most jurisdictions and are reference tools used by most tax authorities in the assessment and adjustment of taxable profits.

The OECD, in conjunction with G20 members,[5] also initiated the Base Erosion and Profit Shifting (BEPS) Project[6] to address the risk of transfer price abuses. The BEPS project is to address the loopholes seen in the existing system. A key aspect of the

---
5. The G20 members in their St. Petersburg Declaration called for changes to the international tax laws in order to ensure that profits are taxed where economic activities occur and value is created.
6. This is particularly helpful for developing countries, where tax revenues as a percentage of GDP are around half of that in OECD countries. Governments across the world rely on five primary sources of tax revenue: personal income taxes, corporate taxes, sales and excise taxes, property and wealth taxes, and payroll taxes.

BEPS Action Plan is country-by-country reporting (CBCR), which "provides a template for multinational enterprises (MNEs) to report annually and for each tax jurisdiction in which they do business the information set out therein."[7] The OECD hopes that, with CBCR, tax administrations where a company operates will get aggregate information annually, starting with 2016 accounts, relating to the global allocation of income and taxes paid, together with other indicators of the location of economic activity within the MNE group. The system will also cover information about which entities do business in a particular jurisdiction and the business activities each entity engages in. The information will be collected by the country of residence of the MNE group, and will then be exchanged through exchange-of-information mechanisms supported by relevant agreements. The first exchanges have started in 2017 and will continue in 2018, using 2016 data. The expectation is that tax authorities will thereby find it easier to recognize and tackle profit-shifting and transfer-pricing abuses.

While the CBCR under the BEPS project has garnered praise, skepticism surrounds its implementation and effective execution. Some have argued that CBCR reports should not be publicly accessible and worry that the more extensive EU plan for public release of the reports would jeopardize the BEPS project agreement altogether. Also, the threshold of EUR 750 million for MNEs to comply with the CBCR may be exclusionary, thus leading to calls for considerable reduction of the EUR 750 million threshold for MNEs to engage in CBCR, claiming that the threshold risks excluding smaller but substantial taxpayers from disclosure.

Another concern is the capacity of developing countries to take advantage of the opportunities present in the CBCR plan. When countries are not able to participate in the CBCR action plan, this may provide further tax maneuvering opportunities for tax planners and MNEs. The OECD, on its part, is working to ensure that the plan's implementation is inclusive, to help countries get to the "right level" and gain access to the information they need. The World Bank is equally collaborating with the OECD and the IMF on the preparation of a G20-mandated toolkit to help developing countries deal with the lack of comparable data in transfer pricing as well as with information asymmetry. Other simplification measures that establish reasonable benchmarks and shift the burden of proof to taxpayers, in order to help administrators lacking information and capacity to establish effective administration of multinational enterprise transactions, have been equally advocated.

[B] Automatic Exchange of Information

Other strides accomplished by the OECD include the multilateral competent authority agreement (MCAA) and the Global Forum. The MCAA, a multilateral framework agreement, provides a standardized and efficient mechanism to facilitate the automatic exchange of information in accordance with the Standard for Automatic Exchange of Financial Information in Tax Matters (the Standard), thus avoiding the need for several bilateral agreements to be concluded.

---

7. http://www.oecd.org/tax/beps/country-by-country-reporting.htm.

The MCAA enables joint audit and automatic exchange of information, thereby promoting transparency and accessibility of information.

[C] Stringent Disclosure Requirements

Another important action undertaken by the OECD involves the peer review processes developed by the Global Forum on Transparency and Exchange of Information (Global Forum). The Global Forum, which 135 jurisdictions have already joined, offers robust peer review that ensures high standards of transparency and information sharing. Perez-Navarro further claims that, "Through all these OECD initiatives, the OECD is leveling the playing field for developing countries, as these countries can now get relevant information from all other signatories to the agreements." There is renewed confidence in the international tax system and calls for optimism. The OECD BEPS project offers encouraging signs for increased tax collection by developing countries. World Bank data reveal that estimated profit shifting by MNEs is reduced by about 50% after a country introduces mandatory transfer-pricing documentation requirements.

Even if international organizations have done much to improve the current international tax system, particularly in recent years, the palliatives introduced by the OECD and other stakeholders fall short of effectively addressing the tax evasion and avoidance practices of multinational companies. This attempt at improving source taxation through the BEPS Action Plans, while protecting the primacy of residence taxation, seems to be plagued with difficulties.

One major reason for this is that the OECD "allegedly, continuously shies away from addressing the right to tax." As constantly posited, developing countries want to base their tax revenues on the "source income," because it allows them to obtain tax revenues from the local operations of foreign companies. While, in contrast, countries of the North want to tax the headquarters' earnings of their companies. This conflicting interest is yet to be addressed in the OECD BEPS project by design and self-interest, this conceptual chasm is not.

Thus, it becomes important to once again undertake structured and collaborative efforts to consider viable alternatives to current practices. The OECD agrees, alongside other stakeholders, that overhauling the global tax system and its practices is fundamental if we are to deliver stronger growth worldwide in the years to come.

§3.07 TAX COMPETITION AND THE NEED FOR BETTER FISCAL COOPERATION IN A GLOBALIZED WORLD

Capital mobility enabled by contemporary globalization puts significant pressure on countries and their citizens to make fiscal choices. With the mobility of capital, sovereign countries lower their tax rates on income earned by foreigners within their borders and provide special tax advantages to some taxpayers, in order to attract both portfolio and direct investment (Avi-Yonah 2001). Tax competition, in turn, threatens to undermine the collection capacity associated with individual and corporate income taxes, which potentially remain major sources of revenue (in terms of percentage of total revenue collected) for all modern states.

Since the mid-twentieth century, many countries at all income levels have granted tax incentives to taxpayers/investors, while also reducing overall tax rates in some cases, on the expectation of attracting new investors (Lent 1967). At times, these incentives were justified as compensation for above-normal capital risks, enhancements of the business climate, or as a way to promote strategic sectors or products. As mentioned, globalization and the mobility of capital increased, and tax competition between countries cause a race to the bottom. This increased mobility has been the result of technological changes and the relaxation of exchange controls (Avi-Yonah 2001). By reducing the ability of developing countries to reach their revenue potential, this type of tax competition impedes long-term economic development and often creates negative spillovers between countries. Ultimately, the winners are those who benefit from a reduced tax rate on an investment they would have made anyway, while the benefits for society as a whole have yet to be accurately measured in many countries.

The growing (mis)use of tax incentives by developing countries to attract FDI has far-reaching effects for their fragile economies. Such tax incentives are often inefficient and ineffective and in some cases associated with corruption. A World Bank survey reveals that most investors would have made their investment in developing countries, such as Rwanda, Mozambique, without the tax incentives granted. To correct the problem of tax incentives, greater transparency and judicious exercise of discretionary powers in the administration of tax incentives, must be ensured and administration of tax incentives should be the sole concern of the Ministry of Finance or a government unit.

Moving away from tax incentives, other issues affecting revenue optimization by developing countries, include: basic problems in the design of the value-added tax (VAT); extending the reach of the personal income tax (PIT); achieving appropriate excises; and ineffective revenue administration. Also, there is the issue of efficiency on the part of the revenue authorities who are yet to optimize their capacities for addressing tax evasion and avoidance at the country level. The World Bank, on its part, has committed to helping developing countries establish "reasonable" systems [systems that are appropriately designed, without creating excess burdens on the private sector.] Other strategies to improve revenue mobilization include: harnessing "tools commensurate with administrative capacity, such as rebuttable presumptions and the use of the popular six method transfer-pricing methodology for the extractive sector." Also, tax aid given by developing countries to developed countries, in the form of incentives and tax holidays, constitutes tools for tax competition among developing countries with adverse effects. Discouraging the use of tax incentives and holidays by developing countries may contribute to leveling the international playing field.

Furthermore, developing countries should be prudent before signing tax treaties. Over 3,000 bilateral tax treaties are active at the present time, and one-third of them have been signed by developing countries (OECD 2014). If those bilateral treaties are not properly renegotiated to reflect current realities, they may not be favorable to developing countries. Moreover, there is evidence that signing tax treaties does not always result in greater foreign direct investment (IMF 2014). Countries may face the possibility of significant revenue losses caused by treaty abuse.

In addition, the use of withholding taxes by developing countries should be further encouraged as they aid the protection of the tax bases of developing countries. Withholding taxes are relatively easy to manage and strengthen the negotiations with multinational companies, if for no other reason than that the government holds the cash. This taxation instrument tends to be relatively simple in its structure, and the language normally used by tax authorities around the world tends to be similar (Pogge and Mehta 2016). Withholding taxes on payments for interest, royalties, dividends, and/or services are already used in developing countries. However, these taxes can often be reduced, even eliminated, through withholding tax limitations or indirectly through tax jurisdiction restrictions.

§3.08 ACHIEVEMENTS AND PERSISTENT CHALLENGES: PROSPECTS FOR TAX COOPERATION AMONG DEVELOPING COUNTRIES

Much remains to be done and, despite the unprecedented level of cooperation among countries all over the world, we are far from a fair global tax system. There is general consensus that the international tax system must be adapted to today's reality, and that fixing it is in everyone's interest. However, reaching a consensus on the appropriate measures requires more cooperation.

There are heightened calls for the establishment of an intergovernmental tax body within the UN. However, this proposal has also been strongly challenged, for example at the 2015 Addis Ababa Conference on development finance. A faction, mostly from the Global North, believes that the OECD should continue to set international standards. They maintain that it is not possible for the UN to attain the level of tax expertise required to establish tax standards, coupled with the fact that the UN has other very difficult work to do at the moment.

Another faction advocates for an intergovernmental tax body within the UN, vehemently opposing claims by those who believe that the UN does not possess the requisite tax expertise to lead the discussions. They call the argument "quite weak and quite false," asserting that if the UN were to put together a platform for tax cooperation, developing countries would send their best experts. It is believed that an intergovernmental tax body within the UN could better bridge the fundamental differences between the Global North (where most international companies are headquartered) and the Global South (whose interest lies in obtaining a fair share of the tax revenues arising from the operations of international companies in its territory).

While this faction, mostly experts from developing countries, sees an urgent need for global cooperation on tax issues, its members believe the necessary discussions and decisions should take shape within the UN and involve all governments. They should not be pursued within exclusive groups like the OECD. The UN is better positioned to address tax competition mechanisms, largely championed by MNEs in the Global North such as: secrecy facilities, provisions, and jurisdictions; secret tax agreements;

low withholding-tax agreements; patent boxes; and regulatory connivance. The OECD's core principle of eliminating tax barriers to cross-border trade and investment contradicts developing countries' desire to receive a fair share of revenue for the exploration and exploitation of their resources. The OECD remains an exclusive membership organization, wherein members negotiate with each other and reach agreements on standards of tax cooperation. This is in contrast to a UN tax body, where all stakeholders would have access to the agenda, the deliberations, and the decision-making.

The OECD in acknowledging that only G20 countries were included initially in the BEPS process, claims that this was done because these countries represent 90% of the economy. It further emphasizes ongoing inclusive projects by the OECD, further reiterating that developing countries are now welcome to implement the BEPS project outcomes, and can work on the remaining BEPS issues, on an equal footing.

Reacting to this late inclusiveness push from the OECD, it is argued that the claim by the OECD of inviting developing countries to participate in the implementation of BEPS "on an equal footing," but according to rules exclusively defined by OECD members, has simply had the effect of increasing developing countries' sensitivity to intolerable tax governance imbalances and intensifying their efforts at self-organization to counter the situation. This view is held, notwithstanding the efforts of global bodies, to amplify the concerns of developing countries. In 2015, the World Bank/IMF Joint Initiative for Strengthening Tax Systems in Developing Countries was launched to strengthen the voice of developing countries in the global debate on tax issues. Through the initiative, the World Bank and the IMF are assembling tools and guidance aimed at addressing developing-economy needs, working to push the concerns of developing countries to the fore and boosting regional cooperation as a counteraction to destructive tax competition.

It is only reasonable that any attempt to reform the global tax system must be inclusive of all jurisdictions from the start, since tax issues have gained global status. Likewise, human rights and public-interest policies must be part of efforts to reform the international tax system and mitigate tax competition. This is because tax evasion and avoidance have today become human rights abuses of interest to the whole world. Thus, inclusiveness is a required condition for arriving at any meaningful reform.

One thing appears certain: There is currently a lack of trust between developed and developing countries in tax matters, and the OECD, perhaps understandably, is the scapegoat for this state of affairs. Thus, to achieve a fair tax system in today's globalized world demands renewed cooperation. For today's borderless financial world to thrive and be fair, the other side of the competition coin is greater cooperation. Delivering an international tax system that supports the efficient operation of global markets is an important part of achieving the fair allocation of taxing rights.

Finally, how developing countries will get a fair deal on tax competition and tax justice is an important question. Tax cooperation is likely to be an idea whose time has come. Developed countries must now "walk the talk" of democracy, good governance, and the rule of law, and support the establishment of an intergovernmental tax body, with the active involvement and participation of the UN. In April 2016, the IMF, the UN, the World Bank Group, and the OECD agreed to set up a global platform to support governments in addressing tax challenges in a better-coordinated manner. While the creation of this platform is laudable, the four organizations must contribute to changing the global tax scene in order to provide a level playing field for developing countries.

REFERENCES

Avi-Yonah, Reuven S. 2001. "Globalization and Tax Competition: Implications for Developing Countries." *Law Quad. Notes* 44 (2): 60-65.

Boyce, James and Ndikumana, Leonce. 2012. "Capital Flight From sub-Saharan African Countries: Updated Estimates, 1970 – 2010." PERI Research Report.

Crivelli, Ernesto, Ruud A. De Mooij, and Michael Keen. 2016. "Base Erosion, Profit Shifting and Developing Countries." *Finanz Archiv* 72: 268-301.

Dietsch, Peter. 2015. *The Ethics of Tax Competition*. Oxford: Oxford University Press.

IMF Fiscal Affairs Department. 2014. "Spillovers in International Corporate Taxation." Washington, DC: IMF.

IMF, OECD, UN, and World Bank. 2011. "Supporting the Development of More Effective Tax Systems: A Report to the G-20 Development Working Group by the IMF, OECD, UN, and World Bank." Available at: http://www.oecd.org/ctp/48993634.pdf.

Keen, Michael. 2008. "Tax Competition." In Durlauf, Steven N. and Lawrence E. Blume, eds. *The New Palgrave Dictionary of Economics*, Volume 6. Basingstoke: Palgrave Macmillan.

Lent, George. 1967. "Tax Incentives for Investment in Developing Countries." *IMF Staff Papers* 14(2): 249-323.

OECD (Organization for Economic Co-operation and Development). 2014. "Part 1 of a Report to the G20 Development Working Group on the Impact of BEPS in Low Income Countries." Paris: OECD.

Oxfam America. 2014. "You vs. Big Business: Will G20 World Leaders Take Your Side on Global Tax Policy?" Oxfam America Politics of Poverty blogs. Available at: http://politicsofpoverty.oxfamamerica.org/2014/11/g20-corporate-tax-evasion/.

Pogge, Thomas. and Mehta, Krishen. 2016. *Global Tax Fairness*. Oxford: Oxford University Press.

Tanzi, Vito and Howell H. Zee. 2000. "Tax Policy for Emerging Markets: Developing Countries." IMF Working Paper. Washington, DC: IMF.

Tax Justice Network. 2013. "Ten Reasons to Defend the Corporation Tax." Available at: http://www.taxjustice.net/wp-content/uploads/2013/04/Ten_Reasons_Full_Report.pdf#13.

Tax Justice Network. 2015. "UNCTAD: multinational tax avoidance costs developing countries $ 100 billion + " Available at: http://www.taxjustice.net/2015/03/26/unctad-multinational-tax-avoidance-costs-developing-countries-100-billion/.

CHAPTER 4
Taxing Multinationals in a Globalized World

Lyne Latulippe[*]

Multinational corporations play a predominant role in trade and investment. As global economic integration intensifies, multinationals' taxation raises a number of issues, and alternatives to tax these corporations are increasingly being discussed. This chapter presents the discussion around the international tax system through the analysis of the paradigm behind it. The chapter first briefly summarizes the debate around corporate taxation and the arguments concerning the consequences and desirability of maintaining such components of tax systems. Then, failures and challenges of the current system to tax multinational corporations are presented in conjunction with the analysis of the dominant international tax paradigm and its possible evolution or replacement.

The fundamental flaws of the current system lie in the fact that multinational corporations are considered as separate entities for taxation purposes, and that, in a global digital world, it is problematic to compute and locate their taxable income. Administrative issues, such as access to relevant tax information and enforcement, also pose important challenges, particularly to developing countries. Structural issues, resulting from an environment where countries use tax policy to compete to attract investment, increase problems with multinationals' taxation and limit the international cooperation necessary to the functioning of the system. The chapter also discusses a range of solutions and their potential impact on the evolution or replacement of the current system and, in particular, it introduces two alternatives developed to address its problems.

---

[*] The author is grateful to Julie St-Cerny Gosselin for great research assistance and to the Research Chair on Taxation and Public Finance for financial support.

§4.01 CORPORATE TAXATION AND GLOBALIZATION

A brief look at some of the arguments in favor and against corporate taxation helps to put into perspective the current debate surrounding this form of taxation and to better understand how internationalization alters this analysis.[1]

First, corporate taxation is an efficient way to collect taxes as it limits collection efforts to a relatively small number of important actors, instead of numerous individuals. It is also a policy tool allowing states to structure, orient, and influence corporations' economic activities.

An argument against corporate taxation is that ultimately only individuals support the price of corporate tax. However, it is not clear which individuals, i.e., shareholders, customers, or employees, bear the burden of the corporate taxes and in which circumstances and proportions. Consequences of lowering existing corporate tax rates may be felt differently among these groups, which are not symmetric to the effects of increasing such taxation. The impact of a reduction or increase is also expected to be different in short and long term.

More generally, corporations exist, generate profit, and accumulate wealth because of the legal and economic framework offered by states (legal entities, protection of property rights, market access, infrastructure and more). In comparison with personal income earners, it could also be argued that corporations have the ability to accumulate more gains due to their corporate structure and economies of scale. Taxes on profit may be seen as a price to be paid for the opportunity to benefit from those elements in order to earn such profit. A well-entrenched perspective identifies shareholder value maximization as the sole purpose of corporations. Therefore, taxes are seen as an appropriation of private property (profits) by the state and corporations are justified to reduce this cost by any legal means. An alternative discourse emphasizes that corporations are embedded in society and they have a broader purpose, which takes into account all stakeholders. This allows seeing taxes differently and may justify corporations and their directors not to use tax planning solely based on an objective to reduce their tax obligations. Furthermore, there are increasing public pressures for corporate actors to adopt a socially responsible behavior, including paying corporate taxes in countries where they operate or benefit from infrastructure (and government-financed public goods such as security, peace or justice), workforce, resources, networks, and/or markets.

A counterargument can be made that corporations (including multinationals) already contribute to society through job creation, development of technology and more generally through the economic growth they generate. On a similar note, the rejection of corporate taxes may be based on the economic distortions generated by this form of taxation. In this perspective, corporate taxes are seen as reducing productivity,

---

1. For more analysis, Mintz, Jack. "The Corporation Tax: A Survey." *Fiscal Studies* 16.4 (1995): 23-68; Avi-Yonah, Reuven S. "Corporations, Society, and the State: A Defense of the Corporate Tax." *Virginia Law Review* (2004): 1193-1255; Brauner, Yariv. "Non-Sense Tax: A Reply to New Corporate Income Tax Advocacy." *Michigan State Law Review* (2008): 591. The author expresses a special thanks to Marc Naccache for prior research assistance on this topic.

investment, and jobs, which is why lowering corporate tax rates is advocated in order to foster global economic growth. No matter how relevant these arguments may sound, it disregards the fact that these investment decisions are dictated solely by the interest of multinationals, which select the industry, research, jobs, location and so on to invest in. While the interest of the multinational may sometimes coincide with or incorporate that of society as a whole, this is certainly not always the case. In addition, local job creation, as well as the distribution of gains within the corporations and how they benefit workers, is a private sector decision, mostly driven by business goals, which may or may not be conducive to growth and equity in a particular host country where the corporation operates. Furthermore, the increased use of financial products, technology and artificial intelligence will continue to widen the gap between the wealth accumulated by multinationals and the economic benefits to society. In that sense, corporate income taxes should be seen as fiscal instruments to contribute to the financing of social programs and public expenditures, public policy choices that are likely to differ from the priorities of corporations and be beneficial for citizens and society as a whole.

The internationalization of business raises an additional question: how much should be paid in taxes and where should those taxes be paid? In the case of domestic-only corporations, taxes are paid to the government in the country where the corporation is operating. Once corporations have activities in many countries, the portion of taxes paid to each jurisdiction needs to be determined. However, where this contribution should be paid is not always obvious, because it may be unclear which proportion of profits arises from which country. And more fundamentally, this raises internation equity considerations, which are of particular importance in reference to lower income countries. If designed according to the ability to pay, the taxation of multinational corporations can be used to stimulate equitable growth and income distribution by avoiding unfair competition vis-à-vis domestic companies honoring their tax obligations, and by implicitly allowing for a transfer of income to lower income segments of the population.

Although an equity-efficiency trade-off is always to be considered, in today's world economic distortions are mainly created because tax rates and systems vary across countries, influencing the allocation of resources and corporate governance, not always towards what is most efficient regionally and globally speaking. Consideration should be given to the fact that an increasing proportion of multinationals' profits are based on rents (especially those benefiting from natural resources) and are generated based on, for example, market power, intellectual property and allocation of profits. Furthermore, the internationalization of businesses adds to the pressures for lower corporate tax given the dominant competitiveness argument. In this context, global cooperation and coordination regarding corporate taxation are constrained.

It is beyond the scope of this chapter to provide an in-depth analysis to explain the resilience of corporate taxation in domestic tax system and its adaptation to the international dimension. A compromise emerging from these contradictory perspectives, tainted by political factors and the need for tax revenues, may have allowed some form of corporate tax component to remain an integral part of tax policy for the past century. The rejection of this form of taxation altogether does not seem to be a foreseeable outcome though. Furthermore, the rise of public awareness of the issues of corporate taxes paid (or not) by multinationals provides further support for this form of taxation at the corporate level. Therefore, if tax systems continue to formally include a corporate tax component, it is essential that it should not informally or formally allow corporations, especially multinationals, to reduce their tax obligations and to avoid paying taxes altogether.

§4.02 PARADIGM, PRINCIPLES AND CHALLENGES

To further the analysis of problems and issues, it is relevant to evaluate them in light of the principles of corporate taxation at the national and international level. Can the difficulties be overcome with administrative or incremental adjustments or are more fundamental changes required?

Corporate taxation had originally taken the legal entity as the unit of taxation, and the tax base has generally been considered the corporate "profits." Since last century, businesses have evolved, and their structures have been adapted to increased possibilities to access markets and move people and capital around the globe. This trend has accelerated in the past decades because of the growing role of technologies and intangibles as vectors of value creation, as well as the innovations of the financial sector.

While international factors have always influenced the domestic choices (unit, base and rate), their importance has grown as multinationals play an increasing role in the global economy. On the one hand, the evolution of the rules for taxing multinationals is affected by their designs at the national level. On the other hand, once there is a consensus on an international tax issue, it becomes more difficult to change the domestic tax regime. Many agree that current issues with multinationals' taxation can only be addressed through global solutions. However, the two-level context is certainly an important challenge in moving towards a revised system.

Central to the existing international tax paradigm is the fundamental role given to legal constructs in determining corporate taxation. The corporate taxation's unit as the legal entity and the tax base as the profit resulting from the computation of revenues and expenses are both characterized and located upon legal arrangements. Major failures appear when the legal status as well as the fiscal residence and contractual agreement disconnect the entity from economic reality. This problem has long been identified, and international tax rules have evolved over the years to take this into consideration. Particularly, this led to the creation of mechanisms to compensate for the discrepancies between economic substance and legal form, such as the arm's length principle with regard to transfer-pricing rules and anti-avoidance rules. So far, these modifications have been adjustments to the existing paradigm. At some point, it may become difficult to maintain the dominance of a paradigm when issues multiply and adjustments amount to bending or even disregarding the fundamental inadequacy of the principles. An accumulation of issues or more fundamental failures may lead to a paradigm shift. Dereje Alemayehu, Chair of the Global Alliance for Tax Justice and Senior Economic Policy Advisor of Tax Justice Network Africa, points out that the time has come to take these legal fictions for what they are, fiction, not reality. Arm's length principle should therefore not be taken as a principle, but rather as a fiction created to fix a problem resulting from flawed principles (Alemayehu, 2016).

[A] Issues with the Unit of Taxation and the Tax Base

Many experts note that using separate legal entities for multinational corporate taxation is a major issue with the existing system. For example, Mr. El Hadji Ibrahima Diop, Director of Legislation and Litigation Studies at the Ministry of Economy and Finance of Senegal, argues that referring to separate accounting to tax a multinational's entities (related entities within the MNE group) generates incentives to shift costs and manipulate transfer-pricing rules. As long as transfer-pricing rules can be manipulated to reduce profitability, he argues that a domestic corporation will always pay relatively more taxes than its international competitor. However, accounting information is now required by many countries on a consolidated basis (IFRS) to accurately represent the operations of multinationals. Regarding transfer-pricing rules, Mr. Alemayehu questions the efficiency of the OECD's BEPS Actions moving forward; for him, as long as multinationals are considered as separate entities there can be no solution to global tax dodging and the erosion of the tax base.

Agreeing that the current tax system's rules are unfit for a global economy, Ms. Rita de la Feria, Professor of tax law at Leeds University and International Research Fellow at the Centre for Business Taxation, Oxford University, notes that the current analysis tends to focus on the manipulation of tax rules by governments (through tax competition), by corporations (through tax planning) and by wealthy individuals (through tax avoidance, tax evasion and some tax planning). However, she argues that the problem is not only about manipulation but also about the fundamentals of the tax system, which need to be reassessed. The territoriality and physicality premises of the corporate taxation no longer refer to something real but are rather artificial. A lot of effort is spent trying to locate profits based on transactions dislocating the production phases in numerous countries. Also, physicality is disappearing as the global economy is becoming mainly digital. In these circumstances, according to Professor de la Feria, the solutions offered, such as anti-avoidance measures, including the OECD's recommendations in the context of the BEPS Action Plan, are a temporary fix to a permanent problem.

[B] Enforcement Issues

Aside from the above fundamental failures, one of the specific challenges addressed is the enforcement of corporate taxation in a globalized world. One of the main challenges in this area is the access to information. Without the relevant tax information, it is impossible to have an efficient tax system. This information may be available in more advanced countries, and it is crucial for developing countries to have efficient tools to obtain it.

For some countries it is also urgent to innovate and modernize tax administrations to face these issues. This implies improving the training of tax inspectors in order to better apprehend the complexity of structures used by multinationals to reduce their taxes. Transfer-pricing arrangements also add to the enforcement challenge, particularly due to the lack of data on comparables to analyze the transfer-pricing positions of multinationals. It requires the development of expertise to ensure the appropriate application of transfer-pricing rules. Tax planning to avoid permanent establishment complexifies the control of compliance (Diop, 2016). Furthermore, the digital world renders this concept obsolete. These enforcement challenges are being dealt with through the BEPS project and other previous or concomitant work, such as the on-request and automatic exchange of information.

[C] Cooperation and Competition

Global economic liberalization reinforces the competitive climate among countries and still fosters a disconnection between official discourse at the international level and domestic policy-making, particularly in the field of taxation. Multinationals' competitiveness arguments contribute to promoting policies that reduce corporate taxes or tolerate (even facilitate) aggressive tax planning (Latulippe, 2016).

The fact that taxation remains national but that businesses are often multinationals is central to issues facing corporate taxation system and renders necessary for countries to cooperate or coordinate their corporate tax systems. Since the early twentieth century, tax cooperation has been occurring to some extent and it has intensified over recent years, particularly to address the enforcement issues. However, cooperation takes place in an economic environment still rooted in competition, among businesses as well as among governments. Competition between countries, particularly through the use of tax incentives, contributes to the challenges of taxing multinationals. In particular, the extractive industry is a salient issue for developing countries: while these countries need foreign investment, the incentives offered to attract extractive companies are very costly.

Tax incentives offered by developing countries should be revisited to end the tax wars, and research shows they are too costly (Tax Justice Network Africa and Action Aid International, 2012) and often not effective (IMF, OECD, UN and World Bank, 2015). However, initiatives to reconsider tax incentives need to be combined with other institutional arrangements such as Investment Treaties and Tax Treaties, as both types of treaties have features tied to tax incentives. African countries should be encouraged to revise their Investment Treaties, which they are also pressured to sign in the context of Official Development Assistance. Some components of Investment Treaties and Tax Treaties may facilitate tax planning and support the development of harmful tax practices as they were signed in different circumstances, at a different time. According to Mr. Alemayehu, all these arrangements should be considered together within each country.

It is necessary to reinvent the international tax paradigm and that cooperation, not competition, is key to achieve this. There are lessons to learn from the many experiences of regional economic cooperation in African countries (e.g., UEMOA, SADC) to work towards establishing workable solutions for cooperation in tax matters. A rethinking of international taxation could create a new global fiscal order for an equitable distribution of the tax base (Diop, 2016).

As for the collaboration process to achieve change, Mr. Alemayehu advises that developing countries need to be involved in the policy-making process "on an equal footing." It is not desirable to design rules and then reach to developing countries for their implementation. He considers that this process could take place within the context of the UN. Efforts towards cooperation need to be maintained and intensified either to find better policy solutions to fix the current paradigm or to replace it.

[D] Public Pressures and Transparency

The protection of commercial secrets and businesses' confidential information should not justify total corporate tax opacity. Over the past decade, public pressures have influenced the reexamination of the international tax system. Greater tax transparency could inform the debate outside the usual circles of tax experts. A first step has been taken towards providing more information to tax authorities and promoting the automatic exchange of information among countries. However, as long as corporate taxation is totally sheltered from public scrutiny, corporations' lobbying can continue to be exerted on governments, without any countervailing argument being voiced or without having to justify their request. On this topic, Mr. Alemayehu calls for the creation of a democratic space where citizens can also put pressure on their respective countries and offer a counterweight to private companies' lobbying. Unless governments are put under pressure to find a common solution to a global problem, each country will be tempted to give concessions to the private lobbying.

§4.03 THE WAY FORWARD

To address the above challenges, a remodeling or a replacement of the system needs to be considered. The OECD's work on BEPS and AEOI is entrenched in the current paradigm. Modifications of rules or policies within a paradigm may reinforce it. However, if the adjustments did not fit well with its principle, the paradigm would be weakened. Also, the dominance of the paradigm and the consensus around it may fade when major principle flaws cannot be fixed. This would shake the foundation of the paradigm, which may nonetheless continue to prevail if there is no viable, credible and supported replacement alternative (Kuhn, 1983, Hall, 1993).

Given there is a global consensus that multinationals should pay their fair share of taxes somewhere, then the key unresolved questions are what is "fair" and where is "somewhere"; a variety of options should thus be assessed to formulate fair and effective responses to these fundamental questions on the design and implementation of multinationals' taxation. Every option should be studied, not only options that fit the current paradigm or that allow it to survive. Many arguments make a case for changing the current international tax paradigm.

To replace a paradigm, the existence of a complete and coherent alternative is necessary. However, at this point, while some alternatives exist, they do not seem to be rooted in an all-encompassing coherent program to lead to a paradigm shift. Unless these proposals are presented as part of a clear paradigmatic framework that articulates a set of coherent standards or a new assemblage of the constitutive elements and which is endorsed by an authoritative voice, or a group of them, it is unlikely that a new paradigm will replace the existing one (Blyth, 2013).

Flaws of the current paradigm have been identified for many years (Graetz, 2000). Options to replace or modify the corporate tax system have been developed, either from a domestic perspective or from an international perspective. Some propositions deal with the tax base, such as profits, cash flow or rents, or offer a different way to calculate the profit (e.g., options not to consider interest (CBIT), or to permit an allowance regarding equity (ACE)). Some of these propositions consider multinational groups as a single entity.

Proposed alternatives deal with the international dimension of the problem by focusing on the allocation of taxing rights. Professor Rita de la Feria and Michael Devereux, among others, suggest a change in the tax base and propose a destination-based corporate cash-flow tax. A cash-flow tax differs from the conventional form of income tax, as it implies the immediate expensing of investment expenditures and inclusion of net financial inflows in the tax base (Devereux and De la Feria, 2014). In essence, this international system of taxing corporate profit is based on the identification of the least mobile element in the value chain: the customers. In their proposal, they argue that locating taxation in the purchaser's place of residence minimizes economic distortions to the behavior of multinational companies, to the ownership of assets and to competitiveness,[2] and also that this basis is less amenable to manipulation by corporations (Auerbach et al., 2017).

In practice, a destination-based cash-flow tax (DBCFT) is a tax on corporate profit that works much like a value-added tax (VAT), except that domestic labor costs are fully deductible from the tax base. However, under DBCFT, the destination is intended as a place of relative immobility, not as a proxy for consumption. It translates into sales being taxed where the purchasers reside, and expenses receiving tax relief where they are incurred ((Devereux and De la Feria, 2014). Its implementation would require a shift in the paradigm governing the international allocation of taxing rights, currently based on residence or source.

Professors de la Feria and Devereux studied how a DBCFT could be designed in order to make it a workable solution, drawing from the experiences of VAT systems in a global environment (Devereux and De la Feria, 2014). Assuming countries wish to cooperate to implement the tax, they find that it would be legitimate for countries to tax

---

2. Under certain conditions, Auerbach and Devereux show that a destination-based cash-flow tax does not create distortions to the location, investment, and financial pricing decisions of multinational companies. *See* Alan J. Auerbach and Michael P. Devereux, 'Consumption and Cash-Flow Taxes in an International Setting' (2012) *Oxford University Centre for Business Taxation Working Paper Series*, WP 12/14.

corporations on the basis of destination (substantive jurisdiction) and that it would be feasible (enforcement jurisdiction).

Some critics argue that a destination-based sales tax is deeply regressive and fundamentally unfair because, like a VAT, it exempts capital from taxation and passes on the entire tax burden to domestic consumers. While it is true that the burden of a DBCFT falls on domestic consumption, because it is equivalent to a VAT combined with a labor tax cut, the tax incidence is actually on domestic consumption financed by other means than wages (Auerbach et al., 2017). As such, it is certainly more progressive than a unique rate VAT, and possibly more so than the current corporate income tax (which may have a direct incidence on wages).

A thorough analysis of the revenue-effect and redistribution effect of a DBCFT still needs to be done, notably concerning its impact on developing countries. As mentioned previously, the burden of a DBCFT falls entirely on domestic residents, while in a source-based system, some of the burden of the tax falls on non-residents. This is a concern for developing countries, whose economies often rely heavily on natural resources, and Auerbach et al. argue to keep source-based taxation for natural resources. According to their calculations, international balance of payments statistics suggests that the DBCFT for non-resource sectors would increase the tax base for most countries, including developing countries. Also, while it is not a perfect solution, it may be argued that destination-based corporate taxation is a possible way to end the race to the bottom and the cycle of anti-avoidance measures that only work temporarily. It is an opportunity to move away from a dysfunctional system: instead of dealing with the symptoms, it eliminates the issues related to the current corporate income tax system.

Other alternatives for an international tax system include the possibility to allocate profits on the basis of a formula factoring in employees, sales, property (formulary apportionment) or based only on a sales factor. A sales factor apportionment (SFA) allocates consolidated profits proportionally to sales. SFA is considered to be the less distortionary option at least for high consumption countries, since companies are susceptible to make tax-motivated decisions regarding the location of employment or investment, but less so concerning the location of sales (Bill Parks and Jerry Wegman, 2015).

SFA requires only information on global sales and global pre-tax profits on a consolidated basis, which is already available since many countries require consolidated financial statements. It prevents multinationals from shifting costs within the group: the location of costs does not matter as SFA taxes a percentage of the company's worldwide income. It makes the tax rate irrelevant for corporate competitiveness purposes and therefore removes the competitive disadvantage associated with high rates. Also, with this system all corporations, multinational or domestic would be taxed equally. If a desirable public policy objective is to help small businesses, SFA could be combined with progressive corporate tax (e.g., lowering the tax rate for the first million dollars of profit). While a coordinated adoption of SFA by many countries may be desirable, according to its proponent it is not a prerequisite for its successful implementation in a few countries, such as the United Kingdom or the United States, also with its relative simplicity and reduced administration and collection costs, apportionment may be more beneficial to developing countries than the current system of taxation (Parks, 2016).

§4.04 CONCLUDING REMARKS

There are important international concerns with how the current corporate income tax system applies to multinationals from both a developing and a developed country perspective. While it seems clear that coordination and cooperation are necessary to solve enforcement issues, other fundamental issues also require global solutions.

It may be central to first recognize fundamental obstacles and then to dedicate time and resources to the complex endeavor of finding appropriate global solutions in the long term. Many experts agree on the identification of the problems with the current corporate tax system. The enforcement issues, including accessing information and controlling tax planning, are challenges which international organizations and states are trying to address to protect the corporate tax system. However, other problems, like using the legal entity as the unit of taxation, are failures of the dominant paradigm. In an integrated, global economy, using separate-entity accounting to attribute profits and costs to individual tax jurisdictions does not make sense (Avi-Yonah, Clausing and Durst, 2008). It may not be possible to find long-term viable solutions within the current paradigm. In parallel with the existing system, a complete and coherent alternative way to tax corporations generally and/or multinationals more precisely may be developed and it may at one point replace the existing paradigm if it gains sufficient credibility and adherents. Patching things within the current paradigm may extend its life for some time; however, patches may not be enough to fundamentally solve the current issues.

So, is a paradigm shift required to maintain a viable corporate tax system for multinationals? There is no simple answer, but it is important to take into account that the current paradigm is suffering from major flaws. Some solutions are recommended, through the BEPS Action Plan for example, and are potential remedies to adjust or remodel the current paradigm. While fixing the current paradigm is necessary for the short term, it may also be necessary to rethink principles themselves to find workable long-term solutions. In that sense, considering MNCs as single entities may be a necessary first step; however, the endeavor needs to be commensurate with the challenges of the constant changing business landscape. To design a viable global alternative it is essential to fully encompass the features of the digital and financial economy and to acknowledge upcoming technological development that will continue to modify the organization of businesses and the way wealth is created. An alternative based on these realities should allocate taxing rights accordingly and be less amenable to manipulation, particularly by MNCs.

Chapter 4: Taxing Multinationals in a Globalized World

REFERENCES

Alemayehu, Dereje. 2016. *Winning the Tax Wars*, Conference World Bank and TaxCOOP, panel "Taxing Multinationals in a Globalised World", Washington, May 23, 2016.

Auerbach, Alan J. 2016. "Destination Based Cash Flow Tax." Available at: https://www.taxpolicycenter.org/sites/default/files/destination-based-cash-flow-tax-proposal-and-development_0.pdf.

Auerbach, Alan J., and Michael P. Devereux. 2012. "Consumption and Cash-Flow Taxes in an International Setting." *Oxford University Centre for Business Taxation Working Paper Series*, WP 12/14.

Auerbach, Alan J., Michael P. Devereux, Michael Keen and John Vella. 2017 "Destination-Bas Cash Flow Taxation." Oxford University Center for Business Taxation, WP 17/01.

Avi-Yonah, Reuven S. 2004. "Corporations, Society, and the State: A Defense of the Corporate Tax." *Virginia Law Review*: 1193-1255.

Avi-Yonah, Reuven S., Kimberly A. Clausing, and Michael C. Durst. 2008. "Allocating Business Profits for Tax Purposes: A Proposal to Adopt a Formulary Profit Split." University of Michigan Law School, Law & Economics Working Papers.

Blyth, Mark. 2013. "Paradigms and Paradox: The Politics of Economic Ideas in Two Moments of Crisis." *Governance* 26(2): 197-215.

Boadway, Robin W., and Jean-François Tremblay. 2014. *Corporate Tax Reform: Issues and Prospects for Canada*. Mowat Centre, Mowat Research #88, April 2014.

Brauner, Yariv. 2008. "Non-Sense Tax: A Reply to New Corporate Income Tax Advocacy." *Michigan State Law Review* (2008): 591.

Devereux, Michael, and Rita de la Feria. 2014. "Designing and Implementing a Destination-Based Corporate Tax." Oxford University Centre for Business Taxation Working paper series, WP14/07.

Diop, El Hadji Ibrahima. 2016, *Winning the Tax Wars*, Conference World Bank and TaxCOOP, panel "Taxing Multinationals in a Globalised World", Washington, May 23, 2016.

Graetz, Michael J. 2000. "Taxing International Income: Inadequate Principles, Outdated Concepts, and Unsatisfactory Policies." Brooklyn *Journal* of International Law. 26: 1357.

Hall, Peter. 1993. "Policy Paradigms, Social Learning, and the State." *Comparative Politics* 25, No. 3 (April 1993): 275-296.

IMF, OECD, UN and World Bank. 2015. *Options for Low-Income Countries: Effective and Efficient Use of Tax Incentives for Investment*. Available at: https://www.imf.org/external/np/g20/pdf/101515.pdf.

Kuhn, Thomas S. 1983. *La structure des révolutions scientifiques*. Paris: Flammarion (translated of augmented 1970 version).

Latulippe, Lyne. 2016. "Tax Competition: An Internalized Policy Goal?" in *Global Tax Governance: What Is Wrong and How to Fix It*, edited by Peter Dietsch and Thomas Rixen, 77-100. Colchester, UK: ECPR Press.

Mintz, Jack. 1995. "The Corporation Tax: A Survey." *Fiscal Studies* 16(4): 23-68.

Parks, Bill. 2016. *Winning the Tax Wars*, Conference World Bank and TaxCOOP, panel "Taxing Multinationals in a Globalised World", Washington, May 23, 2016.

Parks, Bill, and Jerry Wegman. 2015. "Sales Factor Apportionment: A Reform for All Seasons?" *Tax Notes* (January 19, 2015): 395-404.

Tax Justice Network-Africa and Action Aid International. 2012. "Tax Competition in East Africa. A Race to the Bottom." Report. Available at: http://www.actionaid.org/sites/files/actionaid/eac_report.pdf.

CHAPTER 5
Offshore Tax Investigations, Tax Whistleblowing, and Global Tax Compliance

Louise Otis & Brigitte Alepin[*]

§5.01 INTRODUCTION

This chapter questions and reflects on what our understanding of the global tax system would be, without the results of the offshore tax investigations that have recently taken place in the United Kingdom (U.K.), France, the United States (U.S.), Luxembourg, and Panama, given the information revealed by the different leaks and whistleblowing. It argues that to adapt our tax systems to the demands of the twenty-first century, it is crucial to know how tax is treated in the real world, to ensure that all taxpayers pay their fair share, and to use more of these tools to further promote transparency.

Also, this chapter considers the numerous interlinkages between offshore tax investigations, tax whistleblowing, and global tax compliance. Offshore tax investigations and tax whistleblowing are relatively new and powerful practices that are increasingly playing a role in implementing a better system for global tax compliance. The second half of this chapter analyses the present system and proposes thoughts on global tax compliance for the twenty-first century.

---

[*] In collaboration with *Michel Sapin*, Minister of Finance of France and *Alexander Ezenagu*, Doctoral Candidate in International Tax Law at McGill University.

§5.02 OFFSHORE TAX INVESTIGATIONS AND TAX WHISTLEBLOWING

[A] Definitions and Importance

[1] Offshore Tax Investigations

Offshore tax investigation connotes the in-depth inquiry into the affairs of taxpayers to disclose information hidden, intentionally or unintentionally, from the tax authority in a particular country. These investigations can find the facts, increase transparency, help change what is going on in the world, and increase tax fairness.

These investigations are being conducted by States themselves, the media,[1] interest groups, and in some instances individuals (International Consortium of Investigative Journalists (ICIJ) 2013). Sovereign States engage in offshore tax investigations via their tax administrations, which they empower to audit taxpayers. To make these investigations productive, States must collaborate, through their tax administrations, to reveal the consequences of the actions or inactions of taxpayers, individuals, or companies operating internationally. In addition, some States and other political entities, like the U.S., the U.K., Australia, France, and the European Commission, carry out important and popular tax investigations via special committees, probes, and subpoena powers.

In August 2016, for example, the European Commission (EC) ruled that Ireland granted undue tax benefits to the Apple corporation, to the value of EUR 13 billion.[2] This decision spurred legal, economic, and political controversies across the globe. Ireland challenged the EC's decision, claiming that it violated the country's fiscal sovereignty. Meanwhile, States other than Ireland have laid claim to the EUR 13 billion, alleging that part of the profits should have been paid to them, on the basis of their being the host countries where the significant economic activities of the company actually took place.

During the last 10 years, tax journalists working primarily for the media have engaged in important tax investigations. In 2013, Thomson Reuters revealed that, while Google said it didn't sell in countries like Britain and France, it advertised "sales" jobs in London and Paris, which it indicated would involve "negotiating deals" and meeting "sales quotas." These investigations by Thomson Reuters led to raids of Google headquarters in Paris and fines imposed on the company (Rose and Labbé 2016). Similarly, investigations by Thomson Reuters' Tom Bergin revealed that Starbucks had paid just GBP 8.6 million in corporate income tax despite a U.K. turnover of GBP 3.1 billion between 2000 and 2013. The investigations took four months and involved combing through accounts across a dozen countries going back 14 or 15 years (Marsh 2015).

Non-governmental organizations like Oxfam and Tax Justice Network are also very proactive in investigating the taxes that multinationals are or are not paying.

---

1. For example, the offshore tax investigations conducted by the International Consortium of Investigative Journalists.
2. http://europa.eu/rapid/press-release_IP-16-2923_en.htm.

The ICIJ investigations into Luxembourg's tax rulings (LuxLeaks) revealed the tax-avoidance schemes in Luxembourg and contributed to formulating measures aimed at regulating tax-avoidance schemes beneficial to multinational companies. These investigations revealed the active participation of tax administrations, such as the Luxembourg's *Administration des Contributions Directes* (Luxembourg's Inland Revenue or LACD) in the facilitation of tax avoidance by multinational companies. Omri Marian, in what he has described as "investigative journalism at its best," informs us that LACD assisted multinational taxpayers to erode the tax base in jurisdictions other than Luxembourg, without attracting any real investment into Luxembourg. Luxembourg's tax administration served as a conduit, or intermediary agent, between the jurisdiction of the investor and the jurisdiction of the investment, eroding the tax bases, both at source and at residence, in return for fees for tax-avoidance services. LuxLeaks helped reveal the arbitrage manufacturing[3] which took place in Luxembourg. Omri Marian further believes that a contributing factor that enabled arbitrage manufacturing to take place in the LuxLeaks scandal was the fact that the rulings were never made public. He then recommends that "light be equally shone on the practices and laws of governments and their tax administrations … and not just on corporations."

The Panama Papers leaks involved 370 journalists, working in 25 languages, digging into 11.5 million documents to reveal Mossack Fonseca's inner workings. This investigation traced the secret dealings of the firm's clients and revealed the use of shell companies by the rich for fraud, tax evasion, and money laundering, amongst many other lawful or unlawful purposes.

Offshore tax investigations are important, given that most States shift the burden of tax revenue to domestic taxpayers to compensate for the international taxpayers that pay little or nothing in taxes. We should fear the reactions of domestic taxpayers if, in addition to what is frequently felt as an unfair transfer of the tax burden, they have the impression that taxes are administered with more flexibility and less severity for international taxpayers. It is therefore very important for countries to adopt, as soon as possible, their practices in order to efficiently audit and investigate international taxpayers.

[2]   Tax Whistleblowing

Recognition of the fundamental value of whistleblowing has been increasing over the last 30 years. According to the U.S. Government Accountability Project (GAP), a leading organization in whistleblower protection and advocacy, whistleblowing is the disclosure of information providing evidence of illegality, gross waste or fraud, mismanagement, abuse of power, general wrongdoing, or a substantial and specific danger to public health and safety.

Transparency International (TI), a global organization against corruption, has identified whistleblowing as an effective tool in the prevention and detection of

---

3. Omri Marian describes this as a process in which, in return for a fee, a jurisdiction issues a regulatory instrument to a taxpayer who resides outside the jurisdiction, in respect of an investment located outside the jurisdiction.

corruption and tax wrongdoings. As pointed out by TI, the clandestine nature of corrupt behavior means that it may never come to light unless cases are reported by people who discover them in the course of their work. But reporting can come at a high price: whistleblowers often expose themselves to great personal risks in order to protect the public interest. As a result of speaking out, they may lose their jobs, dampen their career prospects, and even put their lives at risk.[4]

Tax whistleblowing is probably as old as tax evasion, but the possibility to stock the tax profiles of millions of taxpayers on one disk has given a new dimension to tax whistleblowing, an enormous power to the whistleblowers, as well as a potentially immense value to the information they obtain. This new reality may oblige policy makers to revisit their traditional treatment of tax whistleblowing. For the purposes of this chapter, this new phenomenon is called "mega tax whistleblowing."

[B] Responses from Governments and International Organizations

Beyond revealing the facts, providing relevant information, and promoting transparency, offshore tax investigations and tax whistleblowing influence the policies and laws of domestic and supranational bodies.

The investigative results of the ICIJ led to the European Commission rulings against Fiat and Starbucks' operations in Luxembourg and the Netherlands, respectively. The active participation of tax authorities of sovereign States in tax evasion and avoidance, brought to the fore by LuxLeaks, amplified calls by other nations for the offending countries to give up their tax havens. Michel Sapin, French finance minister, has urged Britain to go "right to the end" in stamping out tax secrecy in its overseas territories and crown dependencies, which continue to act as tax havens for the wealthy (Chrisafis 2016). Furthermore, French authorities, in clamping down on offshore tax avoidance, sent McDonalds France a EUR 300 million bill for unpaid taxes on profits believed to have been funneled through Luxembourg and Switzerland. The French government has committed to seeking tougher EU sanctions on people who facilitate tax evasion, as well as stronger measures to ensure that countries allowing tax evasion will be subject to coordinated countermeasures by other States.[5]

The Panama Papers revelations likewise elicited strong reactions from governments. U.K. officials have commenced investigations into British taxpayers mentioned in the leaks. The Australian Tax Office is investigating more than 800 wealthy clients of Mossack Fonseca, in conjunction with the Australian police and the anti-money-laundering regulator, AUSTRAC. Panama, for its part, has asked to join the OECD's Multilateral Convention on Mutual Assistance, a move widely praised as a major step towards tax transparency and effective exchange of information.[6] Panama has likewise committed to the automatic sharing of financial and tax data with other countries.

---

4. https://www.transparency.org.
5. http://ca.reuters.com/article/businessNews/idCAKCN0X81YI.
6. http://www.oecd.org/ctp/exchange-of-tax-information/panama-decides-to-sign-multilateral-tax-information-sharing-convention.htm.

Other positive aspects of offshore tax investigations include: Ireland's decision to stop allowing tax residency blanks; the proposed U.S. rule to mandate country-by-country reporting (CBCR); the EU's actions on sweetheart tax deals; and invalidation of some deals as illegal state aid, among others. Dismantling secrecy laws and practices is a necessary step towards ensuring global tax compliance. All relevant actors are enjoined to engage in offshore tax investigations, if we are committed to having a transparent world.

Also of importance is the benefit of whistleblowing in exposing taxpayers' tax frauds or evasion strategies. For instance, Daniel Schlicksup's whistleblowing led to investigations into the activities of Caterpillar and its transfer-pricing practices by both the U.S. Securities and Exchange Commission (SEC) and the Senate Permanent Subcommittee on Investigations. Bradley Birkenfeld blew the lid off UBS' tax-evasion practices, which led to the prosecution of UBS for conspiring to hide USD 20 billion in assets.

Many States have agreed to financially compensate tax whistleblowers. The U.S. pays eligible whistleblowers up to 30% for voluntarily reporting information that leads to a successful judicial or administrative action in which the SEC obtains monetary sanctions of at least USD 1 million.[7] The Canada Revenue Agency in 2014 instituted the CRA Whistleblower Program, also known as the Informant Leads Program. This program encourages whistleblowing and rewards whistleblowers whose information leads to over USD 100,000 in additional federal tax being assessed and collected.[8] The award, which is between 5% and 15% of the federal income tax collected, has led to an increase in the number of informants to the revenue authority. Other countries, like France and Britain, have adopted similar tax whistleblowing programs. However, when it comes to mega whistleblowing, most countries seem to refuse to pay these awards, instead placing emphasis on protections. Australia and France are proposing new whistleblower protections for people who disclose information about tax misconduct. Under these new rules, informants will have their identity protected and will be protected from victimization as well as civil and criminal action for disclosing information.

Blowing the whistle on tax practices of large organizations and their clients is generally felt to be like committing suicide, for the whistleblower. For example, Hervé Falciani's exposure of HSBC Switzerland's conspiracy to commit or enable tax fraud led to his arrest in several countries. Bradley Birkenfeld's and Daniel Schlicksup's whistleblowing led to their arrests and detention. These arrests were carried out, despite the public benefits of their revelations, on the premise that they either were in breach of privacy or revealed legal acts in breach of confidentiality agreements. If we are committed to ensuring global tax compliance, those who lift the lids on the activities of tax gamers and harmful tax planners must be protected, and we should ensure they suffer no harm. This protection must be global.

---

7. https://www.sec.gov/whistleblower.
8. http://taxsolutionscanada.com/cra-whistleblower-program-who-does-it-and-how-it-could-happen-to-you/.

International organizations have produced guidelines and regulations regarding whistleblowing. The OECD (2012) has stated that: "[The] protection of both public- and private-sector whistleblowers from retaliation for reporting in good faith suspected acts of corruption and other wrongdoing is therefore integral to efforts to combat corruption, safeguard integrity, enhance accountability, and support a clean business environment." An adequate whistleblower law for government and corporate employees should possess: sufficient internal and external disclosure channels; opportunities for anonymous reporting; an agency to investigate disclosures and complaints; transparent/accountable enforcement of laws; a confidentiality guarantee; and penalties for retaliators (Worth 2014, 7).

The European Union has resolved to protect whistleblowers who act in the public interest or only in order to expose misconduct, wrongdoing, fraud, or illegal activity in relation to corporate taxation in any Member State. The EU believes that such whistleblowers should be protected if they report suspected misconduct, wrongdoing, fraud, or illegal activity to the relevant competent authority, and also if they report their concerns to the wider public, in cases of persistently unaddressed misconduct, wrongdoing, fraud, or illegal activity in relation to corporate taxation that could affect the public interest.

The United Nations (UN), for its part, guarantees the protection of its staff, interns, or UN Volunteers, from being punished for reporting misconduct or for cooperating with an official audit or investigation.[9] The UN's protection-against-retaliation policy was enacted to encourage staff to report internal corruption, fraud, abuse of authority, and other cases of serious misconduct, so as to protect the integrity and interests of the organization. The Ethics Office and Office of International Oversight Services can take preventive action where a risk of relation has been duly identified.

On a global scale, the UN, through the UN Convention against Corruption, enjoins each State Party to consider incorporating into its domestic legal system appropriate measures to provide protection against any unjustified treatment for any person who reports in good faith and on reasonable grounds to the competent authorities any facts concerning offenses established in accordance with this Convention.[10]

In all organizations, including private corporations, the strength of the protection against reprisal is the foundation of the effectiveness of whistleblowing policies. The establishment of a prevention mechanism could effectively deter retaliatory measures. As soon as the disclosures of certain taxpayers' fraudulent actions or tax-evasion methods have been identified as posing a risk of retaliation, effective measures should be taken in order to prevent or mitigate retaliatory actions against whistleblowers. Being bound by a confidentiality or non-disclosure agreement might not preclude a consultant or an employee from acting as a whistleblower and disclosing tax frauds or evasive tax devices. The reasonable expectation is that confidentiality agreements will

---

9. Protection against retaliation for reporting misconduct and for cooperating with duly authorized audits or investigations. ST/SGB/2017/2.
10. Article 33 of the United Nations Convention on Corruption.

protect the employer against disclosure of trade secrets, proprietary information, and the like.

Confidentiality agreements will not protect corporations from the disclosure of information on illegal acts that may lead to non-compliance with the criminal justice system. If the confidentiality clause is in conflict with the law of the jurisdiction under which the agreement falls, its enforceability can be challenged. In this respect, withholding information on an employer's illegal activity could in itself be illegal. A court might also rule that the unequal bargaining power between the parties provides a basis to challenge the confidentiality clause. Finally, a confidentiality clause in an employment agreement has to be reasonable to be enforceable. Criteria for reasonableness include the public interest. Certainly, disclosing tax frauds or evasive devices of taxpayers will be deemed to be in the public interest.

[C] Guidance in Decision-Making

Offshore tax investigations and mega tax whistleblowing can be significant and useful to balance the books of sovereign States. However, if not carried out with extreme care, both can transform themselves into a threat to the proper functioning of the system.

Although the investigative efforts of media and interest groups are important and appreciated, they should remain an exception, because they can send the signal that tax authorities and governments are not doing their job, or are complicit in the tax gaming, as revealed in the LuxLeaks. In addition, most often, media and interest groups do not have the means and the knowledge that are available to tax administrations and governments to conduct these tax investigations. This can result in technical or judgment mistakes. Once these mistakes are made, and false information is released to the public, it is very difficult to correct the situation and present what should be the real interpretation of the tax situation.[11]

Tax whistleblowing that involves massive tax information, coupled with fraudulent taxpayers' fear of being exposed, can represent a quick fix to the tax system. The work of the ICIJ, for example, can effectively represent a game changer for tax evasion and aggressive tax planning, because the last thing most public figures, multimillionaires, or multinationals wish to see is their name on these lists. However, policy makers have to consider many factors when dealing with this new form of tax whistleblowing.

Beyond protection, the decision to compensate mega tax whistleblowing poses controversies amongst sovereign States. The "against-compensation" group generally explains that it is not acceptable for a sovereign State to encourage something that is in contradiction with the domestic rules of privacy. This group fears the future of a system where a market would be created out of the activities of tax whistleblowers. On the other hand, the "pro-compensation" experts claim that a tax whistleblowing regime is not robust and convincing without financial compensation.

---

11. Albert Einstein said that, "The hardest thing in the world to understand is the income tax." Therefore, we should not expect citizens to be able to differentiate between real and false conclusions of nonprofessional tax investigations.

Now that the whole world knows the nature and extent of illicit activities that deprive nations of critical resources to maintain public services, the time for prospective rhetoric is finished. Nations must act with the same vigor and the same audacity as individuals and corporations who use the deficiencies of the law and state controls to avoid their tax responsibilities. In this, compensation of whistleblowers can be a powerful tool for tracking tax wrongdoers in the highest national and international public interest. Evidently, sophisticated verification measures should guide policy makers before engaging in an incentive payment program.

It would be unrealistic to expect a commitment of all nations before activating a compensation program for whistleblowers. To mark a change, it would be sufficient that the Member States of the OECD, the G20, and the most important developing countries adopt a common policy: (1) setting criteria for remuneration; (2) identifying the nature of the investigative cases that would be subject to disclosure for which protection and payment might be offered; and (3) committing to share the information collected with the nations which may have an interest in the disclosure.

Concluding here, we must be mindful of State-sponsored offshore tax investigations and whistleblowing, which may arm ill-intentioned States or individuals with information detrimental to others. Today's world, faced with terrorism and cyber-attacks, could be spared this evolving menace. Beyond the security issues associated with possession of information, another consideration is the ethical value and ownership status of information obtained through offshore tax investigations and whistleblowing. Should such information be treated as property, with the owner exercising unrestrained rights over it, or should we design international laws limiting the rights and uses of such property? Should an international body be formed to regulate the activities, outcomes, and exercise of offshore tax investigations and whistleblowing, or should a benchmark or framework be created, in the same vein as tax treaties, for offshore tax investigations and whistleblowing?

These are important issues to be considered when implementing a system of global tax compliance. But what exactly is global tax compliance? The next section analyses the present system for global tax compliance and proposes thoughts to improve it in the twenty-first century.

§5.03 GLOBAL TAX COMPLIANCE

[A] Definition

During the early 1900s, experts' main concern was to prevent the double taxation of companies engaged in cross-border activities, seen then and now, and rightly so, as a discouragement to international trade. Thus, countries formulated and entered into treaties to prevent this clogging of the flow of international trade. A few years later, countries returned to the negotiating table to address the menace of double non-taxation of multinational enterprises, tax fraud, and non-compliance.

As far back as October 1936, the Assembly of the League of Nations adopted the following stinging resolution:

The Assembly,

Considering that efforts to reduce the obstacle to the international circulation of capital must not have the effect of increasing fiscal fraud;

… Requests the Fiscal Committee to pursue vigorously its work for the avoidance of double taxation as far as possible, and also its work on the subject of international fiscal assistance, in order to promote practical arrangements calculated, as far as possible, to put down fiscal fraud.

Carl Levin points out that, echoing these words a quarter of a century later, U.S. President John F. Kennedy told the U.S. Congress in 1961:

Recently, more and more enterprises organized abroad by American firms have arranged their corporate structures – aided by artificial arrangements between parent and subsidiary regarding intercompany pricing, the transfer of patent licensing rights, the shifting of management fees, and similar practices which maximize the accumulation of profits in the tax haven … in order to sharply reduce or eliminate their tax liabilities. … I recommend elimination of the tax haven "device" anywhere in the world.

Global tax compliance denotes the adherence by international taxpayers to the tax laws and practices in the jurisdictions where the law requires such adherence. The determination of the duty of taxpayers to tax remittances has been a source of vigorous debate over the years.

Taxpayers take advantage of loopholes to pay reduced tax. This occurs most frequently against the spirit of the law but in compliance with the letter of the law. Omri Marian describes this as an international tax arbitrage (ITA), "a situation in which … taxpayers rely on conflicts or differences between two countries' tax rules to structure a transaction …with the goal of obtaining tax benefit… ."

Carl Levin unapologetically describes such tax-avoidance schemes as "theft – the theft of public services and economic opportunity from all but a few select individuals." He further asserts that "tax dodging contributes to a growing income inequality that shocks the conscience." In the U.S., Senator Levin explained, firms hold USD 2.4 trillion offshore, deferring payment of U.S. taxes of USD 700 billion and denying the U.S. Treasury significant sums needed for physical and social infrastructure.

The effects of these tax-avoidance schemes are felt by both developing and developed countries, although developing countries are worse hit, considering that they are in dire need of revenues to finance physical and social infrastructure required for economic growth and social inclusion. Tax avoidance by multinational companies further increases developing countries' reliance on foreign aid, therefore making them more vulnerable to aid volatility (for further discussion, *see* Chapter 7). Thus, tax-avoidance practices aggravate existing income disparities between developed and developing countries. This is especially disheartening, when one considers the vast natural and human capital resources of developing countries and the economic returns they bring to the world, over against the prevailing poverty and lower human development index often observed in these countries. The UN Conference on Trade and Development, in a 2015 publication, claims that developing countries lose USD 100 billion per year due to tax avoidance by multinational companies and as much as USD

300 billion in total foregone development finance. Between 1970 and 2010, capital flight through tax-evasion and avoidance schemes stood at USD 814 billion, exceeding the official development aid of USD 659 billion and foreign direct investment of USD 306 billion for the same period.

To put this in perspective, from 2009 to 2012, Apple got away with sending USD 74 billion in profits to its Irish subsidiaries, even though Apple products were designed in the U.S., assembled mostly in China, and sold in Europe, Africa, Asia, and the Middle East, with relatively few sales in Ireland. Apple was able to assign USD 74 billion to Ireland, by taking advantage of a secret tax deal with the Irish government, which enabled Apple to pay a total effective tax rate of 1% in Ireland. Although Apple had three subsidiaries in Ireland, each claimed to have tax residency nowhere, which effectively led to tax dodging.

The question is, should duty require compliance with the letter of the law or both the letter and the spirit of the law? What is the letter of the law? What is its spirit of the law? Where should taxpayers pay taxes? Where profit is made, or where they owe economic allegiance? How do we determine the location of profit in today's world of fluid business and mobile money? Should taxpayers be required to pay a fair amount of tax? What is fair, and where is fair?[12] How do we measure fairness? The constitution of many countries refer to "fairness," "proportionality," and "capacity to pay" principles. These countries include Algeria, Benin, Cameroon, Congo, Côte D'Ivoire, the Democratic Republic of the Congo, France, Gabon, Guinea, Italy, Madagascar, Mauritania, Morocco, and Tunisia.[13]

---

12. There are different ways to avoid paying the "fair" tax share that corresponds to a particular taxpayer. First, some tax laws are not enacted according to the "ability to pay" principle, often due to trade-offs between equity and efficiency. Second, it is possible that a taxpayer remits his/her tax obligation according to the law, and yet the tax burden is unfair because of the use of tax-dodging schemes; and third, a taxpayer can avoid the tax law altogether. Tax avoidance and tax evasion correspond respectively to the second and third situations. The first form of tax unfairness is not covered in this chapter.
13. Article 64 of Algeria's constitution provides that everyone should participate in financing the public expenses, *in accordance with his contributory capacity*. It further provides that citizens are equals before the taxes, in the same article.
    Article 33 of Benin's constitution provides that all citizens of the Republic of Benin have the duty to work for the common good, to fulfill all of their civic and professional obligations, and to *pay their fiscal contributions*.
    The Cameroonian constitution incorporates the African Charter on Human and Peoples Rights, which in its Article 29 provides that "The individual shall also have the duty: (6) to work to the best of his abilities and competence, and to pay taxes imposed by law in the interest of the society."
    Article 60 of the constitution of Congo Brazzaville provides that "Every individual shall be expected to work in measure with his capabilities and his possibilities and to pay *his due contribution* fixed by law for the safeguard of the fundamental interests of society."
    In Congo Kinshasa, Article 65 of the Constitution provides that "All Congolese are held to loyally fulfil their obligations concerning the State. They have, likewise, the duty to pay their taxes and duties."
    Article 27 of the Constitution of Cote d'Ivoire provides that "The duty of acquitting oneself of one's fiscal obligations, in conformity with the law, is imposed on all." However, the 2016 draft constitution in Article 43, enjoins the state to fight against tax evasion and avoidance. It provides thus: "*L'Etat prend les mesures nécessaires pour garantir le recouvrement des impôts, la lutte contre l'évasion et la fraude fiscales.*"

The absence of agreed answers to these questions and others create rent-seeking and gaming potentials of the system. Carl Levin further cautions that "people of wealth and profitable corporations should not be able to benefit from the laws, resources, and protections provided by their governments without paying their fair share of the cost. Nor can they be allowed through tax avoidance and tax-evasion schemes to rob their nations of resources to the detriment of everyone else."

[B]   The Present Compliance System for International Taxpayers

Global tax compliance is facilitated by domestic and international laws, policies, principles, and practices. Countries have provisions in their domestic laws requiring resident taxpayers to comply with the laws where they do business. Similarly, through international treaties, laws, principles, and guidelines agreed to by countries, taxpayers are mandated to be responsible global citizens. For example, the model tax treaties developed by the UN and the OECD greatly influence the actions or inaction of multinational enterprises engaged in cross-border activities. Also, the activities of the G7, G20, World Bank, IMF, and other relevant international bodies support developing countries with tax design and implementation, so that multinational enterprises comply with the tax laws in jurisdictions where they operate or derive profit.

However, as shown above, existing tax systems still fail to fully ensure that international taxpayers pay their fair share of tax and to stop tax evasion and avoidance that negatively affects developing countries. It is in response to the call to stamp out rent-seeking by multinational corporations that these complex techniques to avoid taxes have come under unprecedented scrutiny in recent years, and there now exist concerted efforts to address the challenges posed by tax avoidance and evasion.

In Equatorial Guinea, Article 19 of the Constitution provides that *"Every citizen shall pay taxes according to his revenues."*

In Gabon, Article 20 of the Constitution provides that, "The Nation proclaims the solidarity and equality of all before the public charges; everyone must participate, *in proportion to his resources, to the financing of public expense."*

Article 22 of Guinea's Constitution provides, "Each citizen must contribute, *to the extent of their means*, to taxes and must fulfil their social obligations for the common good within the conditions determined by law... ."

Article 36 of the constitution of Madagascar provides, "The participation of each citizen in the public expenditures *must be progressive and calculated as a function of their contributive capacity."*

Article 20 of the constitution of Mauritania provides, "Each must participate in the public charges as a *function of their contributive capacity."*

Article 39 of the constitution of Morocco provides, "All support, *in proportion to their contributive faculties*, the public expenditures [charges] which only the law may, in the forms provided by this Constitution, create and assess."

Article 10 of the constitution of Tunisia provides, *"Paying taxes and contributing towards public expenditure are obligations, through a fair and equitable system. The state shall put in place the necessary mechanisms for the collection of taxes, and to combat tax evasion and fraud."*

Article 13 of the Déclaration Universelle des Droits de L'Homme of France: *"L'impôt doit être réparti entre tous les citoyens en fonction de leur richesse."*

Article 53 of the Constitution of the Republic of Italy: *"Every person shall contribute to public expenditure in accordance with their capability. The tax system shall be progressive".*

The Global Forum on Transparency and Exchange of Information for Tax Purposes, created in the early 2000s by the OECD in response to call from the G20, has 139 members on equal footing.[14] It is the agora for ensuring the implementation of the internationally agreed standards of transparency and exchange of information in the tax area. (*See*, however, the divergent assessments of this mechanism reflected, for example, in Chapter 3 of this volume.)

In 2013, the G20 mandated the OECD to address harmful tax competition and non-compliance by multinational companies. The OECD is at the forefront of such efforts through its Base Erosion and Profit Shifting (BEPS) project, which culminated in the BEPS report of October 2015. This and subsequent proposed efforts seek the inclusion, active involvement, and support of all countries. Central to the OECD's BEPS project is access to information. The OECD initiated, and has successfully persuaded countries to sign, the Multilateral Competent Authority Agreement for the Common Reporting Standards (CRS MCAA), which promotes the automatic exchange of information among signatories to the Convention. Another major step by the OECD is the CBCR requirement of MNEs recommended in the BEPS Action 13 report (Transfer Pricing Documentation and CBCR).

As formulated by the OECD, "With country-by-country reporting, tax administrations where a company operates will get aggregate information annually, starting with 2016 accounts, relating to the global allocation of income and taxes paid, together with other indicators of the location of economic activity within the MNE group. It will also cover information about which entities do business in a particular jurisdiction and the business activities each entity engages in. The information will be collected by the country of residence of the MNE group, and will then be exchanged through exchange of information supported by such agreements as signed today." The OECD expects the first exchanges to start during 2017-2018, based on 2016 information. In the absence of exchange of information based on the CBCR and MCAA models, the OECD believes that the BEPS Action 13 report on transfer-pricing documentation provides for alternative filing so that the playing field is leveled.

For developing countries struggling with tax evasion, the OECD's CBCR model will offer a viable tool for addressing the problem only if they can actually receive and absorb the information that should be provided to them under the framework. To ensure that developing countries are able to take advantage of this opportunity, the World Bank, IMF, and UN, in conjunction with the OECD, are working on enhancing developing countries' capacity to exchange information with other jurisdictions, given the reciprocal nature of the CBCR.

At the European level, the EU has accepted the recommendations to introduce: CBCR of multinationals' activities; common consolidated corporate tax base (CCCTB); better protection of whistleblowers; extension of automatic exchange of information on tax rulings to all tax rulings, which will also be made available to the public; countermeasures towards companies that make use of tax havens; changes to the EU state-aid regime as it relates to tax through binding guidelines; and other measures.

---

14. http://www.oecd.org/tax/transparency/.

Reacting to the LuxLeaks scandal and the claim that the EU loses EUR 50-70 billion a year due to tax avoidance from corporate taxation, the EU is championing claims that corporate taxation should be guided by the principle of taxing profits where they are generated. A CCCTB is proposed for the EU, based on a formula-apportionment method, which reflects the real economic activities of companies and does not unduly advantage certain Member States. Also, the EU proposes to move to a mandatory common corporate tax base (CCTB) for Member States of the Union to cover MNEs and companies with no cross-border activity, with possible temporary exemption for small and medium-sized enterprises. This CCTB will provide a uniform set of rules for companies operating in several Member States to calculate their taxable profits. These recommendations, amongst others, aim to strengthen global tax compliance by multinational companies operating within the Union.

The U.S. has been a leader in the fight against secret bank accounts used to hide assets from tax authorities and ensuring that U.S. taxpayers comply with the tax laws and practices. In 2010, the U.S. enacted the Foreign Account Tax Compliance Act (FATCA), requiring financial institutions around the world to disclose to the IRS large accounts held by U.S. persons, or pay a 30% withholding tax on the institution's earnings obtained in the U.S.. Carl Levin informs us that the 30% hammer has forced financial institutions around the world, nearly 200,000, to agree to disclose to the IRS any large account of a U.S. client. Countries, following FATCA, are setting up similar bank account disclosure systems with global reach. Levin, speaking further on the secrecy that surrounds multinational tax payments, queries why no tax authority in the world, including in the U.S., has reliable, timely information about where a multinational corporation does business, declares profits, and pays taxes.

The OECD's CBCR, the EU's CCCTB, and the U.S.' FATCA, anchored on the availability and accessibility of information that had hitherto been unavailable, are expected to promote global tax compliance by multinational enterprises.

Carl Levin concedes that the international community has made some modest headway in the BEPS project, forging a consensus that multinational corporations ought to pay their taxes and pay them in the countries where they have actual economic activity. However, much more needs to be done, especially to allow developing countries to benefit from new rules and regulations intended to improve tax compliance worldwide.

[C] Global Tax Compliance for the Twenty-First Century

As globalization challenges tax compliance across boundaries, tax policy making and administration must adapt to the new realities and find new ways of enforcing tax laws consistent with economic and social goals. The liberalization of the market economy through globalization and the cross-border trade that has emanated partly from the activities of multinational enterprises must now integrate advances in legal and tax systems worldwide in a coordinated manner. To effectively address global tax compliance issues is a larger discourse. Many questions remained unresolved.

In April 2016, the IMF, the UN, the World Bank Group, and the OECD agreed to set up a Global Platform for tax collaboration, to better support governments in addressing the tax challenges they face in a coordinated manner. The Platform should contribute to changing the global tax scene in order to provide a level playing field for developing countries.

Experts have advised that countries should consider the creation of an all-inclusive global tax body, just as the League of Nations did in the 1920s. The responsibilities of this global tax body should be unambiguous, well thought out, communicated, and adhered to. Omri Marian enjoins that, "Coordinated international efforts should target arbitrage-manufacturing practices." Achieving this, admittedly, is a Herculean task. As Carl Levin rightly notes, "There is nothing easy about tax policy."

The implementation of a well-functioning global tax compliance system adapted to the twenty-first century will necessitate that countries discuss, to a certain degree, how to treat multinationals caught engaging in tax fraud. Currently, each country applies its domestic laws to the specific parts of international tax structures that concern it. In France and Canada, for example, a multinational accused of tax evasion faces criminal punishment, including jail terms for top management officials, revocation of licenses, and restriction of operations. Because it is very long and costly for countries to criminally prosecute a multinational "too big to jail," only a few French and Canadian multinationals have actually been accused by States. The U.S. and the U.K., on the other hand, are proceeding differently. Instead of having the obligation to criminally prosecute the multinationals, they have adopted a system of transactional justice where it is possible to restrict the charges to economic penalties. This system allows these countries to obtain significant sums in economic penalties. For example, Swiss Bank – Credit Suisse was hammered with a USD 2.8 billion fine, after pleading guilty to a criminal charge of having helped its customers elude America's tax authorities. UBS was fined USD 780 million in 2009 for its tax-evasion practices.

CBCR by multinationals should offer many jurisdictions the opportunity to take coordinated actions against tax avoidance and tax evasion by multinational companies. Since citizens and domestic companies have to pay their taxes and respect increasingly complex tax laws, governments must also put in place the necessary measures to take action against international taxpayers that do not respect their laws.

The danger inherent in economic penalties is that it could create a different system for the wealthy and the powerful, where for example an SME found guilty of tax evasion would pay a penalty and see some of its executives go to jail, while an MNE would pay a penalty but avoid jail. In addition, a penalty for a multinational does not have the same connotation as for other taxpayers. Multinationals can hedge the risks and take advantage of the financial market to spread the potential burden of such a fine. Revealingly, Credit Suisse's stock price rose the day the guilty plea was announced and the fine imposed, rather than dipping.

It would be possible to moderate this danger by putting in place a system that:

- Targets and excludes violators from the organization. If clients or other organizations are involved in the criminal activities, the multinationals should be obliged to provide their names. Credit Suisse was not required to hand over

the names of its clients, denying the IRS the opportunity to go after those clients involved in tax evasion. As expressed by Carl Levin, "It is a mystery to me that the U.S. government didn't require as part of the agreement that the bank cough up some of the names."
- Provides stronger penalties for multinationals who reoffend, to make sure that it cannot become a recurrent scenario for a multinational to perpetrate tax evasion and then simply pay a penalty if caught.
- Considers presenting the measure as temporary or experimental. This could provide a window of opportunity, an amnesty for multinationals to clean up their business. Tax amnesties are popular. The U.S. has granted tax amnesty to Americans living in Canada and Offshore who failed to file their taxes for years. India, in its 2016 budget, offered domestic holders of undisclosed income and assets a one-time compliance opportunity to escape prosecution. This four-month window is for holders of unaccounted wealth to come clean by paying 30% tax plus a penalty of 7.5% and a similar percentage of surcharges. However, tax amnesties should remain a temporary comprise to repatriate billions of dollars, because populations are inclined to perceive tax amnesties as being unjust to taxpayers who complied voluntarily with the laws. Also, temporary tax amnesties can create expectations among taxpayers who hope such an amnesty will be granted again.

Clearly, a global tax-compliance system adapted to the twenty-first century must take into account the expected reaction of consumers. Will consumers stop buying the products of a multinational enterprise that fails to respect its legal and moral tax dues? The case of Uber is interesting, as clients in many settings continue to use Uber services, even though it is clear that the company is not paying appropriate taxes.

Finally, in an ultimate effort to bring an end to tax avoidance and evasion, the implementation of an International Tax Court (ITC) could be considered. A global tax court could balance out the inequality between the strength of legal representation at the disposal of multinational enterprises and the more limited resources often available to countries, especially lower-income countries. Such a global tax court, staffed by experts, would presumably be impartial and not easily swayed by the panache of the international legal and accounting firms hired by MNEs. Such a global tax court would be able to adjudicate cross-border disputes and resolve these promptly, a pattern with potentially far-reaching implications for States and other stakeholders.

However, the implementation of an ITC would pose sovereignty issues, given that taxation is still widely considered a matter of national jurisdiction. The statute creating the Court would have to be agreed and ratified by sovereign States, which would then be legally obligated to cooperate with the Court when required.

The composition and organization of the Court and the selection of its judges are not necessarily complex issues to resolve, since there are models emanating from other international courts, such as the International Criminal Court (ICC), the World Court, and various International Administrative Courts (UNAT, UNDT, ILOAT, WBAT) already in existence in international organizations. The independence of the ITC and the impartiality of its judges could be achieved through a thorough process of selection taking into account regional diversity and systems of law. As with most international tribunals, the ITC would establish its jurisdiction through a mixture of the systems of law applicable in civil and common law countries. The procuracy, registry, working languages, and privileges and immunities would all be matters to be agreed among Member States.

The model would comprise a prosecutor's office independent from the Court itself, which would be in charge of investigations, analysis, and prosecutions. The applicable law would reflect principles from the major tax law systems of the world in language as neutral and universal as possible.

§5.04 CONCLUSION

Addressing these challenges of globalization for global tax compliance will bring us closer to tax transparency and fairness in today's globalized world.

This chapter has made clear that, as tax information becomes available to stakeholders and secrecy laws are dismantled, sovereign countries will be better able to enforce their tax rules and regulations. To ensure availability and accessibility of information, offshore tax investigations must be encouraged and whistleblowers protected from victimization, oppression, and discrimination. International laws must also jealously protect the availability and accessibility of information. International bodies such as the UN, the World Bank Group, the OECD, and the IMF, in cooperation with regional tax organizations and bilateral government agencies, can promote tax compliance practices which respond better to modern-day business structures, with adherence to transparency, equity, and fairness.

REFERENCES

Chrisafis, Angelique. 2016. "French minister urges UK to stamp out tax secrecy in its territories." *The Guardian*. Wednesday 11 May. Available at: https://www.theguardian.com/uk-news/2016/may/11/uk-target-tax-secrecy-overseas-territories-michel-sapin-jersey-virgin-islands.

International Consortium of Investigative Journalists. 2013. "Authorities announce tax haven investigation." Blog. Available at: https://www.icij.org/blog/2013/05/authorities-announce-tax-haven-investigation.

Marsh, Bethan Haf. 2013. "How Reuters man exposed Starbucks tax avoidance." *Press Gazette*. February 28. Available at: http://www.pressgazette.co.uk/how-reuters-man-exposed-starbucks-tax-avoidance/.

OECD. 2012. *Whistleblower Protection: Encouraging Reporting*. Paris: OECD.

Rose, Michel, and Chine Labbé. 2016. "Investigators raid Google Paris HQ in tax evasion inquiry." Reuters. May 24, 2016. Available at: http://www.reuters.com/article/us-google-france-investigation-idUSKCN0YF1CV.

Worth, Mark. 2014. "Keeping Pace: Whistleblowing and the Response of Government." International Whistleblower Project: Re-visiting Whistleblower Protection. Paris: OECD.

CHAPTER 6
Tax Competition or Tax Cooperation

Vanessa Houlder

The era of globalization has increased competition among governments for revenues and investment. The lifting of restrictions on trade and capital flows has put downward pressure on tax rates and encouraged a proliferation of incentives. These practices have come under closer scrutiny since the international financial crisis. Some economists argue that the current system is inherently unstable and the corporate tax needs to be redesigned to eliminate the incentive for competitive ratecutting. Despite questions over the willingness and ability of governments to coordinate tax policy, there has been a push to secure greater cooperation in the collection of revenues in recent years. A G20-led initiative to tackle "base erosion and profit shifting" has drawn up recommendations to reduce arbitrage and competition for highly mobile profits. A number of regional initiatives are aiming to strengthen cooperation on tax matters. Tax authorities are also preparing for more joint action on matters such as tax audits and information sharing.

§6.01 INTRODUCTION

The trend towards greater economic integration of the last few decades has sparked fierce competition between countries for tax revenues and investment. Governments find themselves participating in what some perceive to be an unsustainable race to the bottom, involving the proliferation of tax incentives, repeated cuts in tax rates, a reliance on secrecy and the lax enforcement of tax laws. These practices have come under much closer scrutiny in the last few years, as governments attempt to rebuild their finances after the international financial crisis. Concerns about the effectiveness of tax incentives have intensified, particularly in the light of the problems faced by developing countries in collecting sufficient revenue to fund public services. The challenges faced by cash-strapped governments across much of the world have reignited the debate about the impact of tax competition, prompting renewed interest in more cooperative approaches.

This chapter discusses how governments view tax competition and cooperation. It examines how countries can better protect their tax sovereignty and the challenges involved with protecting their tax base. It also looks at the challenges and achievements of some of the international and regional initiatives aiming to promote the coordination of tax policies.

§6.02 TAX COMPETITION

[A] Definition

When applied to corporate taxation, the term is usually taken to mean the competition between countries that use their tax systems to attract inward flows of capital. But it can take other forms. In recent years, competition for taxing rights – or "paper profits"– has often been as significant as the competition for the operations that generate the profit. Tax competition also comes into play when governments offer tax advantages to multinationals headquartered in their countries that give them an edge over foreign rivals when they compete abroad.

The statutory tax rate is only one among many corporate tax parameters that countries can manipulate. The pervasiveness of tax incentives is thought to be at least in part a response to tax competition.

Academics often use game theory in their analysis of the phenomenon. They describe tax competition as a game between two or more countries that do not cooperate in the design of tax policies that influence the allocation of an internationally mobile tax base.

[B] Importance and History

Tax competition has existed for hundreds, if not thousands of years, but the phenomenon has become a far bigger issue over the last few decades as greater economic integration increased the cross-border flows of trade and investment.

Tax rates have plummeted. Between 1983 and 2015 the average statutory corporate tax rate of 28 G20 and OECD countries fell from nearly 50% to below 30% (Bilicka et al. 2012). The falls have been most significant in Europe and Central Asia and somewhat less in Sub-Saharan Africa and Latin America (International Monetary Fund (IMF) 2014).

In the aftermath of the financial crisis, the rate cuts have been relatively small, sparking speculation by some tax experts that the decline is leveling off.[1] But in 2016, the Paris-based Organisation for Economic Co-operation and Development reported that rate reductions "seem to be picking up again," in a sign that the trend appeared to be "gaining renewed momentum" (OECD 2016).

---

1. https://www.ft.com/content/7132769c-d228-11e3-97a6-00144feabdc0.

Pressure is likely to intensify if the United States (U.S.) reforms its tax regime. A recent working paper published by the IMF urged policymakers not to cut the U.S. rate below the current statutory OECD median of 25% because of its effects on global tax competition. It said: "Indeed, any reduction in the US corporate income tax rate will likely cause some rate-lowering response in other countries" (Clausing et al. 2016).

There is strong evidence that governments' ability to set their own tax policies is affected by tax policy changes elsewhere. For OECD countries, a 1 percentage point decrease in the statutory corporate tax rates of others has been found to generate, on average, a cut of 0.7 percentage points in response (Devereux et al. 2004). Analysis by the IMF concluded that a typical country's corporate tax base would be reduced by 3.7%, following a one-point reduction in corporate tax rates in all other countries. It said: "With corporate tax rates having fallen, on average, by 5 points or so over the last 10 years, this implies a sizeable effect" (IMF 2014, *supra*).

There is also evidence linking the growth of tax competition to the lifting of restrictions on trade and capital flows. Companies have been increasingly able to access markets in countries where they have no substantial operations. They have expanded through cross-border mergers, weakening their links with individual countries, which account for an increasingly small share of their sales and shareholders. As they restructured their supply chains to take advantage of their wider international footprint, they became increasingly willing and able to consolidate key activities in tax-advantageous locations.

The impact of these changes has been particularly felt in regions struggling to collect enough tax. A 2011 IMF report on revenue mobilization in developing countries said: "Increased mobility of goods and factors means, to a large degree, increased mobility of tax bases, and hence, potentially, downward pressure on tax rates and revenues. With levels of domestic resource mobilization already low relative to spending needs, this is liable to be an especially significant concern in Sub-Saharan Africa" (Keen et al. 2009).

Tax competition has been felt particularly keenly in Europe, especially after the accession of 10 states in 2004, the largest single expansion of the European Union (EU). In a sign of the tensions associated with this trend, Nicolas Sarkozy, former French President, repeatedly criticized the new accession countries for cutting their tax rates shortly after joining the EU. He threatened their EU aid payments saying that "nations can't claim to be rich enough to do away with taxes while also claiming to be poor enough to ask other nations to provide funds for them" (Davies and Voget 2011).

While cuts in tax rates may be the most visible sign of tax competition, other facets of tax policy are also involved. In a 2006 report, KPMG, one of the four biggest firms of professional advisers, explained the changing climate for competition, particularly as it affected Europe. "The progressive lowering of trade barriers particularly in the EU, and the increasingly sophisticated supply chain options available to large, global companies provide credible alternatives for locating investments so exerting constant downward pressure on headline rates. But although important, economically and symbolically, statutory corporate income tax rates are not, of course, the only considerations for companies seeking low tax jurisdictions.

A low tax rate does not necessarily mean a low tax burden. An apparently high tax jurisdiction can be attractive for investment if its effective rate is significantly lower than its statutory rate. Other tools in government armories include special regimes for particular types of investment, such as headquarter companies, treasury companies and research and development, and shifting the burden to indirect taxes.

More subtle competitive variables include the attitude of governments and their tax authorities to corporate tax payers, ranging from aggressive policing to promoting business collaboration; tax certainty or the lack of it (deriving from such factors as complexity of tax law and the availability of binding agreements) and the efficiency or otherwise of tax administration and the costs it imposes on tax payers. In time as tax competition progressively erodes differences in rates, such factors are likely to assume more importance and one of the keys to tax competitiveness could become the 'business friendliness' of a nation's tax environment."[2]

Europe provides many examples of these points, including lax practices involving rulings which are now under scrutiny for potential breaches of state aid rules. There has also been intensifying tax competition in the EU aimed at mobile profits, such as royalty payments on patents which can be easily moved between countries. By the end of 2014, a dozen EU countries were competing for this income through "patent boxes," which charge reduced tax rates on income earned by certain types of intellectual property.

While some of these trends have been particularly pronounced in Europe, the proliferation of tax incentives has been a global phenomenon and is particularly problematic in developing countries. Tax breaks aimed at foreign direct investment – largely to multinationals domiciled in big industrialized countries – have significantly undermined revenues of many developing countries. A 2012 working paper published by the IMF reported that "a race to the bottom is evident among special regimes, most notably in the case of Africa, creating effectively a parallel tax system where rates have fallen to almost zero."

There is evidence that such incentives are not a stable source of investment but governments often feel they have little choice in the matter. A report by the IMF, OECD, United Nations and World Bank in 2011 said: "Developing countries sometimes believe – often correctly – that an attempt to hold the line against multinational enterprises negotiating for 'necessary' tax breaks will simply drive the investment in question into a neighboring country. This sort of bargaining frequently results in a 'race to the bottom,' in which countries in a region are made collectively worse off, to the benefit of the multinational investors" (IMF 2011).

Even subtler aspects of tax competition, including a tolerance of certain avoidance strategies, have also become more important in recent years. Pascal Saint-Amans, the top tax official of the Paris-based Organisation for Economic Co-operation and Development, said in 2012: "The aggressive tax planning of the last 20 years was achieved with the complicity of governments themselves to cope with tax competition."[3]

---

2. http://people.stern.nyu.edu/adamodar/pdfiles/articles/KPMGtaxratesurvey.pdf.
3. https://www.ft.com/content/0dc00990-5be0-11e2-bef7-00144feab49a#axzz2I1wxwcUG.

Tax planning became an increasingly important driver of the lower effective tax rates paid by U.S. companies around the turn of the century, according to 2006 research by Rosanne Altshuler and Harry Grubert (Altshuler and Grubert 2006). While tax competition by governments competing for foreign direct investment was the main driver of the reduction in effective tax rates paid by U.S. companies from 1992 to 1998, tax avoidance became more important after 1998. It was increasingly driven by aggressive tax planning made possible by tax provisions passed by the multinationals' home governments, as well as the host countries where they were operating. The researchers concluded that: "The results illustrate the importance of including both company tax planning and the cooperation of home and host governments in an accurate depiction of any race to the bottom."

The prime example of a measure passed by a home government that helps its multinationals compete overseas is a U.S. rule known as "check the box." Passed in 1997, the measure was originally designed to be a simplification, but it soon became clear that it opened up opportunities for companies to shift income to tax havens. Companies had a new incentive to strip taxable profits out of high-tax countries in which they operated – often through payments of interest or royalties– pushing down the average overseas tax rates of U.S. businesses. The Treasury mounted two attempts to reform the rules but the business community successfully pushed back, saying changes would put them at a disadvantage when competing abroad.[4]

A more recent example of a government setting out to help its multinationals compete abroad was the U.K.'s "finance company partial exemption" that introduced a very low tax rate – a quarter of the full rate – for subsidiaries in tax havens that provided finance for other parts of a multinational group. While the government saw it as a way of attracting more multinational headquarters, critics feared it was an invitation to strip other countries tax base. Action Aid, a charity, said the rule could cost developing countries up to GBP 4billion of tax revenues.[5]

[C] Responses of Governments

Many governments see tax competition as a major problem. Ricardo Ortega, Colombia's former tax director, emphasizes the unfairness of the phenomenon. "As an economist one always believes that competition is virtuous – it is part of our mantra – but for competition to make sense, you have to talk about competition as a game within a legal framework. The lawyers are the ones that are ruling the game and most of the time they are winning.

There are many jurisdictions being used to undermine the system as a whole and many of the players do not have the tools nor the political strength to make this a more fair game. The international community is the only hope for things to go in a better direction."

---

4. https://www.ft.com/content/69703dfe-e82e-11e0-9fc7-00144feab49a.
5. https://www.ft.com/content/a8e0dfbc-3dfb-11e0-99ac-00144feabdc0.

He also highlights another risk of tax competition. In his experience in Colombia, special zones – with tax advantages purportedly designed to boost foreign investment– were exploited by organized crime, fueling money laundering, corruption and the drugs industry.

Cristina Duarte, the former finance minister of Cabo Verde, also experienced the pressures of tax competition. She describes it as "a global game with unfair and unbalanced rules." In her experience, the pressure to cut taxes came from fellow members of her government, as well as international businesses. As part of her regular Budget preparations, she would routinely receive 10 to 15 tax-cutting proposals from each of her colleagues.

She says it is crucial that a finance minister shows leadership in resisting this pressure – and gets the support of the head of the government in doing so. Otherwise, a country can get locked in a vicious circle in which fiscal policy is employed to compensate for the inefficiencies of various sectors. That hurts the mechanisms of resource allocation which, as a result, hurts the competitiveness of the country.

But the decisions about tax rates need to be deeply rooted in an understanding of the structure and competitiveness of individual sector. Only then can a finance minister understand the weight and the role of tax in determining a country's appeal to businesses. Ms. Duarte says she carried out extensive analysis before removing the reduced rate of value added tax on tourism services – resulting in a rise from 6% to 15% in 2014 – and says she is sure her actions did not jeopardize Cabo Verde's competitiveness.

At the other end of the scale are the governments that view tax competition as a positive tool they can use to bring jobs and revenue to their country. One example is the U.K. government that came to power in 2010, with a goal of bringing back some of the 24 companies that had recently shifted their headquarters out of the U.K. for tax reasons.

It made sweeping cuts in corporate taxation, which it partly justified on the grounds that corporate income taxes are the taxes most harmful for growth, citing 2008 work by the OECD on growth-oriented tax reform (OECD 2010). It also sought to attract more headquarters and other activities, by introducing a patent box and a special tax rate for offshore finance income.

George Osborne, then Chancellor, was frank about his willingness to fuel tax competition. In 2013 he said, "nothing beats having the most competitive business tax system of any major economy in the world." Citing a ranking of competitive tax regimes by accountants KPMG he said: "Three years ago, we were near the bottom of that table. Now we're at the top. But in this global race, we cannot stand still."[6] In 2016, he announced another corporate tax rate cut, taking the rate– which had been 28% in 2000 to 17% by 2020, saying: "Britain is blazing a trail – let the rest of the world catch up."

---

6. http://www.telegraph.co.uk/finance/budget/9942779/George-Osbornes-Budget-speech-in-full.html.

§6.03 TAX COOPERATION

[A] Definition

International tax cooperation is a way of reducing or even neutralizing the effects of tax competition. It can take many different forms, including taking practical steps to help other countries tackle evasion and avoidance.

Coming up with common rules is another long-standing goal for many regions. These can involve agreements on minimum tax rates, a common approach to tax incentives and a ban on certain types of preferential regimes.

Attempts to harmonize tax systems entirely are far less common. Harmonization involves three elements: an equalization of tax rates, a common definition of national tax bases and a uniform application of agreed rules. Without uniform application of the rules, there can be a subtle form of tax complication involving lax application of regulations, such as low audit rates.

[B] International and Regional Initiatives

[1] International Initiatives

Until recently the biggest international effort of this sort was the OECD's "harmful tax competition" initiative launched in 1998. It sought to discourage countries from pursuing policies that were thought to harm other countries by unfairly eroding their tax bases. From the start, it acknowledged there were difficulties in defining tax competition. Countries that were remote or lacked natural resources frequently considered that they needed special tax incentives to offset non-tax disadvantages. It said: "Tax competition and the interaction of tax systems can have effects that some countries may view as negative or harmful but others may not."

Despite the challenges, it floated the possibility of sanctions against countries that operated as tax havens. Its suggested definition of a tax haven involved low or zero tax rates, lack of tax information exchange with other countries, bank secrecy and lack of real economic activity.[7]

But after heavy lobbying, the Bush administration in the U.S. withdrew its support from the OECD's initiative to stamp out harmful tax competition. Paul O'Neill, Treasury secretary announced that "the U.S. does not support efforts to dictate to any country what its own tax rates or tax systems should be, and will not participate in any initiative to harmonize world tax systems."[8]

After that, the OECD largely abandoned its original aim of dealing with harmful competition for mobile capital and instead pursued the exchange of tax information on request. It made slow progress, not least because several OECD countries were themselves bastions of bank secrecy. According to Martin Sullivan of Tax Analysts in

---

7. http://www.oecd.org/tax/transparency/44430243.pdf.
8. https://www.treasury.gov/press-center/press-releases/Pages/po366.aspx.

2007, "the OECD efforts to curb 'harmful tax competition' slowly dissolved into a series of toothless pronouncements, a mixture of cheerleading and scorekeeping."[9]

Since then, the battle against bank secrecy has scored important successes. A string of tax evasion scandals, against a backdrop of the financial crisis, prompted the U.S. to introduce sweeping legislation requiring the transfer of tax information from overseas banks under its 2010 Foreign Account Tax Compliance Act.[10] It proved a catalyst for other governments to take similar steps, creating the "common reporting standard" for cross-border flows of tax data between more than 100 countries – though not yet including the U.S.

Another global initiative was the assault on "base erosion and profit shifting" that was initiated by G20 countries in 2012 in response to public anger about corporate tax avoidance.[11] The BEPS initiative was, in some respects, a return to the earlier attempt to crack down on "harmful tax competition." However this time the OECD made clear that it was not against tax competition on tax rates, so long as it concerned real activities rather than paper– or highly mobile– profits. In a 2014 interview, Pascal Saint-Amans, the OECD's top tax official said: "We are in favor of lower tax rates on corporate income tax, as long as you have broad bases. And the fact that countries want to compete on this is not a problem, as long as they don't do it in a harmful manner, meaning ring-fenced or too aggressive on some sectors where it's highly mobile."[12]

One example of the BEPS project's attack on harmful tax practices was the decision to require substantial activities for any preferential regime. After a standoff between Germany and the U.K. in 2014, a compromise was agreed. It determined that the low tax rates offered by "patent boxes" should only be applied in cases where taxpayers engaged in research and development in countries where they benefited from these regimes.

One of the potential challenges to the legitimacy of the BEPS project was the restricted number of countries involved in the decision-making. Following the agreement of the BEPS action plan by leaders of the G20 countries in late 2015, there has been an effort to involve a much wider group of countries in reviewing and monitoring the implementation of the package. A meeting in Japan in June 2016 was the first time that a broad range of countries, representing varying levels of development, came together on an equal footing in the OECD's Committee on Fiscal Affairs, marking what it described as "a new era in international tax co-operation."

At the United Nations, which many developing countries view as the most appropriate forum for setting international tax rules, there has also been renewed interest in facilitating "an inclusive and broad-based dialogue on international tax cooperation." In 2013, its Economic and Social Council agreed to hold a special meeting

---

9. http://www.taxjustice.net/cms/upload/pdf/Tax_Notes_0707_Lessons_from_the_war_on_tax_havens.pdf
10. https://www.irs.gov/businesses/corporations/foreign-account-tax-compliance-act-fatca.
11. http://www.oecd.org/tax/beps/.
12. https://www.pwc.com/gx/en/tax/tax-policy-administration/beps/assets/pwc-tax-interview-transcript.pdf.

annually "to consider international cooperation in tax matters, including, as appropriate, its contribution to mobilizing domestic financial resources for development and the institutional arrangements to promote such cooperation."[13]

A willingness to share information is emerging as one of the big themes of international cooperation. Many tax authorities think the biggest achievement of the BEPS initiative will be the spotlight shone on multinationals' tax arrangements by new "country by country" reporting rules, requiring them to share information with tax authorities about where they earn their profits and pay their taxes.

This initiative will provide information on how companies allocate their taxable income in a standardized format, helping tax administrations get a better understanding of the structures of multinationals. Many tax authorities are planning to use sophisticated digital technologies and analytical techniques to identify high-risk taxpayers that require further investigation but not all have access to these tools. In addition, some developing countries are likely to face restrictions on getting access to the data, according to a Tax Justice Network report for the Financial Transparency Coalition. It argues that this creates a "risk that the inequalities in taxing rights faced by lower-income countries may actually be exacerbated" (Knobel and Cobham 2016).

Another example of growing cooperation between tax authorities is the Joint International Taskforce on Shared Intelligence and Collaboration (JITSIC). JITSIC began in 2004 as the Joint International Tax Shelter Information Centre, a joint initiative of the revenue authorities of Australia, Canada, the U.K. and the U.S. to facilitate their work in countering abusive tax schemes and tax avoidance structures. Its membership was gradually expanded and its focus broadened, before being renamed in 2016. It now has 36 members including Australia, Russia, South Africa, the U.S. and many EU countries. Its larger membership provides greater scope for tax administrations to exchange information and undertake collaborative casework.

[2] Regional Initiatives

[a] The European Union

From the beginning of the EU, its leaders concluded that economic integration would require the removal of tax barriers and greater cooperation in the collection of revenues.

After two reports studied the issues in 1962 and 1970, a number of initiatives were designed to achieve a limited degree of harmonization of the corporate tax system. Proposals for directives were put forward by the Commission in 1975, 1984 and 1985, which were later withdrawn. In 1988 there was a draft proposal for the harmonization of the corporate tax base but it was never tabled, due to the reluctance of most Member States.

In 1992, a committee under the chairmanship of Onno Ruding, which had been asked to examine the distortions caused by corporate tax regimes in the EU, suggested

---

13. http://www.un.org/ga/search/view_doc.asp?symbol=E/RES/2013/24&Lang=E.

the introduction of a minimum rate of 30%. At the time it was seen as a modest proposal although the recommendation was soon overtaken by the continuing downwards movement of rates. In 1997 the Commission took a new approach which was a voluntary code of conduct aimed against "harmful" tax competition. It took issue with some preferential regimes but overall it did little to tackle the practices that facilitated multinationals' tax avoidance.

In 2001, the Commission came up with a new approach: a plan to harmonize the base and apportion profits between Member States using a formula. Governments failed to agree on the plan but in 2014, the Commission announced plans to relaunch the proposal, using a phased approach. It said the idea, known as the common consolidated corporate tax base, was a "holistic solution" that would make it simpler and cheaper for companies to operate cross-border, while serving as a powerful tool against corporate tax avoidance. The EU has also put in place a directive to ensure that the OECD anti-BEPS measures are implemented in a coordinated manner. Some finance ministers have also voiced support for the idea of a minimum tax rate (Turner 2015).

The insistence of Member States on their sovereignty over direct tax matters has seriously limited attempts to harmonize taxes. In cases where Brussels has been able to use the law to force governments to change their tax rules, its impact has been much bigger.

The 1957 Treaty of Rome has had a big impact on tax systems because it barred governments from discriminating against cross-border businesses – although it was not until a series of rulings from the European Court of Justice this century that its full impact was felt. The Commission's recent string of "state aid" cases in which it has accused governments including Ireland, the Netherlands and Luxembourg of giving preferential tax treatment to multinationals such as Apple, Starbucks and Amazon is also likely to have a significant impact on some countries' tax regimes.

[b]   West Africa

The degree of tax coordination in West Africa is one of the most advanced in the world. Under the 1994 treaty setting up the West African Economic and Monetary Union, eight countries–Benin, Burkina Faso, Cote d'Ivoire, Guinea-Bissau, Mali, Niger, Senegal and Togo – have agreed to work towards greater regional integration. The countries have agreed to coordinate the setting of tax rates and bases for the major taxes through regional directives. They also made plans for the convergence of the tax revenue-to-GDP ratio to at least 17%.

Research published in 2013 by the IMF found the union might have succeeded in improving revenue mobilization but that special tax regimes were the 'Achilles' heel of tax coordination' in WAEMU states. The framework allowed unfettered tax competition through investment incentives, as long as it was done outside countries' main tax laws. This, in turn, made tax systems opaque, increased their complexity and contributed to a culture of "tax negotiation" (Mansour and Rota-Graziosi 2013).

[c] East Africa

The East African Community, which was reestablished in 1999, paved the way for a customs union involving Kenya, Tanzania, Uganda, Rwanda and Burundi which meant that companies based in any of the countries could get access to their markets. Countries increased investment incentives to attract foreign direct investment, resulting in what Action Aid, a charity, estimated in 2012 were losses of up to USD 2.8 billion a year from tax incentives for Kenya, Uganda, Tanzania and Rwanda. It reported that many governments in East Africa were pledging to reduce or eliminate tax incentives, amid growing concerns about the ineffectiveness of the policy.[14]

A follow-up report by Action Aid in 2016 found mixed results. It said that governments had taken some positive steps to reduce tax incentives, especially those related to the VAT. This was increasing tax collection and providing vital extra revenues that could be spent on providing critical services. But they were still failing to eliminate all unnecessary tax incentives, including tax breaks for corporations.

It said the East African Community countries had shown that there was regional political will towards ending harmful tax incentives to multinationals. But it added: "However, what seems to have not been understood is that it takes more than just political will to achieve this. Stronger policies need to be further implemented at both country and regional levels to make sure that they effectively seal loopholes, and that the region is able to get its rightful share of lost tax revenue."[15]

[d] Southern Africa

The Southern African Development Community (SADC), established in 1992, is a group of 15 Member States committed to regional integration and poverty eradication within Southern Africa. In 2002, finance ministers signed a memorandum of understanding in which they set out their intentions to reduce the tax competition that damaged the region's revenue mobilization efforts. It said they would "endeavor to achieve a common approach to the treatment and application of tax incentives" and ensure they were only provided for in legislation. Progress has been limited but reducing tax competition on incentives remains an important theme.

In 2013 it agreed another program to support regional economic integration which set out to support "a common approach to tax incentives to avoid harmful tax competition between Member States, whilst encouraging sustainable investment and avoiding unnecessary revenue given away."[16]

---

14. http://www.actionaid.org/sites/files/actionaid/eac_report.pdf.
15. http://www.actionaid.org/publications/still-racing-toward-bottom-corporate-tax-incentives-east-africa.
16. http://www.sadc.int/themes/economic-development/investment/tax-coordination/.

[e]   Southeast Asia

The Association of Southeast Asian Nations (ASEAN) was formed in 1967 to promote economic growth and regional stability. On December 31, 2015 its 10 Member States– comprising Indonesia, Malaysia, Philippines, Singapore, Thailand, Brunei, Laos, Myanmar, Cambodia and Vietnam– formally launched the ASEAN Economic Community (AEC), with the aim of creating a single market with minimal economic barriers.

In the run-up to the launch of the single market, there were sharp falls in corporate tax rates and an expansion of the tax incentives used to attract foreign direct investment. The explanation offered by KPMG, professional services firm, was that: "With an ASEAN single market in goods and services, taxation becomes one of the policy tools still available for national governments to compete for investment."[17]

But there have also been pressures pushing in the opposite direction. The cuts in tariffs that accompanied the creation of the AEC "should exert pressure on national budgets and increase the need for cooperation on the tax side" according to a report by the International Tax Compact, a development policy initiative funded by the German government (Büttner et al. 2013).

Tax cooperation played a relatively limited role in the early plans of the AEC, although the 2007 blueprint for the community committed Member States to work towards completing double tax agreements and tackling certain withholding tax issues. The focus on these issues intensified in 2011, when finance ministers set up the ASEAN Forum on Taxation in recognition of "the importance of addressing tax-related impediments to integration."

As the community looks ahead to 2025, tax cooperation is likely to play a bigger role. The Blueprint 2025 mentions the commitment to "discuss measures to address the issue of base erosion and profit shifting to ensure fiscal health." In the view of KPMG, this opens the door for discussions about the "potential detrimental effects of tax competition within the region."

[3]   **Responses of Governments**

Cristina Duarte, the former finance minister of Cabo Verde, says she is "very skeptical" regarding tax cooperation, particularly at a time when governments' willingness to cooperate has been tested by recession. "It did not happen during the 'fat period' before the international crisis. Will it happen during the biggest international crisis in the past 75 years? I have my doubts."

Her skepticism is partly based on the repeated failure of the EU – despite its strong institutions and commitment to integration – to coordinate policy. She thinks governments will inevitably struggle to coordinate tax policy in an era when globalization and aggressive tax planning by multinationals is eroding the tax base.

She argues that political will, a willingness to fight any lack of transparency and a determination to withstand lobbying, is a precondition to tax cooperation. She says:

---

17. https://home.kpmg.com/sg/en/home/insights/2016/07/the-asean-economic-community.html.

"The political class need to recoup their sovereignty in relation to their countries' multinational companies and stop functioning as an extension of the marketing department of the multinationals." In her view, the other important preconditions for tax cooperation include an active civil society to take its share of responsibility; internal and international accountability; and policy consistency and progressive reforms.

Michael Sell, head of the German tax department, puts particular stress on the value of cooperation between tax authorities on matters such as tax audits and information sharing.

He argues that increased use of joint audits for multinationals should be made part of "BEPS 2.0," namely, the implementation phase of the project aimed at tackling base erosion and profit shifting. This approach to audits, piloted by Germany and some of its neighbors, stands in contrast to what is currently the norm, in which a multinational may be subject to separate audits for the same transaction by different countries, sometimes many years apart.

[4] Responses of Non-governmental Organizations and Academics

Campaign groups often argue that tax competition is a result of lobbying by the groups that benefit from it. Action Aid, an international charity, says: "Big business is far from being a passive taker of tax rules. Corporate lobbyists constantly argue for lower taxes and tax incentives and warn politicians and the public that without them, job-creating foreign investment will flow elsewhere."[18]

In a similar vein, Christian Aid says tax competition policies "have not contributed to improving citizens' welfare, with most of the benefit accruing to the elites, multinationals, their tax advisers and corporations' shareholders."[19]

Tax Justice Network, an international campaign group urges countries to disengage from tax competition, saying that what keeps them in the race is usually "false ideology, and lobbying." It says that: "International co-ordination on these things is useful, for sure, but another way is possible: countries can unilaterally opt out of the race."[20]

The Independent Commission for the Reform of International Taxation argues that: "Developed nations, possibly through the OECD, should take the first step to stop the current race to the bottom in corporate taxation, by agreeing on a minimum corporate tax rate." This group, established by a broad coalition of civil society and labor organizations, argues that the system of taxing the global profits of multinational corporations is broken and that the rules and institutions governing the international corporate tax system must change. It says that inclusive international cooperation for reform is essential.[21]

---

18. https://www.actionaid.org.uk/sites/default/files/publications/levelling_up_final.pdf.
19. http://www.christianaid.org.uk/Images/christian-aid-tax-justice-strategy-2013-2016.pdf.
20. http://foolsgold.international/optimistic-about-the-state-martin-wolfs-searing-attack-on-the-competitiveness-agenda/.
21. http://www.icrict.org/about-us/.

But some campaigners, representing a different set of interests, take a very different view of tax competition. They say lobbying by interest groups spurs governments to overspend and tax competition provides a useful constraint– although this argument is less often applied in the case of developing countries where there is widespread agreement that governments need to collect more revenue. The Cato Institute says: "If plans to stifle tax competition gain ground, growth will be undermined, governments will grow larger, and economic freedom will be curtailed."[22]

A group of 20 free market and taxpayer advocacy groups wrote to Congress in 2016 to protest about the OECD's BEPS initiative. In it, they said: "Reducing tax competition results in an overall higher tax environment and a weaker global economy. Without the checks on political greed that competition affords, taxpayers inevitably suffer."[23]

Academics are also closely engaged in the arguments over tax competition. Some are highly critical of governments that promote tax competition. Edward Kleinbard, professor at the University of Southern California Gould School of Law, described the U.K.'s recent approach to tax competition as "a trade war by another name – fought with income tax policies rather than tariffs."[24]

Lawrence Summers, former secretary of the U.S. Treasury and professor at Harvard, has called for "responsible nationalism," in which countries are expected to pursue their citizens' economic welfare as a primary objective but where their ability to harm the interests of citizens elsewhere is circumscribed.

He argues that means more scope for international cooperation. He says: "For example, tax burdens on workers around the world are as much as a trillion dollars greater than they would be if we had a proper system of international coordination that identified capital income and prevented a race to the bottom in its taxation" (Summers 2016).

But researchers have identified many difficulties in both practice and principle in tackling tax competition. Michael Devereux and John Vella of the Oxford University Centre for Business Taxation argue that the problem is inevitable given the current structure of the corporate tax system. The issue is one of incentive compatibility, they say. "If countries acting in their own interests believe that they have an incentive to undermine the international consensus, then that international consensus cannot provide a stable long-run system. There is ample evidence that countries have been doing precisely that. Furthermore, quite beyond the current uncertainty surrounding the outcome of the OECD BEPS initiative, even if it is successful on its own terms the BEPS initiative will not eliminate these competitive forces (Devereux and Vella 2014)."

James Hines, a professor at the University of Michigan, thinks that tackling BEPS may end up intensifying tax competition on rates. "Reducing BEPS increases tax burdens but does little, if anything, to reduce the competitive pressures that countries

---

22. http://www.cato.org/research/international-tax-competition.
23. http://freedomandprosperity.org/2016/news/press-releases/coalition-for-tax-competition-letter-urges-congress-to-defund-the-oecd-oppose-beps/.
24. https://www.ft.com/content/a7de48b8-c3bc-11e2-8c30-00144feab7de.

face in attempting to attract and foster business activity; as a result, tax rates are likely to decline – possibly by quite a bit" (Hines Jr. 2014).

Some academics argue that there may be risks from attempting to harmonize taxes. Brigitte Unger of Utrecht University and colleagues have argued that regions that harmonize their tax policies will be at risk from neighboring states that undercut them. They have an incentive to attract investment by freeriding on the "cartel" formed by the other states. In the case of the EU, even if its members agreed to tax harmonization policies, neighboring countries – such as Switzerland, Norway and Turkey – could benefit from a geographical closeness to the EU and a significantly more competitive tax rate. They concluded: "In the world of globalization, the proposal of tax harmonization can therefore be seen to pose an existential threat to the European Union" (McCarthy et al. 2008).

Another potential downside to the harmonization of taxes is the loss of individual countries' ability to tailor their tax regime to their particular circumstances. "To the degree that national tax differences reflect sensible and purposive choices in response to differing situations and political preferences, tax coordination threatens to undermine the benefits that such choices may offer," according to the Mirrlees Review, a collaboration by a high-profile group of international experts. It concluded that the "potential gains from international tax coordination are likely to be rather small and unevenly distributed across countries" (Griffith et al. 2010).

A literature review conducted by Michael Keen of the IMF and Kai Konrad of the Max Planck Institute for Tax Law and Public Finance in 2012 suggested that research did a better job in explaining why a concerted action may be difficult than in suggesting, even in broad terms, what actions might be both desirable and feasible. It concluded that agreeing minimum tax rates was likely to be a more fruitful path to coordinating away from inefficient outcomes than agreeing on common rates (Keen and A. Konrad 2012).

In the short term, increasing transparency over tax matters is likely to be a fruitful approach, according to a 2015 paper on fiscal policy and long-term growth published by the IMF. It argued that international cooperation should be encouraged: "In a world of increasing tax competition, all countries may end up being worse off." But it noted "the difficulty of achieving and enforcing effective cooperation." In view of that, it suggested that coordination could initially focus on smaller steps, such as promoting transparency by publishing data on tax expenditures arising from tax incentives (IMF 2015).

Radical reforms, involving fundamental changes to the structure of corporate tax, might be needed to stabilize the tax system, according to a paper by Alan Auerbach of the University of California Berkeley, Michael Devereux, Michael Keen and John Vella (Auerbach et al. 2017). They argued the tax system could be stabilized by moving to a "destination-based cash flow tax" (DBCFT) which would require profits to be taxed in the country where the sales are made.

The proposal – a version of which was proposed in 2016 by U.S. House Republicans – would reduce the tax rate on domestic source income to zero. The idea, which sparked intense debate over its potential impact on business, trade and currencies, could be seen as the "ultimate move" in the tax competition game concerning the traditional corporate tax, the authors said. It would provide a "powerful incentive" for other countries to follow suit, although countries with natural resources would be advised to retain their taxing rights.

The authors said that countries that adopted the DBCFT would not face competition over tax rates. "In that sense the acceleration of one tax competitive game also puts a stop to another and would provide long term stability for the adopting state free from destabilizing tax competitive forces."

§6.04 CONCLUSION

The impact that one government's tax policies can have on other countries' ability to collect revenues has hugely increased over the past 30 years. The globalization of trade and investment and the expansion of international financial markets put pressure on both countries and companies to compete on tax. Governments have felt a need to create a business-friendly climate and have adjusted their tax systems to reduce barriers to investment. In many countries, the influence of multinationals over corporate tax policies has significantly increased.

At a time when governments are desperate to create jobs and growth, many are continuing to bring down taxes to stimulate growth and attract investment from abroad. But at the same time, there is a growing awareness of the intensity of tax competition and the possibility of mutual harm from a country's efforts to make its tax system more attractive than its neighbors. The difficulties shared by governments as they try to raise revenues and attract investment have prompted political leaders to push tax matters high up the international agenda.

When it comes to transparency, an era of unprecedented international cooperation is now underway. There is now a common – though not comprehensive– approach to information sharing that will underpin global efforts to tackle tax evasion. An international drive to tackle base erosion and profit shifting is set to reduce the scope for avoidance and competition for highly mobile profits.

These achievements are a sign of a greater political willingness to cooperate on certain aspects of tax policy. But the ability of these measures to solve deep-rooted problems remains in doubt. Some economists argue the incentives that lead to competitive rate-cutting stem from deep flaws in the corporate tax system. To stop a race to the bottom, they believe that governments will be forced to undertake a radical rethink of the corporate tax.

REFERENCES

Altshuler, Rosanne and Grubert, Harry. 2006. "Governments and Multinational Corporations in the Race to the Bottom": Tax Notes.
Bilicka, Katarzyna and Devereux, Michael, 2012. "Corporate Tax Ranking": Oxford University Centre for Business Taxation.
Büttner, Wolfgang et al. 2013. "Mapping Taxation in Selected Asian Developing Countries": International Tax Compact.

Clausing, Kimberly et al. 2016 ."U.S. Corporate Income Tax Reform and Its Spillovers": IMF Working Paper.

Davies, Ronald and Voget, Johannes. 2001. "Tax Competition in an Expanding European Union": Oxford University Centre for Business Taxation.

Devereux, Michael and Vella, John. 2014. "Are We Heading Towards a Corporate Tax System Fit for the 21st Century?" Oxford University Centre for Business Taxation.

Devereux, Michael et al. 2004. "Do Countries Compete over Corporate Tax Rates?": University of Warwick.

Griffith, Rachel et al. 2008. "International Capital Taxation": Institute for Fiscal Studies.

Hines, James. 2014. "How Serious Is the Problem of Base Erosion and Profit Shifting?" Canadian Tax Journal.

Knobel, Andres and Cobham, Alex. 2006. "Country-by-Country Reporting: How Restricted Access Exacerbates Global Inequalities in Taxing Rights": Tax Justice Network Report for the Financial Transparency Coalition.

Mansour, Mario and Rota-Graziosi, Grégoire. 2013. "Tax Coordination, Tax Competition, and Revenue Mobilization in the West African Economic and Monetary Union": IMF Working Paper.

McCarthy, Killian et al. 2008. "Globalisation, Tax Competition and the Harmonisation of Corporate Tax Rates in Europe: A Case of Killing the Patient to Cure the Disease?" Utrecht School of Economics.

CHAPTER 7

Experts Debate: What Is Better for Low-Income Countries, Tax Competition, or Tax Cooperation?

Allison Christians

On May 23, 2016, as part of the "Winning the Tax Wars" conference, a debate was convened to explore a set of three resolutions regarding the effect of tax competition on developing countries. First, the debaters considered whether tax competition harms developing countries by reducing their capability to raise fiscal revenue to finance physical and social infrastructure needed for economic growth and social inclusion. Second, the debaters considered whether tax competition increases developing countries' reliance on foreign aid, making them more vulnerable to aid volatility. Finally, the debaters considered whether tax competition aggravates existing income disparities between developed and developing countries.

Arguing the "affirming side" of each resolution was Alison Holder of ActionAid. Arguing the "opposing side" of each resolution was Veronique de Rugy of the Mercatus Center at George Mason University. Evidence from all jurisdictions was admissible. The emphasis was on persuasive, clear, and logical argumentation. The debate proceeded in four rounds and was moderated and judged by Louise Otis of McGill University and Jay Rosengard of Harvard University. After the debate, the judges deliberated while the online audience entered their votes. The majority of those polled voted in favor of supporting tax cooperation as the better strategy for low-income countries. The judges held that, in principle, tax competition is good because, as in other areas, competition should bring down prices and improve services. However, competition is not good in all cases and forms; the judges called for constructive competition, with cooperation to mitigate the race to the bottom that can result from tax competition, and that impedes societies from realizing their collective goals.

Following is an edited transcript of the debate, with corrections for clarity.

§7.01 INTRODUCTION

Today, the enhanced mobility of capital, goods, and people has not only increased international economic integration but also resulted in more mobile tax bases. As national authorities attempt to spur investment by offering more favorable treatment than is available elsewhere, the result is increasingly aggressive tax competition. A main goal of international tax policy is to maximize the utility of goods and resources while also ensuring fundamental fairness. But there is much disagreement on how to go about achieving these goals, especially with respect to tax competition.

On the one hand, those who argue against tax competition maintain that such policies favor only high-income countries and their corporate interests and that low- and middle-income countries are forced into a "beggar-thy-neighbor" situation, deprived of revenue necessary, indeed vital, for developing infrastructure, social programs, and communities.

This disparate effect is exacerbated by the fact that high-income countries, through the OECD and the G20, have globalized the tax policy discourse, developing consensus on a set of mutually agreeable tax norms, suited to their own interests. The countries with the lowest incomes, most of which are in sub-Saharan Africa, have been all but missing from this global dialogue, and it's not clear how these countries may make their voices heard, even in a more inclusive framework. Thus, many of the biggest tax-related challenges faced by the world's poorest countries are not necessarily a reflection of the shortcomings or capacity issues of a particular tax administration. Rather, these challenges reflect the international community's failure to consider how the globalization of tax policy norms affects vulnerable nations.

On the other hand, those in favor of tax competition maintain that tax competition follows real competition – that is, foreign investment. And tax competition policies represent, through deference to the market, a fair and efficient allocation of income and investment, which will generate the highest returns for high, low and middle-income countries. They further maintain that the returns sought by foreign investors are the minimum required to produce direct investment. So it does not follow that, if tax competition is discontinued, the levels of investment currently enjoyed by countries with lower tax rates would remain the same. Overall, those in favor of tax competition posit that artificial limitations placed on the market would reduce trade with an investment in the countries that need it the most, thus slowing the growth and development of low- and middle-income countries.

The debate proceeds with introduction of resolutions by the judges and responses by each debater in turn.

§7.02 FIRST RESOLUTION

The broad theme for this event is: What is better for developing countries, tax competition or tax cooperation? The debaters will argue three proposed resolutions in three rounds and conclude with a round of open debate. The first resolution is as follows: *Be it resolved that tax competition harms developing countries by reducing their capability to raise fiscal revenue to finance physical and social infrastructure needed for economic growth and social inclusion.*

[A] Response to First Resolution by Alison Holder

This debate should start with a distinction between developed and developing countries, and too often debates about tax competition take place in developed countries with only the voices of developed countries represented. As an international development NGO, with offices in 45 countries, most of which are in the global south, ActionAid is well placed to bring the experience of developing countries to bear.

The situation of fiscal revenue raising for public goods in OECD countries is a pretty uniform picture. All OECD countries have extensive public services, state-funded infrastructure supported by tax revenues, much of which could not exist purely on a for-profit basis. Total taxation in OECD countries is typically around 35%–45% of GDP, and corporate income tax is a significant source of revenue, around 8%, but there are also many other sources of revenue.

The situation in developing countries is very different. In most of these countries, tax to GDP ratios tend to be somewhere between 10% and 20%, and corporate income tax accounts for more like 16%. So that's compared with 8% in OECD countries. And when we take into account other revenues such as natural resource royalties and trade taxes, the contribution of corporations to the public finances in developing countries can be far higher than that. With developing countries, we are talking about countries that mobilize far smaller revenues in proportion to the size of their economies, and where corporate tax including income tax and other kinds of contributions are a much bigger proportion of those revenues. In developing countries, almost by definition, public services and infrastructure are undersupplied, and in many countries, there are large areas with very few public services at all. Does tax competition harm the ability of developing countries to raise fiscal revenues and make the necessary investments in economic and human development? The answer is an emphatic yes.

Tax competition is too commonly thought of as just being about the lowering of tax rates, but it's about much more. It is about the lowering of tax rates, but it is also about the erosion of the tax base, whether through profit shifting, granting generous exemptions and incentives, or unfair tax treaties, just as a few examples.

So how do we know that tax competition harms developing countries? Well, first we have research showing that it does, and some of that research comes from this very institution or its close cousin down the road. We have estimates of revenue lost by developing countries because of base erosion and profit shifting, a phenomenon that is only possible in a world where tax competition is rife. IMF research has estimated these losses at about USD 200 billion each year for developing countries, and these are just the legal outflows. So the 200 billion doesn't include illegal outflows due to tax evasion, which are also likely to be substantial. The illegal outflows are less related to the phenomenon of tax competition, but the fact that tax havens and secrecy jurisdictions exist makes tax fraud more attractive, because the profits of it can be laundered and stashed in tax havens.

So we have 200 billion dollars lost due to legal tax avoidance for developing countries, and a system of tax havens and secrecy jurisdictions that enable illegal tax evasion from developing countries. Moreover ActionAid research shows the amount of corporate tax revenue foregone by developing countries because of tax breaks. The cost is startlingly large: just under USD 140 billion every year because of generous tax breaks offered to companies by developing countries. Another study looked specifically at Sierra Leone and found that it had given up revenue equivalent to eight times its national health budget on tax incentives for large companies in 2012 alone.

Another form of tax incentive offered by some developing countries is the weak or unfair tax treaty. More ActionAid research shows that Bangladesh is losing approximately USD 85 million every year just from one clause in its tax treaties that severely restricts its right to tax dividends. Remedying this alone could pay for health services for 3.4 million people. In country after country, the same assumption on the part of politicians is stated: to bring investment, we must offer tax breaks. This assumption will be challenged directly in the next resolution.

To summarize my arguments affirming resolution one: debates about tax competition are often based on assumptions which are not valid for developing countries, which have pressing needs for more revenue to spend on public services, and which depend more heavily on revenue from corporations. Two: tax competition harms developing countries by causing them to raise less revenue than they otherwise might, and the scale of the revenue foregone is likely to be substantial. And three: tax competition is a major enabler of corporate tax avoidance, which also has a disproportionate effect on developing countries.

[B] Response to First Resolution by Veronique de Rugy

Tax competition is a process. It's a process that actually sends a fundamental and important signal to governments about their own domestic policy. For instance, if you have massive amounts of capital flow out of a country, it actually serves as a signal that this country should change its tax policy and, sometimes, its institutions. And it's not because you don't like the signal that is being sent that you should actually squash competition. We would do a lot of disservice to governments who have the tendency, if we understand public choice economics, to overspend, overtax, and never try to actually implement the type of policies that are actually conducive to economic growth, because as you said, this is what we are after.

Now, the other thing is that many developing countries aren't first and foremost suffering from tax competition, they're suffering from corruption, a weak rule of law, and weak institutions that fail, basically, to allow entrepreneurship and prosperity. Unfortunately, big government policies will only enable more corruption. An interesting paper was produced by the World Bank in May 2015 that talks about the consequences of disclosure, especially in developing countries. And when you know that a lot of the attempt by high taxation to squash tax competition has been done through, something we call collaboration, but actually bullying, to disclose and engage in automatic exchange of information, it is important. The conclusion of this paper says, "Disclosure also leads to significantly higher levels of corruption faced by firms. Once firm information is disclosed, the threat of government expropriation is widespread. Information disclosure has allowed rent seeking by bureaucrats, to gain access to disclosed information and use it to extract bribes. With more information about firms available, government expropriations become more severe, especially in countries with poor property rights." This is important to keep in mind. Corruption is a problem.

Second, the underlying assumption is always that tax competition works against developing countries, but it doesn't have to actually be the case. With the right type of institutions, tax competition can become extremely beneficial to developing countries, especially as developed countries continue to oppress capital owners and investors.

Finally, it is worth noting that no country has ever become rich through big government policy. In the West, during the 1800s and 1900s, which is the time of the explosion of economic growth and countries in the Western world becoming rich, the size of government was actually small. And in fact, for most of these countries they didn't even have an income tax. So, government spending for most of these countries at all levels was roughly 10% of GDP. And even as late as 1913, the public sector only consumed an average of about 12% of GDP in those major Western nations. In other words, there wasn't big government to misallocate the economic output, and there weren't high tax rates to discourage economic output.

Now, obviously fiscal policy is not the only thing. You need good trade policy, good monetary policy, and good regulatory policy. But the idea that the solution for developing countries is a larger amount of revenue, as opposed to the right institutions, the right policy, and the right tax code is as important. As Alison has said, taxes are fairly high in these countries, even though they fail to raise revenue. I wonder why. And when you look at the IMF data about developing countries, for instance in Sub-Saharan Africa, the average spending per GDP in these countries is 27%. It isn't far from our level currently, and it is way too far, way too big, to trigger the kind of economic growth that we would expect.

Finally, discouraging tax competition around the world also won't help. Foreign investment is key and essential to the developing world, and tax competition is the way to get more of it. Any successful attempt by a high-tax nation to tax companies more onerously would mean that foreign companies wouldn't have nearly as much incentive to create jobs and growth in the developing world. Let's not forget the developing world is a high-risk investment, making it more difficult won't help. Now the best recipe for the developing world and prosperity is one that has worked in the West, as we said before, and it's called small government and free market. Thank you.

§7.03 SECOND RESOLUTION

The second resolution for debate is as follows: *Be it resolved that tax competition increases developing countries' reliance on foreign aid, making them more vulnerable to aid volatility.*

[A] Response to Second Resolution by Alison Holder

Thank you. So it would be impossible to work for an organization like ActionAid, traveling and working with colleagues across the developing world, and fail to see that developing countries are in grave need of a massive boost in public finance. I've just come from a trip to rural Kenya, where I visited a primary school in Kongelai that teaches hundreds of children every day without any kind of physical structure, just a few trees and a teacher with a simple chalkboard that she holds up, teaching hundreds of children. They have 17 girls boarding at this particular primary school who sleep in an area of about 10 by 10 feet, with no mattresses or mats, just hard mud ground.

The UN has shown that developing countries may need to increase expenditure by some 1.4 trillion dollars each year in order to reach the new Sustainable Development Goals, and a report from Government Spending Watch last year found that domestic public finance currently funds 77% of the spending on the Millennium Development Goals. Not only that, but the report finds that this domestic public finance has been more stable, more aligned to government priorities, and easier to manage than donor-funded aid spending. The need for greater public finance in developing countries needs to be seen in light of the global inequality crisis. And the very broad consensus – including from the World Bank and the IMF – is that rising inequality is bad for all of us. And inequality is not just a rich-country problem. Research from Oxfam showed that seven in 10 people live in a country where inequality is rising. Public finance and progressive tax-and-spend policies are essential to curb the inequality crisis and to ensure that the proceeds of economic growth are shared equitably. Further, a majority of the world's poor are women, and tax-funded public services are vital to their economic empowerment, not to mention their fundamental human rights. Aid is a necessary, but not sufficient, source of financing for many developing countries.

Now it's not a straightforward *either* domestic resource mobilization *or* aid equation, but there are many reasons why developing countries don't want to rely heavily on international aid. One of these reasons is that aid that doesn't conform to aid effectiveness principles can break the social contract between citizens and their government: a social contract that should be based on the principle that, "I pay you tax, and you deliver me public goods in return."

Aid also has a tendency to be unpredictable. In spite of commitments made by donors to improve aid predictability, most research shows that the amount of aid that is actually dispersed varies widely from what was actually committed and that these gaps are widest in the poorest and most aid-dependent countries. And especially since the financial crisis, aid is increasingly skewed in favor of developed countries' own economic and political interests. The OECD aid stats for 2016 show that aid spent on refugees in host countries, so that's in the donor countries themselves, more than doubled in real terms between 2014 and 2015.

My final argument in favor of this resolution is that tax competition doesn't bring investment benefit to compensate for the foregone tax revenue, which further reinforces the point that tax competition makes developing countries more reliant on international aid. We established in the first resolution that tax competition is causing developing countries to lose tax revenue, but now we need to challenge the assumption that the foregone revenue, because of tax competition, is somehow compensated for by the benefits of inward investment.

So the story goes, we heard from Veronique, the story goes that governments will attract investment by cutting tax rates or narrowing the corporate tax base, either as a whole or for particular sectors. The assumption is that doing that will attract investment and that the benefits of that – jobs, economic spillovers, enhanced tax revenue from other sources – will outweigh the cost in foregone revenue. And governments commonly adopt this assumption as a matter of faith. It is hard to test empirically, but most governments don't even seem to try.

The World Bank's own research has found that tax incentives are not effective in attracting foreign direct investment in countries with weak investment climates. And we could argue that the vast majority of developing countries have weak investment climates to some degree. The findings are that in these weaker investment climates, investors put emphasis on other factors besides tax, such as access to financing, or good infrastructure. So the big risk is that we have tax breaks that subsidize an investment that would have been profitable anyway, or conversely, that never would have been profitable without subsidy. So in general, we're seeing some emerging recognition that the costs of tax competition outweigh the benefits, but there is not yet a willingness to give up tax incentives as a tool of investment policy, in spite of what the evidence tells us.

To summarize my arguments affirming resolution two: Developing countries have a great need for finance, and much of it must be public finance in order to reverse the damaging effects of rising inequality. Aid is necessary, but it's not sufficient, to make up the financing gaps. It can be unpredictable, and is often driven by donors' own political and economic agendas. Developing countries do need to attract the right kind of inward investment. That's long-term investment that brings decent jobs, where you're sourcing inputs from within the local economy, and where you have technical and skills transfer. But tax competition is a decidedly bad way to incentivize this kind of investment. The evidence points to the costs in terms of foregone revenue outweighing the benefits for developing countries.

[B] Response to Second Resolution by Veronique de Rugy

The resolution states that tax competition is to blame for increased reliance on foreign aid. This may be true but it is pointing at the wrong target. There is a case to be made, of course, for rich nations to try to help poor nations, however, while we are often very clear on the goal, we stop thinking for a second whether the government and rich countries' governments are actually the best suited to achieve this role. And, case in point, foreign aid definitely isn't.

It has long been believed that directing money to stagnant communities would jumpstart the economy, and to that effect, rich nations have actually spent, since 1962, over 4 trillion dollars in foreign aid. Unfortunately, numerous studies have found little evidence that foreign aid actually leads to greater economic growth. Economists like

Daron Acemoglu and James Robinson, Dambisa Moyo and Bill Easterly, several of them who have actually worked in international bureaucracies, specifically looking at foreign aid, have shown very effectively that foreign aid has a terrible track record and too often only makes matters worse. So, for instance, Moyo wrote in her 2009 book, "Stuck in an aid world, of no incentive, there is no reason for government to seek other, better, more transparent ways of raising development finance." She writes, "A constant stream of free money is a perfect way to keep an inefficient government or simply bad government in power." Acemoglu and Robinson wrote for instance that, "When aid is given to governments that preside over extracting institution, it can be at best irrelevant, at worst downright counter-productive. Many kleptocratic dictators, such as Congo's Mobutu, have been prompted by foreign aid." All of these problems that developing countries have were created by foreign aid and not by tax competition. And, as we've been, as Moyo has explained, if you actually want to increase the amount of spending from developing governments, you need to take away all the things that get in the way, and foreign aid is one of these.

It is worth noting that millions have been moved out of abject poverty around the world over the last six decades, but this has nothing to do, or little to do, with foreign aid. Rather, it had a lot to do with economic growth in countries which received little aid, in Asia in particular, and likely encouraged by the pressure of tax competition. The fastest way to faster economic growth and prosperity, as we know, thanks to Lord Peter Thomas Bauer, is through opportunities for private profit, not government planned. Of course, governments have the limited and crucial role of protecting property rights, enforcing contracts, and treating everybody equally before the law – but also keeping tax low. So, we need to actually be clear that we are using the target of tax competition when there are actually way bigger problems that are facing developing countries, and one of them is foreign aid. The question of the increased reliability of these countries is hardly the problem; it's their reliability on it in the first place that is the problem, and it's something that we absolutely need to address.

§7.04 THIRD RESOLUTION

The third and final resolution is as follows: *Be it resolved that tax competition aggravates existing income disparities between developed and developing countries.*

[A] Response to Third Resolution by Veronique de Rugy

It was an interesting proposition, considering that this is one that we hear all the time about in the United States (U.S.). However, I reject the premise that income disparity is a problem. Rather the problem is big and bad government policies in the developing world that lead to stagnation. In fact, data from the St. Louis Federal Reserve Bank now shows that all low-income nations, not all low-income nations have actually stagnated. You don't want stagnation, you want convergence, but you want convergence in the right direction.

We've seen rapid and persistent relative income growth in previously poor countries like Hong Kong, Singapore, Taiwan, Ireland, in the beginning of the 1960s all through the early 2000s to catch up or converge to the higher level of per capita income in the U.S. That shows to me that it is not a curse of all developing countries to stagnate and stay far behind the U.S. level. In sharp contrast, per capita income relative to the U.S. remains constant and stagnant at 10%-30% of U.S. income in the group of Latin American countries, which remains stuck in the middle-income trap and shows no sign of convergence to higher income levels. The lack of convergence is even more striking among low-income countries. Countries such as Bangladesh, El Salvador, Mozambique, and Niger are stuck in a poverty trap where their relative per capita income is constant and stagnant, at or below 5% of the U.S. level. If you want convergence, and less disparity for relatively poor countries, you should allow them to liberalize their economy by shrinking government and reducing intervention. In fact, data from the Economic Freedom of the World gives us a good roadmap for whether nations will grow. As economic freedom increased in Hong Kong, Singapore, Taiwan, and Ireland, these countries converged towards the U.S. These jurisdictions have pursued, at least to some extent, pro-market policies. In fact, they all rank among the world's top 18 nations for economic growth. And by the way, for the last few years, it was even higher than the U.S.. While economic freedom stayed flat in nations such as Mexico and Brazil, so did their prospect of converging toward the U.S.

Finally, you won't help poor countries by penalizing rich countries, and we've talked a lot about harmonizing taxes in rich countries in the name of helping low-tax countries. The risk of penalizing rich countries is that you will get convergence towards the bottom. And it's not the kind of convergence that you want. Instead, we should all be putting our eggs in a "Let's turn poor countries into capitalist heavens." It has happened before and it can happen again.

Finally, all tax competition can be eliminated but the countries that are stuck at the bottom will be stuck at the bottom, if we don't address the much bigger and fundamental question of their institutions, terrible tax policy, corrupt governments.

[B]   Response to Third Resolution by Alison Holder

Having established that tax competition affects developing countries by reducing the tax revenue they could otherwise collect, that the costs of this are unlikely to be compensated for by the benefits of additional inward investment, and that tax competition increases the reliance of developing countries on international aid in a way that's harmful in the long term, we now need to establish that tax competition affects developing countries more than it does developed countries. And in fact the research tells us that this is true. Tax competition places downward pressure on government revenues in developing countries and this effect is larger than in developed countries. Again, research from the very institutions that we're hosted by today, IMF research from 2014 showed that if all countries cut their tax rates, then the typical country loses tax base. But the losses are two to three times greater for developing countries than for

OECD countries. This shouldn't surprise us hugely because international tax competition is a problem created largely in developed countries. The most significant tax havens are in OECD countries or dependencies of OECD countries. This came through clearly in research done by the International Centre for Tax and Development last year, which shows a clear pattern of a small number of what the authors call profit-haven countries, benefitting from profit shifting by U.S. multinationals to the detriment of lower-income countries. The top five profit-haven countries that benefitted most in this study were the Netherlands, Ireland, Luxembourg, Bermuda, and Switzerland.

Put simply, tax competition both reveals and complicates existing imbalances of power in the global system. Developing countries are disadvantaged by unequal power relations on a number of fronts. First, developing countries are disadvantaged vis-à-vis large and powerful multinational corporations, and Donald Kaberuka, the former president of the African Development Bank, told an interesting story which he said was a very familiar story in Africa, which is that of a large company that flies in to meet a Minister of Finance in an African country and says, "Yes, we'll invest in your country, but here's the list of tax breaks that we will require, oh and by the way, we are flying on to your neighboring country next, so you've got three hours to decide."

Second, developing countries are in a weak position when it comes to resisting advice that is pushed by the international financial institutions. And there is a concern that in the past the IFIs have put too much emphasis on their policy advice on raising indirect taxes and not enough emphasis on taxing corporate profits, and that this is one of the reasons that some developing countries now have extensive and complicated regimes of tax breaks for corporations.

Finally, developing countries are disadvantaged by not having an equal seat at the table where the tax rules are set, and we heard about that in one of the previous panels this afternoon. Richer countries have a greater say in how to respond to tax competition – or not to respond to it, as the case may be – because of the imbalance of power in global governance, more generally, and because of the dominance of the OECD as the institution that is currently most influential in setting tax norms.

We can see the impact of the fact that developing countries don't have an equal seat at the table, if we look at the outcomes of the OECD BEPS project. And ActionAid would argue that a fundamental problem with the OECD BEPS project is precise that it hasn't attempted to systematically address the problem of tax competition. And it wasn't able to. It's a member-based organization, and some OECD countries are enthusiastic practitioners of tax competition.

The issue of lack of democratic governance of the global tax system dominated the Financing for Development Conference in Ethiopia last year. With the G77 countries and civil society calling for a global tax body under the auspices of the UN, where every country has the chance of equal representation in debates about global tax rules. This demand for fair global governance of international tax rules is not one that is going to go away.

To summarize my arguments affirming resolution three: All countries stand to suffer from tax competition, or shall we say the vast majority of countries. By definition, no country can win, because even if the policy succeeds, it can be undone in the long term by another country undercutting it with more tax cuts or tax breaks.

Although all countries stand to suffer, developing countries stand to suffer more, because of their greater reliance on corporate taxes.

Tax competition reveals and complicates existing imbalances of power in the negotiation of tax norms, and in sum, tax competition is a global problem which stands to affect all countries, but it affects developing countries more. And the imbalances in international institutions mean that they're generally in a weaker position to do anything about it.

§7.05 CLOSING REMARKS

[A] Final Remarks by Veronique de Rugy

Is there any time where tax competition would be counter-productive? A consumer shopping around for the highest quality and the lowest price will like having firms competing with one another. Firms are likely to state that, no, it's actually really not great, this competition, and in fact, you see a significant amount of efforts done in the developing world, and especially in the developed world, to actually try to squash competition, against consumers. The same is true for competition. Do countries that are actually trying to raise revenue on a captive audience, *like* tax competition? No, they don't. However, from their point of view, if your goal is to grow government without much constraint, without actually having to be accountable for the right type of investment, for actually funding the right role of government that would be conducive to economic growth, you may not like this. If you're in a developing country, and what you want is to serve special interests at the expense of your people, yes for you, tax competition is counter-productive.

What we've seen over time, considering that the propensity for government to overtax and overspend – this is certainly the case in higher taxation in the developed world, for sure – tax competition is maybe the only way to actually impose some sort of constraints on these governments. Consider what France's economy would look like without any tax competition. If high-income French people didn't actually vote with their feet and move to Belgium when the French government, always in dire need of more revenue, decided that it was okay to impose a 75% marginal tax rate on high-income earners, consider what would have happened. So it really depends on how you think about it, and whom you ask.

[B] Final Remarks by Alison Holder

Are there any conditions that may, under which tax competition might be beneficial for developing countries, my answer to that question is no. What may be beneficial for developing countries are the very policies that have enabled the rich countries to develop over time. That very same toolbox of policy should be available to developing countries. This isn't anything to do with being anti-market or anti-competition in general, but just because competition works in the private sector, and it works in the provision of goods and other items, doesn't mean that it works for tax.

It was interesting that Veronique, earlier in her talk, talked about first of all the early history of the rich countries, like the U.S., and there is no greater argument in favor of big government than the early experiences of our countries. Very directed industrial policy, and the economist Ha-Joon Chang talks about the idea of kicking away the ladder, that the rich countries today try to prevent developing countries from using the very same policies that they used to become rich, so actually those are the kind of policies that developing countries should have at their disposal.

And the other interesting example that Veronique used was the example of mass reductions in poverty which can be attributed largely to east Asian countries over recent years, and again no greater argument in favor of big government being able to direct industrial policy are the exact kind of policies that developing countries should have at their disposal. Tax competition is not the best way of producing economic development strategies that will also bring human development benefits, not just.

§7.06 JUDGES' CONCLUSION

According to the audience polls, the sympathies of the audience seem to be with a call for more cooperation over the current system of somewhat destructive competition.

The judges consider that, in principle, tax competition is good, because as in other areas, competition should bring down prices and improve services. In this case, competition should bring down taxes and improve expenditure efficiency and effectiveness – but – sometimes, competition can be counter-productive, and lead to a race to the bottom, and it's a race to the bottom without any glass-bottom boat, so you crash, and everybody loses, and as we have heard, that race to the bottom can be extremely costly. During the interview with the Finance Minister from France, we heard about how essential taxes are to provide the basic goods and services from the public sector, to enable the private sector and the community to prosper. To paraphrase Oliver Wendell Holmes, "Taxes are the price we pay for civilized society." Thus, governments need more cooperation to achieve more constructive competition. We accordingly disagree with the notion that there is no positive role for competition, but we also disagree with the claim that all competition is good.

And we see interventions to try to mitigate the negative or unintended effects of destructive competition. For international trade taxes, we have treaties, some bringing tariffs down to zero, some also trying to deal with non-tariff measures, once you have zero tariffs. For VAT, there are some general protocols we agree on, for example tax imports not exports, so that at least it's common around the world, and you're looking at a similar tax base. We heard some very good suggestions today on corporate taxation. We heard about a common definition of the tax base, with perhaps a minimum tax, so that you're ensured some minimal level of government revenue. Within that, what you want is for corporations, who have gone from fear of double taxation to the bliss of double non-taxation, however you define it, is that the corporations should pay their fair share, somewhere. And so the devil is in the details, trying to figure out what that fair share is, where that somewhere might be, and that's where we are looking, tomorrow, for a lot more suggestions on how to mitigate the negative consequences of destructive tax competition, and move towards more constructive cooperation, where it might lead to a more efficient and more equitable corporate tax system.

CHAPTER 8
Wealth Taxes in Developing Countries

Blanca Moreno-Dodson, Richard Murphy & Eric M. Zolt

§8.01   INTRODUCTION

Growing inequality throughout the world has spurred renewed interest in wealth taxation as an instrument to raise revenue and reduce disparities in income and wealth. While levels of inequality have increased in most countries, the timing and the size of the increases vary by country. Countries also vary in their ability to use tax and spending measures to reduce inequality. Experts routinely look at estimates of pre-tax and pre-transfer inequality and after-tax and after-transfer inequality, such as Gini coefficients, ratios of top deciles or quintiles to lower groups (such as 90/10 and 90/50 ratios), and the share of income or wealth held by the top 1%. These measures confirm that levels of inequality have increased greatly over the last 30 years (Atkinson, Piketty and Saez, 2011). While the primary focus has been on income inequality, in many countries, the levels of wealth inequality are twice as high as the levels of income inequality (Saez and Zucman, 2014).

Scholars have identified several factors that may contribute to increased inequality, including globalization, skill-biased technological change, decline in labor market protection, increased migration from rural to urban areas, and changing demographics (including the aging of populations and the rise of single-person households). While one can list potential factors that may result in higher levels of inequality, establishing a causal connection between these factors and actual increases in inequality is more challenging. What is likely is that factors influencing changes in levels of inequality vary by country and that, within each country, the individual determining factors have different consequences for different segments of the population.

While scholars have extensively examined the role of income and consumption taxes in both developed and developing countries, less attention has been given to the role of wealth taxation.[1] This chapter examines the increased role of wealth taxation in the fiscal architecture of developing countries.

Recent developments provide a strong basis for increasing the role of wealth taxes in both developed and developing countries. Throughout the world, greater political awareness exists about high levels of income and wealth inequality as well as the tax avoidance and evasion strategies of multinational corporations and high-wealth individuals. Recent OECD initiatives on automatic exchange of information, greater use of registries on beneficial ownership of financial assets, greater access to bank information (resulting from the United States' (U.S.) and other countries' efforts to require banks to disclose foreign accounts), and the decline in bank secrecy laws should provide taxing authorities with greater ability to monitor the income and wealth of individuals residing in their countries. Technological advances have also made it easier for taxing authorities to identify and value assets, and emerging technologies will dramatically improve governments' abilities to track them.

For developing countries, increased use of wealth taxation provides an opportunity to improve the progressivity of the tax system and to raise additional revenue to fund public social spending programs targeted to reduce rising inequality. Wealth taxes may also mitigate increasing intergenerational transmission of inequality and the growing inequality of opportunity. This chapter seeks to highlight key issues about wealth taxation and to further the debate about the increased role of wealth taxes in raising revenue and reducing inequality.

§8.02 WHY ARE WEALTH TAXES DESIRABLE?

Several factors support higher taxes on the wealthy (including annual wealth taxes on specific assets), especially in times of increasing inequality. The discussion below highlights the common arguments that support the increased use of wealth taxes, as well as some of the qualifications and challenges that might apply.

[A] Equity Justifications

Higher taxes on the wealthy are often justified based on the "ability to pay" principle and the "benefit" principle. In determining the relative ability to pay, wealth taxes can play an important role in supplementing income taxes, especially in those countries where the income tax plays a relatively minor role in redistributing income. As wealth is essentially multi-year accumulation of income, countries could address extreme

---

1. At the "Winning the Tax Wars" conference 2016, Eric M. Zolt (Michael H. Schill Distinguished Professor of Law, UCLA School of Law), Richard Murphy (Professor of Practice in International Political Economy, City University, London), and Joe Thorndike (Director of the Tax History Project at Tax Analysts and contributing editor for *Tax Notes* magazine) presented some preliminary thoughts on the fundamentals of wealth taxes. They discussed why wealth taxes might be desirable on equity and efficiency grounds, and the political and economic challenges of increasing use of wealth taxes. They also highlighted how recent economic, political, and technological changes likely increase the desirability and administrative feasibility of expanding wealth taxation.

concentration of wealth by taxing income more progressively. For countries that do not tax income from capital effectively, wealth taxes (whether in the form of annual wealth taxes on specific assets or an estate or inheritance tax) can serve to improve the fairness of the tax system by increasing the tax burden on accumulated capital. In addition, because an individual's tax capacity reflects both income and net wealth, using both income and wealth taxes may better approximate an individual's ability to pay than just using personal income taxes. Equity concerns may also support wealth taxes where a disproportionate share of a country's economic gains are received by the wealthy or where the wealthy have used tax avoidance and evasion strategies to minimize their tax liability under the personal income tax.

The benefit principle also provides support for the use of wealth taxes. The creation of private wealth depends on governments providing public goods and services such as security, protection of property rights (including intellectual property rights), infrastructure improvements, and education and health services to develop and support a qualified workforce. Murphy observes that those at the high end of the income and wealth distribution benefit greatly, and perhaps disproportionately, from these government-provided goods and services. In many countries, there is also a strong perception that the wealthy have benefitted from government policies for their financial advantage. As Murphy notes, the wealth tax can be justified as a tax on the economic rents that wealth enjoys from government protection.

While fairness concerns may justify higher taxes on the wealthy, Zolt emphasizes that it is not clear what approach countries should follow in increasing the tax burden on the wealthy. For some countries, introducing a new annual wealth tax on specific assets (or strengthening an existing wealth tax) may be the best strategy for improving the level of equity in the tax system. For other countries, there may be greater payoff from improving the taxation of income from capital under the personal income tax system or increasing the tax rates and effectiveness for current taxes on real estate, rather than adopting an annual wealth tax on specific assets.

[B] Efficiency Justifications

Experts, in analyzing the possible efficiency justifications for wealth taxes, contend that wealth taxes can result in more productive use of assets by encouraging owners to develop under-utilized assets. Increasing the tax costs of holding portfolio assets in low- or no-tax jurisdictions may also create incentives to invest resources domestically. Wealth taxes may also be less distortionary than other types of taxes. To the extent the burden of wealth taxes falls primarily on economic rents, the distortionary effects will be small. But wealth taxes also generate efficiency costs. For example, they create incentives to move assets out of the country and to use offshore entities and other opaque legal structures to disguise ownership.

However, it is difficult to determine the economic consequences of wealth taxes without a better understanding of who actually bears the economic burden of these taxes. It must be noted that the incidence of wealth taxes likely varies by the type of wealth tax as well as by country-specific factors.

[C] Political Economy Benefits

Adopting wealth taxes in a country presents political and social economic gains. Since the nineteenth century, scholars have examined the effects of income inequality on a country's prospects for democratization. In his recent book *Capital in the Twenty-First Century*, Thomas Piketty highlights the dangers of excessive wealth concentration, including that high concentration of wealth may increase the risk of capture of the political system, with adverse implications for the proper functioning of a modern democracy (Piketty, 2013).

Even the appearance of progressive taxation (whether in the form of progressive tax rates or wealth taxes) plays an important role in establishing the social legitimacy of the tax system. This is essential to promote social and political cohesion and improve levels of tax compliance. Thorndike highlights that the success of wealth tax initiatives has relied on desirable social objectives: the reallocation of fiscal burdens, the fairness of the tax system, and the minimization of wealth concentration. These are all crucial components in building an enduring democracy.

[D] Administrative Gains

The adoption of a wealth tax on specific assets and increasing effectiveness of existing taxes on real estate and improvements may also result in significant administrative gains. Wealth tax systems generally require taxpayers to provide a listing of certain assets and to value those assets. The collection of this information will be useful to tax authorities in administering income and consumption taxes. Disclosure of assets will allow taxing authorities to match reported taxable income with accumulation of assets, information that will prove helpful in identifying tax avoidance and evasion strategies used by taxpayers. Wealth taxes may also be a useful tool for anti-corruption efforts, particularly in those countries that require political candidates and government officials to file reports disclosing personal and family assets.

§8.03 WEALTH TAXES

[A] Types of Wealth Taxes

Wealth taxes come in various forms and sizes (Gordon and Rudnick, 1996; Ernst and Young, 2015). They could cover such assets as cash and cash equivalents, corporate stock, corporate and government debt, privately held businesses, owner-occupied housing, commercial real estate, collectibles, retirement assets, and life insurance. A narrow view of wealth taxes would include annual taxes on real property and improvements, annual wealth taxes on other types of investment assets, and estate or inheritance taxes (including supporting taxes on lifetime transfers). A broader view of wealth taxes could include any tax on assets, including taxes on income from capital under the personal income tax and corporate income taxes.

At a general level, three categories of wealth taxes exist: taxes imposed on the holding of assets; taxes imposed on the transfer of assets; and taxes imposed on the appreciation of assets:

(1) *Taxes on the holding of assets* include taxes on real property and other types of investment assets. Countries generally assess these taxes on an annual basis, but in some cases, countries assess taxes as a one-time charge or on a temporary basis during periods of war or financial crises.
(2) *Transfer taxes* include estate or inheritance taxes on death (levied either on the decedents' estate or on the beneficiary of property received) as well as on certain lifetime gifts. Transfer taxes also include taxes related to transfers of real property and certain other financial assets (real estate transfer taxes, stamp taxes, and financial transactions taxes).
(3) *Taxes on the appreciation of assets* include capital gains taxes on realized gains under the personal income tax system. Some countries also treat transfers on death or gift as a realization event for income tax purposes (Evans, 2013).

Countries differ greatly in their experience with taxing wealth. Taxes on real property and improvements are the most common type of wealth taxes. Many countries assign these taxes to subnational governments. While taxes on real property raise a relatively small percentage of total tax revenue, they are often the largest source of local discretionary revenue and therefore a critical resource in the provision of local public infrastructure and services. Several possible explanations exist for the relatively small revenue yield, including the unpopularity of property taxes, challenges in determining and collecting property taxes, challenges in valuing property, and the lack of political will to increase significantly the tax burden on real estate (Norregaard, 2013). Because real property and improvements likely represent a large percentage of wealth in many developing countries, any meaningful wealth tax reform would require achieving political consensus to improve the administration of real property tax systems and to increase the tax burden on such property.

Murphy notes that other forms of tax on the holding of assets are rare, but he believes that introducing such taxes merits consideration. He also suggests that a self-assessment basis of valuation with penalties for under-valuation could improve compliance rates.

Experts generally acknowledge the many challenges associated with transfer taxes in both developed and developing countries. While compliance rates are relatively high in many developed countries because of effective enforcement mechanisms, in other countries the levels of avoidance and evasion are sufficiently high to undermine the legitimacy of these taxes. Murphy further notes that estate and inheritance taxes are unpopular and widely avoided, through transfer of assets either during the owner's lifetime or through use of trusts and offshore arrangements. In many countries, transfer taxes create incentives to drive transactions underground or to misreport the true value of the transferred assets, sometimes in collusion with tax officials and public notaries.

Taxes on capital gains are an important part of most tax systems, but the revenue yields are generally relatively low. In many tax systems, the primary role of capital gains taxation is not to raise revenue but to prevent leakage from the personal tax system. In recent years, many countries have reduced capital gains tax rates to spur investment and entrepreneurship, despite the lack of any clear evidence about the effectiveness of such measures.

[B] Role in Tax System

At a general level, there are three major bases for taxation: income, consumption, and wealth. Zolt highlights that countries can use wealth taxes to either supplement existing income or consumption taxes or to replace existing taxes. For example, countries can retain current taxes on income and consumption but impose an additional wealth tax targeted at certain assets or high-wealth individuals. The combination of wealth taxes and income taxes may allow countries to use revenues from a wealth tax to reduce marginal tax rates under the income tax. Countries can also use wealth taxes to tax certain investment assets on a presumptive basis or as a minimum tax for income tax purposes (for individuals and corporations).

Scholars have proposed using wealth taxes to replace existing taxes (Schenk, 2000; Shakow and Shuldiner, 2000). For example, countries could combine a progressive consumption tax with an annual wealth tax to replace the income tax. Countries can also de-link the taxation of income from labor and income from capital (Bird and Zolt, 2011) and consider using wealth taxes to tax income from capital either on a mark-to-market taxation basis or as a retrospective tax on capital.

Zolt notes that the Netherlands' tax on portfolio income provides an interesting example of a wealth tax as part of the personal income tax system. In 2001, the Netherlands adopted a schedule approach in their personal income tax system dividing income into three boxes:

> Box 1: Taxable income from labor and homeownership taxed at progressive rates;
>
> Box 2: Taxable income from substantial business interest taxed at a flat rate; and
>
> Box 3: Taxable income from portfolio investments taxed at presumptive tax rates.

The presumptive tax rate for Box 3 assumes that net assets generate a return of 4% and are subject to a 30% tax rate. While this is part of the personal income tax system, it is effectively a wealth tax on portfolio investments taxed at an annual tax rate of 1.2%.

[C] Design Issues in Adopting a Wealth Tax

Some of the major design issues in adopting an annual tax on assets include: determining the scope of the tax, identification and disclosure of assets, valuation of assets, treatment of liabilities, and addressing liquidity concerns.

The initial question is determining who is subject to the tax and what assets are included. For example, Zolt notes that countries could assess an annual wealth tax of specific assets on individuals, households, families, or entities. For many closely held businesses, ownership interests are spread among many different family members. It will often be easier to determine the valuation of the entire business than in valuing the interests held by a single individual. Particularly in developing countries, using the family (broadly defined) as the unit of taxation may make it easier to impose wealth taxes on large family enterprises.

Determining which assets are subject to a wealth tax may depend on several different factors, including valuation challenges, challenges in identifying assets, political resistance, and effectiveness in taxing high-wealth individuals.

Another important issue in designing wealth taxes is the treatment of debt used to acquire or hold assets. Countries could impose taxes on a gross basis (e.g., taxes on real property) or on a net basis that provides for offsets for debt incurred on the acquisition or holding of assets (such as some annual wealth taxes on investment assets). While allowing an offset for debt would be more effective in taxing the net wealth of the taxpayer, allowing adjustments for debt presents additional challenges in administering a wealth tax. Because of the fungibility of money, allowing debt adjustments will encourage taxpayers to allocate debt to those assets that are subject to the wealth tax, even if the debt is not related to those assets.

Finally, policy makers may need to consider some measures to address challenges related to liquidity for those taxpayers who have substantial assets but lack the cash to pay the taxes. While liquidity challenges most often arise with respect to estate or inheritance taxes imposed on the value of closely held businesses and family farms, it is still a concern with respect to annual real property taxes, particularly for elderly taxpayers.

§8.04 CHALLENGES IN ADOPTING WEALTH TAXES

This section examines some of the challenges and risks of adopting wealth taxes. These include the political challenges in taxing wealth, the lack of popular support for wealth taxes, and administrative challenges facing developing countries.

[A] Political Challenges in Taxing Wealth

Countries vary greatly in their relative use of tax instruments to fund government operations and in their ability to impose higher taxes on the wealthy. With some exceptions, the percentage of tax revenue raised by income taxes in developing countries is much lower than the percentage in developed countries (Bird and Zolt,

2005). The variation is even greater if one examines the relative revenue raised by personal income taxes, especially the relative revenue collected under the personal income tax system on income from capital.

Several possible explanations exist for the relatively low tax burden on the wealthy in developing countries. These include administrative challenges facing tax authorities in collecting taxes on income from capital (held both domestically and abroad) and the tax avoidance and evasion strategies used by high-net-worth individuals in avoiding tax liability. However, a major reason for the low levels of taxation is the lack of political feasibility to increase taxes on the wealthy (Bird, 1991; Ardanaz and Scartascini, 2011).

While countries continue to impose annual taxes on real property and transfer taxes on property (and in some countries, financial transactions), relatively few countries impose annual wealth taxes on specific investment assets, and several countries have abolished these types of taxes over the last 30 years. Similar trends exist for abolishing or reducing inheritance and estate taxes. Even in those countries that use wealth taxes, the tax revenue generated from annual wealth taxes on specific investment assets, property taxes, and inheritance or estate taxes is remarkably small compared to revenue generated by other types of taxes.

[B] Lack of Popular Support for Wealth Taxes

While few taxpayers like income and consumption taxes, wealth taxes rank at or near the bottom in terms of popularity, even among those who will likely never have to pay them. In his examination of the development of early forms of property and estate taxes in the U.S., Thorndike outlines important political and economic factors that influence the rise and fall of these taxes. Box 1 sets forth Thorndike's historical account of the U.S. estate tax. He finds that arguments based on the fair allocation of tax burden are more likely to be persuasive with voters than arguments based on redistribution. While increasing inequality may have played a role in the debates about wealth taxes in the U.S., Thorndike finds that inequality concerns are of limited importance in influencing tax policies.

Box 1: Uneasy Invention: The Politics of Wealth Taxation in the United States
Joseph J. Thorndike

In the U.S., estate and inheritance taxes have been the principal instruments for taxing wealth for a long time. Early American experiments with wealth taxes were precipitated primarily by wars and crises. In the wake of a quasi-war with France, a small estate tax, called the stamp tax, was adopted in 1797 for the purpose of funding military operations. It set a graduated property tax, ranging from a rate of 0.2% on houses, land, and slaves worth USD 100, up to 1% on property worth more than USD 30,000. However, the measure was plagued by heavy administrative costs. It was repealed in 1802.

Chapter 8: Wealth Taxes in Developing Countries §8.04[B]

> To help pay for the Civil War, Congress imposed a "legacy tax" in 1862. It applied to the transfer of property after death and imposed a gradual tax, ranging from a low of 0.75% to a high of 5%, depending on the degree of kinship. The measure was, however, considered a failure. It generated lower revenues than expected and was easy to evade. Though arguments continued about its successes and shortcomings, it was repealed in 1870. There was a rising momentum in Congress to cut taxes, culminating in the repeal of transfer taxes, as well as legacy and succession taxes, until another war.
>
> Taxation of inherited wealth found a foothold in the law again in the wake of the Spanish American War of 1898. Congress imposed a new gradual estate tax, levied on the value of all personal property in an estate. Though it is considered a success, lawmakers repealed the measure in 1903.
>
> The early history of wealth transfer taxes in the U.S. is a story about revenue and not reform. Measures were designed to address the particular challenge of funding wars and were not based on a solid economic rationale. As a result, such taxes were not firmly integrated in the fiscal architecture. The progressivity of estate taxes aimed to ensure that wealth paid its fair share of the overall tax burden.
>
> September 2016 marked 100 years since the modern-day U.S. estate tax was introduced by the Revenue Act of 1916, which also created the country's modern income tax. Revenue generation was still the driving force in the wake of World War I. In addition to the main concern to raise revenue and achieve a fairer distribution of the burden of taxation, some members of Congress also began to argue that these taxes had a redistributive role.
>
> In 1935, the estate tax was raised. Issues of concentration of wealth and the inherent distaste for the transmission of inequalities across generations predominated among arguments favoring an increase in the tax. President Franklin Delano Roosevelt affirmed: "The transmission from generation to generation of vast fortunes by will ... is not consistent with the ideals ... of the American people." Roosevelt also cautioned about the subsequent "perpetuation of great and undesirable concentration of control in a relatively few individuals." The subsequent history of the estate tax in the 1990s and 2000s was largely dismal, however.

Whether recent economic and political developments will change popular perception of the desirability of different types of wealth taxes is uncertain. As discussed below, in many countries, the chances for adopting wealth taxes to raise revenue and reduce inequality are likely higher now than in the last several decades.

[C] Administrative Challenges

The administrative challenges of designing and implementing wealth taxes depend primarily on the type of wealth taxes adopted and the tax environment within specific countries. Murphy emphasizes that wealth taxes generally require tax authorities to locate the asset, to identify the owners, to value the asset, and to collect the tax. He states that countries that have access to high-quality information on investment income, automatic information exchange regimes with key financial hubs and offshore financial centers, and relatively high rates of compliance with regard to declaring investment income under personal tax regimes will have a much easier time collecting and enforcing wealth taxes than those countries that do not.

An annual wealth tax on specific assets also raises identification and disclosure issues. Challenges exist in identifying a taxpayer's assets, as taxpayers can physically hide assets (such as gold, diamonds, and fine art), and use many techniques to obfuscate ownership (including the use of shell corporations, trusts, foundations, and family partnerships). There are also challenges in getting taxpayers to disclose ownership of assets. While many types of assets are subject to registration requirements (such as real property tax registries and financial asset registries), other types of assets are not included. As Murphy notes, any wealth tax system would need to provide for higher penalties for failure to disclose assets, perhaps in the form of additional assessments for failure to disclose or higher tax rates for undisclosed assets under either capital gains taxes or inheritance taxes.

Substantial challenges also exist on valuing assets. Assets can be divided into three general categories: (i) those assets that are easy to value, such as publicly traded stock; (ii) those assets that are somewhat difficult to value, but where estimates of value would fall within some reasonable range (e.g., most types of real estate); and (iii) those assets that are hard to value, including stock of closely held corporations and complex financial instruments (Shakow and Shuldiner, 2000). Improvements in and the greater availability of online markets and online valuation platforms (such as Zillow and Redfin) give taxing authorities greater ability to check estimates of taxpayers' valuation. In those countries where the markets for certain assets are less robust, this may limit the type of assets that could be subject to wealth taxes. In all countries, taxpayers will become more aggressive in holding assets in different ownership structures (such as trusts, family partnerships, and offshore entities), which will result in increased difficulties in identifying and valuing assets.

A good predictor of a country's likely success in administering a wealth tax is the relative effectiveness of collecting taxes on income from capital under the personal income tax regime and collecting taxes on real property and improvements. Those countries with relatively low revenue yields and high levels of non-compliance under these taxes will have significant difficulties in administering many types of wealth taxes. Additional challenges exist in those countries where domestic bank secrecy laws or practice limit the tax authority's access to taxpayer-specific financial information. Finally, some developing countries may lack sufficiently robust capital and real estate markets to allow for effective valuation of different types of non-publicly traded property.

§8.05 THE CHANGING ENVIRONMENT FOR WEALTH TAXES

The desirability and feasibility of wealth taxes have increased significantly in recent years, in both developed and developing countries. Greater popular and political awareness of high income and wealth inequality, combined with exposure of the tax avoidance and evasion strategies used by multinational corporations and high-net-worth individuals, provide a window of opportunity for countries to reform their tax systems to increase the tax burden on the wealthy. These developments have created greater support for tax reform than existed just a few years ago. But challenges remain in achieving the political consensus to adopt wealth taxes. In all countries, the wealthy are politically powerful and they have incentives and resources to resist higher wealth taxes.

Key to the successful implementation of any tax is access to information. Recent global developments, such as the Lux Leaks and Panama Papers, have improved taxing authorities' ability to access information about individuals' income and wealth, and further make it harder for wealthy individuals to hide their assets in tax havens. Other factors that increase countries' ability to implement and enforce different types of wealth taxes include: recent OECD initiatives on automatic exchange of information; greater use of registries on beneficial ownership of financial assets; increased disclosure by financial institutions of accounts held by non-residents; the decline in bank secrecy laws, both domestically and in tax-haven jurisdictions; and the greater willingness of the international community to challenge practices in tax-haven countries that facilitate tax avoidance and tax evasion. Recent technological improvements also give taxing authorities greater ability to identify and value assets. Other emerging tools, such as block chain technology, will dramatically enhance asset tracking.

Finally, several countries in the last few years have adopted tax amnesty programs under the personal income tax. Such programs encourage wealthy individuals to declare assets to tax authorities rather than face harsher tax penalties. The information acquired under tax amnesty programs will provide taxing authorities with a strong foundation for taxing these assets either through a separate wealth tax or through a Netherlands-style presumptive tax on wealth included in the personal income tax system.

§8.06 CONCLUSION

In both developed and developing countries, rising levels of inequality and the need for additional tax revenue have policy makers evaluating options for increasing the tax burden on the wealthy. One key component is to increase the tax burden on capital, either through the personal income tax system or through separate taxes on wealth. While the political, economic, and administrative environments vary greatly among countries, the desirability and the administrative feasibility of wealth taxes are much greater now than even just a few years ago.

For Murphy, the changing global environment provides an exciting opportunity for developing countries to use wealth taxes to raise revenue and reduce inequality. If properly designed and administered, wealth taxes can generate substantial revenues that can serve to reduce aid dependency and reclaim tax sovereignty. This additional source of revenue could fund social spending programs to reduce inequality.

Zolt shares Murphy's enthusiasm for increasing the use of wealth taxes but lacks Murphy's optimism. For some countries, adopting annual wealth taxes on specific assets and adopting or strengthening estate or inheritance taxes may be the best approach to reduce inequality and raise revenue. Here, the revenue and political benefits from adopting wealth taxes exceed the political, economic, and administrative costs associated with these taxes. In other countries, however, there may be greater revenue gains from improving existing personal income taxes (especially taxes on income from capital) and making more effective use of taxes on real property and improvements. For example, several options exist for increasing the tax on capital under the personal income tax system. These include increasing the capital gains tax rate, increasing the tax rates on dividends and interest income, adopting a mark-to-market system that taxes accrued but not realized gains, and treating transfers by gifts and inheritance as realization events under the personal income tax (Kamin, 2015).

Rather than adopt a new tax regime for taxing wealth, countries may be able to raise more revenue from changes to their income and property taxes. This additional revenue could fund public social spending programs targeted to reduce levels of inequality. This approach does not preclude countries from including "wealth-type" taxes under the personal income tax, either as a minimum tax or as a Netherlands-style presumptive tax on income from portfolio assets.

For both Murphy and Zolt, what matters is not the progressivity of the tax system but the progressivity of all government policies, whether on the tax or expenditure side (Zolt, 2013). To reduce inequality, government policies are needed to make the poor richer. Redistributive tax policies are only part of the solution. In all countries, the toughest challenge is how to reduce pre-tax and pre-transfer levels of inequality. Here, more effective and well-targeted spending programs on health, education, and other social services are necessary to reduce inequality and poverty and increase economic mobility.

REFERENCES

Ardanaz, Martín, and Carlos Scartascini. 2011. "Why Don't We Tax the Rich? Inequality, Legislative Malapportionment, and Personal Income Taxation around the World." Working Paper IDB-WB-282, Inter-American Development Bank, Washington DC.

Atkinson, Anthony B., Thomas Piketty, and Emmanuel Saez. 2011. "Top Incomes in the Long Run of History." Journal of Economic Literature 49 (1): 3-71.

Bird, Richard M. 1991. "The Taxation of Personal Wealth in International Perspective." Canadian Public Policy 17 (3): 322-334.

Bird, Richard M. and Eric M. Zolt. 2005. "Redistribution via Taxation: The Limited Role of the Personal Income Tax in Developing Countries." UCLA Law Review 52 (6): 1627-1695.

Bird, Richard M. and Eric M. Zolt. 2011. "Dual Income Taxation: A Promising Path to Tax Reform for Developing Countries." World Development 39 (10): 1691-1703.

Ernst & Young Global Limited. 2015. Wealth Under the Spotlight 2015: How Taxing the Wealthy Is Changing. London.

Evans, Chris. 2013. "Wealth Taxes: Problems and Practice Around the World." Briefing Paper, CHASM (Centre on Household Assets and Savings Management), Birmingham.

Gordon, Richard K., and Rebecca S. Rudnick. 1996. "Taxation of Wealth." In Tax Law Design and Drafting, ed. Victor Thuronyi. International Monetary Fund, Washington, DC.

Kamin, David. 2015. "How to Tax the Rich." Tax Notes. January 5, 2015: 119–129.

Norregaard, John. 2013. "Taxing Immovable Property: Revenue Potential and Implementation Challenges." Working Paper WP/13/129, International Monetary Fund, Washington, DC.

OECD. 2008. "Growing Unequal? Income Distribution and Poverty in OECD Countries." OECD, Paris; and OECD, Income Distribution http://www.oecd.org/social/income-distribution-database.htm (last visited February 24, 2017).

Piketty, Thomas. 2013. Capital in the Twenty-First Century. Translated by Arthur Goldhammer. Cambridge, MA: The Belknap Press of Harvard University Press.

Saez, Emmanuel and Gabriel Zucman. 2014. "Wealth Inequality in the United States since 1913: Evidence from Capitalized Income Tax Data." Technical Report, National Bureau of Economic Research.

Schenk, Deborah. 2000. "Saving the Income Tax with a Wealth Tax." Tax Law Review 53 (3): 423–475.

Shakow, David, and Reed Shuldiner. 2000. "A Comprehensive Wealth Tax." Tax Law Review 53 (4): 499-585.

Zolt, Eric M. 2013. "Inequality in America: Challenges for Tax and Spending Policies." Tax Law Review 66 (4): 641-693.

CHAPTER 9
Taxing to Promote Public Goods: Carbon Pricing
Adam Koniuszewski[*]

§9.01 INTRODUCTION

Amid the euphoria surrounding the December 2015 Paris Climate Agreement and its remarkably rapid entry into force on November 4, 2016, there is a sobering reality: implementation of the accord is largely voluntary and, even if all parties' Intended Nationally Determined Contributions (INDCs) to climate action are fulfilled, the world will be far above the emissions levels needed to hold global warming under 1.5°C to 2°C. We may still pass climate-tipping points with catastrophic and possibly irreversible consequences.

With 16 of the 17 hottest years on record occurring since 2000, the news from COP22 in Marrakech in December 2016 offered both alarm and hope. On the one hand, it is known that 2016 was the hottest year yet and brought deadly heatwaves, floods, and forest fires; on the other, delegates were welcomed with the news that global CO_2 emissions have been stable for the past three years, indicating that economic growth and development can be decoupled from rising carbon emissions. We are finally moving in the right direction, but – in the face of unprecedented global temperatures – we need to go faster, further, and remain vigilant toward forces that threaten to derail progress.

---

[*] With many thanks to the World Bank and TaxCoop for the invitation to address the opportunities offered by carbon pricing in a context of intensifying tax competition, and special words of appreciation to Corrine Lepage, former Environment Minister of France and former Member of the European Parliament, François Damerval, elected representative (conseiller régional) of Ile de France (Paris region), and William Becker, Executive Director of the Presidential Climate Action Project and former Central Regional Director for the U.S. Department of Energy for contributing their insights and experience to the contents of this chapter.

Another major multilateral achievement of 2015 was the launch of the ambitious 2030 Agenda for Sustainable Development to succeed the Millennium Development Goals (MDGs). The new 2030 Agenda includes 17 Sustainable Development Goals (SDGs) aimed at "Transforming the World," for example by ending poverty and hunger, protecting the environment, and reducing inequality. But the SDGs will be impossible to achieve if climate change continues unabated, and any progress made by 2030 will unravel in the face of more extreme weather, drought, insecurity, and forced migration.

Urgent and transformational change is needed. Economies must decarbonize and should already be moving toward the goal of zero net greenhouse gas emissions by the second half of this century. Negotiators and policymakers around the world have trouble understanding that the longer we wait, the faster we have to achieve net-zero emissions and that the window of opportunity is closing fast. Governments and private enterprise must accept that the majority of all known fossil-fuel reserves can never be burnt. However, despite almost universal recognition of these imperatives, the global consumption of fossil fuels is not only far too high, but it also continues to be widely, and heavily, subsidized.

What appears to be a paradox is, in reality, the predictable consequence of the lack of market incentives to encourage the shift away from fossil fuels. Activities that cause carbon-intensive pollution remain cheap and profitable; the burden is instead borne by the millions of victims of air and water pollution, the communities already suffering the effects of climate change, and the publicly funded services required for their care. Looking ahead, the highest price will be paid by future generations. As former World Bank chief economist Nicholas Stern warned a decade ago, climate change is "the greatest market failure the world has ever seen"; it will transfer an externality cost of USD 40 trillion to future generations, a figure that will continue to escalate the longer we delay action.

It is vital that the real price of carbon emissions be paid at the source, where choices that result in carbon pollution are made. This will shift the social costs of climate change to those responsible for its cause, encouraging the reduction of emissions and investment in alternatives and allowing innovation to flourish, while simultaneously raising domestic resources. A sufficiently high and steadily rising carbon price implements the "polluter pays" principle increases the costs of greenhouse gas (GHG) emissions and makes carbon-intensive forms of energy unattractive.

Carbon pricing is among the most cost-effective, rapid, and flexible means of driving down carbon emissions and triggering the large-scale transition to clean energy that is urgently needed. Fortunately, after many years of reluctance, more and more governments in high-income, emerging, and low-income countries are getting on board, and coalitions of governments, investors, and businesses are helping to encourage and guide them.

The business case for an effective carbon pricing as a central element in comprehensive global, regional, and national climate strategies is increasingly compelling. Accumulating evidence confirms that a realistic and responsible price on carbon can help mobilize market forces for the transition to a low-carbon future and help unlock the multiple co-benefits of climate action. This chapter will present encouraging and cautionary lessons from existing carbon pricing schemes.

Carbon pricing can help fill the gaps between current global and national efforts to address climate change. It can advance low-carbon alternatives and help achieve the SDGs – securing key global public goods, as defined by the multi-stakeholder international community. This chapter reflects the contributions made at the conference and expands and furthers the discussion on carbon pricing. Despite some unavoidable setbacks, this chapter shows the growing momentum in favor of carbon pricing today.

§9.02   THE CASE FOR CARBON PRICING

The case for a price on carbon is simple and compelling. By setting a carbon price that reflects the actual cost of CO_2 emissions – including climate-change impacts and the health care costs associated with air pollution – governments internalize the many negative externalities associated with fossil fuels, sending a clear market signal to stimulate private-sector investment in clean technology and innovation and accelerate the reduction of emissions. As the cherry on the cake, the revenue raised can be used for an array of productive purposes, including to offset the impact of higher energy prices on lower-income citizens, finance the transition toward more efficient and renewable energy use, and support communities and countries affected by climate change. Alternatively, some governments may want to reduce taxes in other areas or support other programs to fulfill their social contract. This is often referred to as the "double dividend," allowing governments to both raise tax revenue and make the economy more efficient by internalizing negative externalities.

When the carbon price captures the true cost externalities of burning and releasing fossil fuels, the co-benefits that accrue are largely felt domestically. Most significant is the potential for reducing the air pollution crisis that is taking a toll on both health and government budgets across the world, especially in and around large cities in emerging low- and middle-income countries (LMICs). A new UNICEF report states that 2 billion children are breathing toxic air. Around 620 million live in South Asia, primarily northern India, 520 million are in Africa, and 450 million live in East Asia, mainly China. Of the global total, 300 million children, including 220 million in South Asia, are exposed to pollution levels more than six times the standards set by WHO. This is a global public health emergency: 600,000 children under 5 across the world are dying every year from air pollution-related diseases. Thus, reducing CO_2 emissions and eliminating the most polluting fossil fuels is essential for stemming global climate change, but the first and most direct benefits will be felt much closer to home (Parry, Veung, and Heine 2014).

Carbon pricing can be implemented in two different ways: as a carbon tax which places a direct levy on the carbon content of fossil fuels or by introducing an emissions trading system (ETS) which caps the total level of emissions permitted and lowers it over time. Under the first system, the price of carbon is set (and ideally increased over time), and the market determines the level of emissions; under an ETS or cap-and-trade system, the level of emissions is set and the market determines the price. It is also possible to combine the two approaches. The success of any scheme depends on getting the price right, whether by setting a high enough tax, or by correctly allocating and administering emissions permits, and on the effective monitoring of actual carbon emissions. The difficulties experienced by the European Union ETS are a case in point (*see* the Lessons Learned section of this chapter).

While there is no silver-bullet solution to climate change, as part of a comprehensive package of policies, carbon pricing can help fill a number of glaring gaps: the emissions gap, the climate finance gap, the energy transition investment gap, and the development finance gap.

[A] Closing the Emissions Gap

The emissions gap is the difference between the GHG-emission levels consistent with full implementation of the INDCs, and the levels required to limit mean global temperature rise to below 2°C in 2100. In a report published to mark the entry into force of the Paris Agreement in November 2016, UNEP estimates that by 2030 that gap will stand at 12-14 gigatons (GT), meaning that, even with the Paris pledges achieved, the world is on track for a calamitous 2.9-3.4 degree rise this century (UNEP 2016). The emission gap rises still further if we want a reasonable chance of reaching the 1.5°C target recognized in Paris and recommended by most scientists. To put this in perspective, we have already used up 1°C of the allocated warming allowance, and just 1 GT of emissions is equivalent to the EU's annual emissions of all forms of transport. UNEP insists that the world must take emergency action to cut a further 25% from predicted 2030 emissions.

Ramping up pre-2020 action is identified as a key way to begin filling this emissions gap and to prevent further lock-in of carbon-intensive technology. A recent OECD report on Effective Carbon Rates found that 90% of emissions in 41 OECD and G20 states are not priced at a level that reflects even a conservative estimate of the climate damage they cause, and 60% of carbon emissions from energy use are completely unpriced (OECD 2016). For this analysis, an effective carbon price was defined as at least EUR 30 per ton of CO_2e (carbon equivalent which includes the impact of other greenhouse gases), a very low bar which does not take other externalities, such as mortality and ill health caused by air pollution, into account. The fact that only 10% of emissions in these countries, which together account for 80% of global CO_2 emissions, are priced at an effective rate provides a major opportunity for either introducing carbon prices or raising them to effective levels, to harness the potential of market forces to accelerate climate action.

Carbon pricing is a powerful instrument for climate-change mitigation; it can be the primary market tool to rapidly drive the much more ambitious and rapid reductions needed to close the emissions gap. The Global Commission on the Economy and Climate, an initiative led by 24 former heads of states and finance ministers, heads of international organizations, and business leaders, projects that an average carbon price of USD 75 per ton of CO_2e in high-income countries, and USD 35 per ton in low-income countries, could reduce annual emissions in 2030 by 2.8-5.6 GT (Global Commission on the Economy and Climate 2015). This one measure would represent a major step toward reducing the emissions gap.

[B]   Closing the Low-Carbon Investment Gap

The transition to a low-carbon economy will not be possible without trillions of dollars in new investments, the majority of which will need to take place in emerging and low-income economies. Both public and private funds will be essential. According to one recent estimate, the energy sector, including investments in energy efficiency, will require around USD 50 trillion in core infrastructure investment over the next 15 years (Global Commission on the Economy and Climate 2016). In another analysis, additional low-carbon resilient (LCR) infrastructure needs – including power, transport, and water/sewage, as well as investments in energy efficiency – between 2015 and 2030 present a USD 900 billion a year finance challenge (Meltzer 2016).

Private capital must play a central role in meeting this challenge and could provide half the finance needed for the additional low-carbon infrastructure. But there are several barriers preventing the mobilization of these resources, including, on the policy side, distortions created by continued fossil-fuel subsidies and the lack of effective carbon pricing. As stressed by John Roome, Senior Director for Climate Change at the World Bank Group: "Pricing carbon pollution will help stimulate innovation and cut emissions, and also give governments the funds they need to help drive investments for a low-carbon future."

Introducing a strong, predictable, and rising carbon price will stimulate innovation and catalyze the investment needed to finance the transition to low-carbon infrastructure and greater energy efficiency. As government commitments to climate action become stronger, progress is already underway: UNEP reports that global investment in energy efficiency increased 6% in 2015 to reach USD 221 billion.

[C]   Closing the Climate and Sustainable-Development Financing Gap

Alongside triggering the economy-wide low-carbon transformation, carbon pricing generates additional revenue from the taxation of CO_2 and/or the auctioning of emission allowances. How best to use these new and additional fiscal resources is up to the authorities, and the existing schemes outlined later in this chapter show a wide variety of options. It has, however, been widely suggested that they could be allocated, at least in part, to financing climate mitigation and adaptation, and supporting the SDGs – all priorities for LMICs.

In this context, earmarking carbon pricing revenues for development, infrastructure, and innovation inside a state's own borders can also help make emission reduction pledges more palatable and even attractive. Well-designed carbon pricing and appropriately allocated revenue spending mean that countries can use climate action to stimulate economic activity, development, and job creation – in other words, to support the decoupling of economic development from CO_2 emissions.

The revenues available to any government will depend on how the carbon price is structured, the levy itself, and how widely it is applied. A study prepared for the 2016 Global Economic Symposium presented a hypothetical scenario in which a price of USD 50 per ton was applied to the 36 GT of global CO_2 emissions in 2015, generating USD 1.8 trillion annually. That is equal to 2.3% of global GDP (Mercator Research Institute 2016).

As the cost of providing universal access to clean water, sanitation, and electricity is estimated at USD 1 trillion per year, a widely applied carbon price could significantly contribute to meeting the SDGs. And all contributions are welcome. UNCTAD estimates that the additional finance needed for infrastructure related to the SDGs in all developing countries will reach at least USD 2.5 trillion per year by 2030. This will have to come from multiple sources – public, private, and international – but, as was the case for the MDGs, the majority of SDG investment will ultimately come from domestic public finance. A fiscal shift toward taxing "bads" like GHG emissions, and eliminating the distorting subsidies that encourage them (in particular fossil-fuel subsidies, which are discussed later in this chapter), can generate significant revenues, and provide greater stability, than depending on foreign donors and investors.

However, one specific and important area where low-income countries require increased support is in redressing climate injustice. This was stressed in the introductory remarks to the conference session on carbon pricing. The historical responsibility for causing climate change rests largely with high- and middle-income countries, but its first victims are the poor and vulnerable in low-income countries. Of the 50 countries most affected by global warming, 36 are located in sub-Saharan Africa. Climate justice calls for rich nations to honor their responsibility to support low-income states in adapting to climate change and achieving low-carbon development. A USD 100 billion/year commitment to advance climate justice was first agreed in Copenhagen in 2009, then reconfirmed in Paris in 2015. Failure to meet this funding target starkly illustrates the struggle to fulfill these key obligations.

As of March 2017, the Green Climate Fund created in 2009 had raised the equivalent of just USD 10.1 billion in pledges from 43 different governments – a mere 10% of the amount promised. The pursuit of climate justice was not one of the successes of the Paris Climate Summit, and climate finance retains what has been characterized as its "Wild West" status: unpredictable, poorly defined, and chronically inadequate.

This unacceptable situation is exacerbated by the fact, made clear at the "Winning the Tax Wars" conference, that low-income nations are caught up in a race to the bottom from international tax competition. Increasingly, their revenue base is eroding due to the power of multinationals and rich individuals to reduce their tax remittances. This leads to a relatively heavier reliance on poor and middle-income taxpayers and the perception that tax systems disproportionately penalize the poor and vulnerable. It has been suggested that high- and middle-income nations allocate a portion of the tax revenues they receive from carbon pricing to the Green Climate Fund.

Honoring climate finance obligations would boost trust between developing and developed states, making international climate negotiations less fraught, support climate-resilient development, and allow the Green Climate Fund to be an enabler for achieving the SDGs. After all, climate finance can play a role in meeting all 17 Global Goals, from low-carbon transport, to addressing ocean acidification, to water management and enhancing health. Nicholas Stern warned in 2015 that the "radical separation of finance for development and climate finance could be deeply damaging. It is a serious mistake to see action on climate and action on development as in conflict, or action on the former as a plot to slow the latter" (Stern 2015). The two agendas are indivisible, and each is unachievable without the other.

In these many, interrelated ways, carbon pricing can provide the market signals, incentives, tools, and financing required to catalyze the fundamental transformation needed to tackle climate change, evolve into a low-carbon economy, and meet the SDGs – and it can provide these contributions at a relatively low cost and a rapid pace. For these reasons, pricing carbon has raised the attention of prominent figures, including Pope Francis. In his 2015 Environmental Encyclical, *Laudato Si*, the Pope, emphasized the need to price externalities and indicated a clear preference for a tax solution to avoid the moral dilemma of seeing speculators profit from the climate crisis and human suffering.

Carbon pricing is the most efficient policy available to consign the massive market failure of climate change to history. Although the conceptual and empirical case for carbon pricing is compelling, as this chapter endeavors to show, there are many economic and political reasons why some countries – including the United States (U.S.) and Russia – remain reluctant to implement carbon pricing, including concern over the potential loss of competitive advantage without international policy coordination and full stakeholder compliance, and an over-emphasis on short-term effects instead of long-term benefits. Later in this chapter, a comparison is drawn with the long battle to introduce taxation and regulation on tobacco products, which has also met with heavy resistance despite clear evidence of its benefits for population health. The carbon pricing debate is more recent, but the argument is just as clear. The current challenge is for more governments, local authorities, cities, and private corporations, encompassing a far greater proportion of global CO_2 emissions, to overcome their reservations (and political obstacles) and take the essential step toward introducing effective carbon pricing. Fortunately, there is considerable ongoing movement in this direction.

§9.03 THE PARIS CLIMATE AGREEMENT AND CARBON PRICING MOMENTUM

Firm resistance by a number of states ensured that there is no explicit mention of a carbon price or tax in the text of the Paris Agreement. However, this did not prevent progress in this direction from receiving a boost before, during, and after COP21. More than 100 countries included reference to ETSs, carbon tax, or other pricing mechanisms in the national plans submitted to COP21, and the World Bank reports that the historic summit has galvanized global support for carbon pricing.

Insisting on a reference to carbon pricing or tax in the text of the Paris Agreement itself threatened to derail the negotiations and was therefore foregone in favor of reaching a global consensus. There is explicit recognition only in the United Nations

Framework Convention on Climate Change (UNFCCC) Paris Decisions document, paragraph 137 of which stresses "the important role of providing incentives for emission reduction activities, including tools such as domestic policies and carbon pricing."

The weakness of the Paris outcome in this area demonstrates the profound difficulty that surrounds any proposal to introduce an international carbon pricing system from the top down. Today, there is simply no international organization – including the UN and the World Bank – capable of imposing a worldwide carbon tax and no global agreement on the need for one.

However, in what has been called a "minor miracle," the contentious markets-related Article 6 of the Paris Agreement was agreed to in midnight negotiations on the very last night of COP21 and includes important provisions open to ongoing interpretation. Paragraph 6.3 refers to "internationally transferred mitigation outcomes" (ITMOs) and the ability to use these transfers, which are essentially ETSs, to meet NDCs. It does not limit the use of these provisions to units/outcomes issued through specific mechanisms related to the COP or require that permission be obtained through the Conference of the Parties (CMA) or any other body. Rather than actually establishing either a market or a price for carbon, Article 6 bestows the ability to create an international market if any Parties to the Agreement wish to, on an entirely voluntary basis. In this sense, it is a quintessentially bottom-up approach, but which opens the way for the linking of ETSs between countries or regional groups (Marcu 2016).

Another important market provision, contained in paragraphs 6.4-6.7, is a new mechanism to contribute to mitigation and support sustainable development. In this case, the mechanism does operate under the authority of the COP, and the mitigation outcomes produced can be used to fulfill a state's own NDC or that of another Party. This new sustainable-development mechanism could incentivize private-sector actors to develop emission reduction and related sustainable-development projects.

Although it was not possible for the states to agree even to mention the possibility of a carbon price sometime in the future in the Agreement itself, these new provisions and mechanisms still give a substantial impetus to, and boost expectations for, new and improved carbon markets. This has become stronger still since the Paris Agreement's entry into force on November 4, 2016.

The highest-profile carbon pricing "moment" at COP21 was the official launch of the Carbon Pricing Leadership Coalition by the chiefs of the World Bank, IMF, and OECD, with the heads of state or government from Canada, Chile, Ethiopia, France, Germany, and Mexico. The goal of the Coalition is to expand the use of effective carbon pricing policies that can maintain competitiveness, create jobs, encourage innovation, and deliver meaningful reduction of emissions. World Bank President Dr. Jim Yong Kim said at the launch: "Unless we drastically cut emissions and do more to help countries adapt, the effects of climate change could push an additional 100 million people into poverty by 2030. The most direct and certain path to zero net carbon emissions before the end of the century is through carbon pricing … .This is the right time to set the right price on the true cost of carbon on our planet." More states (including several middle- and low-income countries), organizations, and businesses

Chapter 9: Taxing to Promote Public Goods: Carbon Pricing   §9.03

have since joined the Coalition, which now includes over 20 government partners and dozens of companies and institutions from around the world.

Since the Paris Agreement, momentum on carbon pricing has continued unabated. According to the latest World Bank analysis (World Bank 2016), at the end of 2016, 40 national jurisdictions and over 20 cities, states, and regions are now pricing carbon. This includes seven out of 10 of the world's largest economies. The extent of the world's emissions covered by carbon pricing initiatives has increased threefold in the past decade, and now stretches to 7 GT CO_2e, or 13% of the global total. The number of initiatives implemented or scheduled for implementation jumped from 9 to 42 over the same period (*see* Figure 9.1). However, it is important to recall the OECD report on effective carbon rates and stress that not all emissions are priced high enough. In 2015, governments generated about USD 26 billion in revenues from their carbon pricing initiatives, which is a 60% increase compared to 2014. This figure is projected to nearly double in 2016.

Figure 9.1   The Diversity of Current Carbon Pricing Initiatives

INTERNATIONAL CARBON PRICING INITIATIVES		
101 INDCS include carbon pricing (domestic and/or international)		58% of global GHG emissions are covered by these INDCs
40 NATIONAL	24 SUBNATIONAL	42 CARBON PRICING INITIATIVES
Jurisdictions with carbon pricing initiatives		implemented scheduled for implementation
COVERING ANNUAL GLOBAL GHG EMISSIONS OF 7 GtCO_2e = 13%		
PRICES IN THE IMPLEMENTED INITIATIVES USD 1-131/tCO_2e 75% of the emissions covered are prices < USD 10/tCO_2e		
Carbon pricing revenues raised by governments in 2015 were USD 26 billion 60% increase compared to 2014		Annual value of carbon pricing initiatives in 2016 is just under USD 50 billion Similar to the 2015 value
INTERNAL CARBON PRICING INITIATIVES		
over 1,200 COMPANIES are using or planning to use internal carbon pricing in the coming two years		83% of these companies are located in jurisdictions with (scheduled) mandatory carbon pricing initiatives
INTERNAL CORPORATE CARBON PRICES ARE IN THE RANGE OF USD 0.3-893/tCO_2e		

Source: World Bank 2016, 24.

Milestones in 2016 included the launch or expansion of several new carbon pricing schemes. In the Canadian province of British Columbia, the existing initiative was extended to include a price on liquefied natural gas plant emissions. Australia implemented a safeguard mechanism that requires large emitters to offset excess emissions when they exceed set limits.[1] South Korea introduced an ETS covering two-thirds of the country's emissions.

Looking to the near future, France announced in May 2016 that it intends to apply a domestic carbon price floor of EUR 30/tCO$_2$e for the power sector in 2017 by taxing carbon at the level needed to make up the difference between this new floor and the price generated by the EU ETS. Mexico launched a one-year pilot cap-and-trade scheme in late 2016, in advance of an expected national carbon market in 2018. The Western Climate Initiative launched by Quebec and California in 2014 will expand to include Ontario in 2017. Chile and South Africa are scheduled to introduce carbon taxes, and Canada is planning to launch a nationwide carbon pricing scheme, building on the experiences in Quebec and British Columbia. The national initiative, announced by the Canadian Prime Minister in October 2016, will begin in 2018 with the introduction of a national minimum carbon price. Provinces have until 2018 to adopt a carbon pricing scheme, if they do not already have one, or the federal government will intervene to impose one. The proposed initial minimum price is CAD10 per CO$_2$t, and will rise by CAD 10 per year to reach a maximum of CAD 50 in 2022.

A breakthrough is expected to occur in 2017, when China implements a national ETS that will be the largest carbon pricing initiative in the world. This will increase world carbon pricing coverage to 20%-25% of global emissions, raising the worth of carbon pricing to USD 100 billion. As Figure 9.2 shows, carbon pricing initiatives are expanding to cover more and more of the globe, including a growing number of emerging and developing states.

---

1. Australia's move is all the more important, because it breaks with an earlier, politically motivated backward step. In 2014, under a previous government, the country had repealed its carbon tax legislation.

Chapter 9: Taxing to Promote Public Goods: Carbon Pricing §9.03

Figure 9.2 Existing, Emerging, and Potential Regional, National, and Subnational Carbon Pricing Initiatives

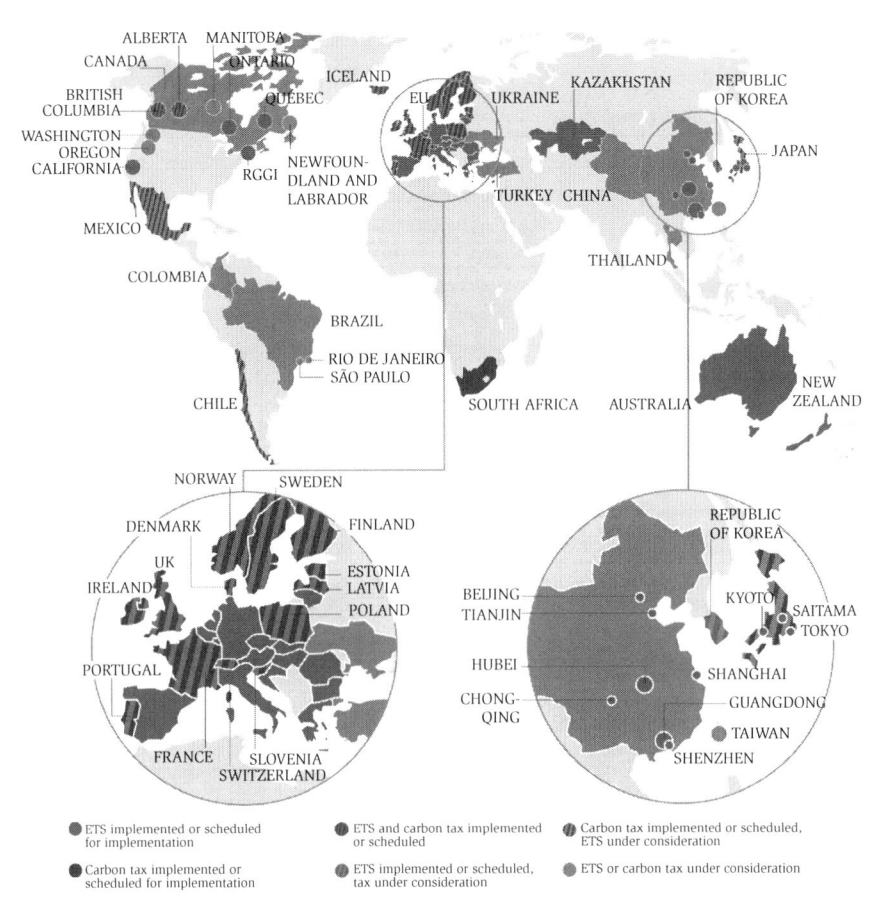

Source: World Bank 2016.

The private sector is also stepping up to the carbon pricing plate, an essential development, as 69 of the world's largest 100 economic entities are corporations (Global Justice Now 2015). Since 2014, the number of companies using, or planning to introduce, an internal carbon price has tripled to reach 1,200 in late 2016; 437 firms are already using an internal carbon price. Prices vary, but 80% are within the range of USD 5 to USD 50 per ton of CO_2e and can be much higher, as with one corporation using an internal carbon price as high as USD 800 per ton.

Finally, another positive development since COP21 is the (long- and hard-fought) agreement reached in October 2016 by the 191-nation International Civil Aviation Organization to cap its emissions at 2020 levels. This global, market-based measure will reduce carbon pollution by an estimated 2.5 billion tons over the first 15 years of implementation. It also signals that, even in an industry where there was strong and widespread resistance, the momentum toward climate action, using market tools, is prevailing.

While celebrating these achievements and positive trends, it is important not to overstate them, or forget that there is a long way to go. Two very big gaps in the carbon initiatives map, the U.S. and Russia – the second- and fourth-biggest carbon emitters – have no plans to introduce nationwide carbon pricing. The last attempt to institute nationwide carbon trading in the U.S. failed to pass Congress in 2009, and there is no chance of success in this regard at the federal level in the foreseeable future. Failure to pass a Washington State carbon tax initiative in late 2016, despite support from organizations and individuals like Audubon, scientist James Hansen, and actor Leonardo DiCaprio, is also a notable setback. In addition, it is important that carbon pricing be aligned with broader climate-mitigation policies, most specifically the phasing out and elimination of distorting fossil-fuel subsidies. Progress on this front has been much slower.

Phasing out fossil-fuel subsidies is the other side of the carbon pricing coin. It sends contradictory messages to the market and to consumers to introduce carbon taxes or ETSs, while continuing to subsidize the most polluting fossil fuels in amounts that dwarf the revenues generated by carbon pricing. The IMF estimates that post-tax energy subsidies in 2015 reached USD 5.3 trillion, or 6.5% of global GDP (Coady et al. 2015). That is a staggering USD 700+ per person on the planet, more than the total global spends on human health. To a great extent, the subsidies reflect externalities, namely the high environmental costs created by fossil fuels, including carbon emissions, health costs due to human exposure to pollution, and impacts on water supplies and agriculture, all of which are a huge drain on domestic fiscal resources. Due to its high environmental damage, coal accounts for the biggest subsidies, and coal use would be most impacted by their removal.

These perverse subsidies are high in both advanced and developing countries, but rise to truly dramatic proportions in certain areas: in emerging and developing Asia, the Middle East, North Africa, and Pakistan (MENAP), and the Commonwealth of Independent States (CIS), fossil-fuel subsidies amount to 13%-18% of GDP. By contrast, in advanced countries, where energy taxes are higher and air pollution emissions rates are relatively low, post-tax subsidies are "only" about 2.5% of regional GDP. The IMF calculates that eliminating post-tax subsidies in 2015 could raise government revenues by USD 2.9 trillion (3.6% of global GDP), cut global CO_2 emissions by over 20%, and reduce premature air pollution deaths by more than half. It is vital to stress that the majority of energy subsidies stem from a failure to effectively charge for the huge cost of domestic environmental damage, with only about 25% related to climate change. This means that even unilateral reform of energy subsidies is in a country's best interests, although progress can be greatly strengthened through global coordination.

As the evidence of the negative effects of fossil-fuel subsidies becomes starker, the momentum for fossil-fuel subsidy reform has been growing, and many governments have begun to reshape their energy policies. A key example of the successful repeal of important fossil-fuel subsidies is Indonesia. Having already banned industry and power generators from consuming subsidized diesel in 2005 (Savatic 2016), Indonesia introduced further major reforms to its fossil-fuel subsidies in December 2014, by removing subsidies for gasoline (except for distribution costs outside of the central islands of Java, Bali, and Madura) and introducing a "fixed" subsidy per liter for diesel. Combined with the drop in world oil prices, these reforms led to huge fiscal savings, equal to USD 15.6 billion. This allowed for major investments in social welfare and infrastructure through budget increases for ministries, state-owned enterprises, and transfers for regions and villages – a true win-win outcome (Pradiptyo et al. 2016).

But, despite such success stories, the need to reform fossil-fuel subsidies remains a global emergency. This is reflected in the 2030 Agenda, in which SDG12.c. calls on states to: "Rationalize inefficient fossil-fuel subsidies that encourage wasteful consumption by removing market distortions, in accordance with national circumstances, including by restructuring taxation and phasing out those harmful subsidies, where they exist, to reflect their environmental impacts." In 2016, the G7 committed to eliminate "inefficient" fossil-fuel subsidies by 2025. There is pressure for the G20 to agree to a similar pledge at their July 2017 summit in Hamburg. The fiscal, environmental, and welfare benefits of eliminating these distorting, damaging subsidies would be enormous, as would be the catalytic impact on the transformation of low-carbon development.

§9.04 LESSONS LEARNED FROM EXISTING CARBON PRICING INITIATIVES

Twenty-five years of experience with carbon pricing in the developed world offer interesting lessons, including for low- and middle-income economies looking to introduce such measures. While cases such as Sweden, Quebec, and British Columbia show that a properly designed and implemented carbon pricing initiative can simultaneously reduce emissions and raise significant revenues, the problems faced in other cases – most importantly the EU ETS – can help states avoid dangerous design and implementation pitfalls. These cases also illustrate the wide variety of options available when it comes to allocating revenues from carbon pricing. Every country is different and must take its own circumstances, risks, and priorities into account, but the successes and failures of existing systems can be a useful guide.

The first-ever carbon pricing scheme, launched in Sweden in 1991, is often referred to as the gold standard. Sweden today imposes the world's highest carbon tax, at EUR 100 (USD 106) per ton of carbon, but neither the country's growth nor its competitiveness has suffered. Since the tax was introduced, emissions have dropped by 23% while real GDP has risen by 58%, making Sweden the poster child for decoupling growth from CO_2 emissions.

Canada's first carbon levy was introduced in British Columbia as part of a provincial Climate Action Plan in 2008, with a tax on fuel use that covers about 70% of the province's total greenhouse gas emissions. The launch price was CAD 10 per ton, which rose by CAD 5 per year to reach CAD 30 per ton in 2012, where it has remained ever since. The tax is credited with causing an additional 5%-15% reduction in emissions between 2008 and 2013, compared to business-as-usual (about three times more than in the rest of Canada), and with sparking a decline in gasoline consumption five times greater than predicted (Murray and Rivers 2015). The carbon tax has not had a negative impact on the region's overall economy and is described as "revenue neutral," as it has been accompanied by cuts to other personal and business taxes, based on the amount collected by the carbon levy. Due to this fiscal shift, British Columbia now has the lowest corporate and personal income tax rates in Canada. The province's carbon tax scheme is widely praised as the most effective and transparent example of carbon pricing in the Western hemisphere.

However, key features of any successful carbon pricing initiative are continuity, predictability, and maintaining a sufficiently high and steadily rising price. Since the 2012 price freeze, British Columbia's emissions have been rising. The province is now at risk of reversing the emission reduction progress made during the early years of the initiative, because the carbon price is not even keeping pace with inflation, and there is no longer a sufficient incentive for businesses and consumers to make lower-carbon choices. There is considerable pressure on the province's Government to raise the carbon tax in order to meet Canada's Paris commitments and British Columbia's own legislated 2020 target to cut its emissions by one-third from 2007 levels. In October 2015, the Climate Leadership Team recommended that British Columbia recommence annual increases in the carbon tax in 2018, when the current carbon tax freeze ends. Their modeling indicates that annual increases in the range of CAD 10 per ton will be required until 2050 in order to achieve British Columbia's emission targets.[2] This call was echoed in March 2016 in an open letter penned by over 130 businesses from across the province, urging the Premier to commit to unfreezing and strengthening the province's carbon tax, and specifically to increase it by CAD 10 per ton per year, starting in July 2018.[3] This would send a strong signal to the private sector and stimulate investment in low-carbon innovation.

In 2016, British Columbia was awarded the UNFCCC Momentum for Change award in recognition of its climate tax policy's game-changing contribution to climate

---

2. British Columbia Climate Leadership Team, chaired by Mike Bernier, Parliamentary Secretary for Energy Literacy and the Environment. "Recommendations to Government." October 31, 2015, p. 10.
3. "More than 130 B.C. businesses call for a stronger carbon tax." March 2016. http://www.pembina.org/media-release/bc-businesses-call-for-stronger-carbon-tax.

change action. Unless the province addresses the current emissions rise by reintroducing a regular, predictable schedule for increasing the price of carbon, this momentum and British Columbia's reputation as a climate-change leader will be at risk.

Quebec has had a cap-and-trade system in place since 2013, and in 2014 set up a carbon market linked with California through the Western Climate Initiative. Prices are relatively low at CAD 16.40 per ton, although the scheme is interesting, as its entire proceeds are channeled toward programs and initiatives that stimulate innovation and support businesses and citizens to transition to a low-carbon economy. Revenues generated by Quebec's carbon market are estimated at CAD 3.3 billion by 2020, much of which is being invested in the electrification of the transport sector and is already producing a leveraging effect on private investments. Several types of electric vehicles are now being produced in Quebec, boosting the economy and creating sustainable jobs. Financial assistance is also being provided to replace fossil-fuel heating systems with renewable energy alternatives, which also reduces household bills.

Another promising example in North America is the Regional Greenhouse Gas Initiative (RGGI) which spans nine northeastern U.S. states as an example where a variety of jurisdictions successfully collaborate on carbon pricing. Between 2012 and 2014, RGGI collected USD 1 billion in carbon credit auction revenues, which were invested as follows: 59% to enhance energy efficiency; 15% in renewable energy; 13% to help low-income households with higher electricity bills; 12% on other GHG reduction programs; and 1% dedicated to research and development (R&D) in clean energy.

During this period, the nine RGGI states were able to spend less on buying fossil fuels from outside the region, instead keeping the money in their own economies to produce a multiplier effect. The regional economy has grown by more than USD 2.3 billion. RGGI is credited with creating or saving nearly 18,000 jobs, and there has been no "leakage" (i.e., businesses leaving or floods of cheaper imports from lower carbon price areas). GHG emissions in the region are already down by 15%-30%, and by 2020 the emissions cap established by RGGI is projected to result in a 45% reduction in power-sector emissions compared to 2005 levels. This achievement demonstrates how much can be done at the subnational level, especially in a federal system, even when the national government resists carbon pricing.

Significantly more complex and fraught with problems is the EU ETS, by far the world's biggest carbon pricing initiative, which is currently being reformed following years of crisis. Launched in 2005, it is a flagship program intended to promote the reduction of GHG emissions in a cost-effective and efficient way. It caps the volume of emissions permitted for energy-intensive industry and power producers at a level set by the EU, and companies either receive or buy individual allowances. The cap is reduced over time, so that the amount of emissions gradually decreases. However, structural flaws and unforeseen developments have undermined and discredited the system, causing it to fail to deliver the promised transformation.

Essentially, an oversupply of carbon credits, due to a weak 2020 emissions target and exacerbated since 2009 because of the financial crisis, led to a collapse of the carbon price to ridiculously low levels incapable of ensuring the competitiveness of low-carbon projects, or of driving emissions cuts. Another fundamental flaw of the EU

ETS is the ability to use overly cheap international "offsets" as a means of shifting domestic responsibilities by funding climate-mitigation projects in other countries. This dubious system was further tarnished by revelations about the detrimental effects of some of these projects in developing countries. Furthermore, too many free allowances and exceptions during the early phase meant no money coming in either to help finance the energy transition, invest in low-carbon technologies, or support the development of struggling regions of the EU.

The potential for leakage is a concern of all carbon pricing initiatives and a major preoccupation of the EU ETS. However, experience and analysis indicate that the risk may be significantly lower than feared, which should also serve to reassure other states and regions considering carbon pricing. Ninety percent of global emissions sources are not at risk of losing market share to international competition. The five carbon-intensive industries most impacted by carbon pricing are ferrous metals, nonferrous metals, non-metal minerals, paper and pulp, and basic chemicals, and targeted steps can be taken to reduce the risk of leakage in these sectors. Such measures include increasing energy efficiency and using increasingly competitive renewable alternatives and using carbon tax revenues to reduce other taxes and labor-related costs. Another option is to require all imports to meet carbon intensity standards equal to those applied to domestic producers, thereby avoiding unfair competition from imported goods and providing stability and predictability for the private sector to plan long-term low-carbon investments. In the EU, free emissions allocations are issued to industries that are most vulnerable to leakage, though it is important to limit these allowances and exceptions, or the entire ETS is undermined.

Deep reforms of the EU ETS are needed and are the subject of extensive, ongoing negotiations. The success of carbon pricing depends entirely on the robustness of the scheme's design, the absence of loopholes, and proper checks and balances to prevent leakage and abuse. A market stability reserve (MSR) has already been created to correct the huge surplus of emissions allowances and make the EU system more resilient to supply-demand imbalances, i.e., avoiding the "backloading" that has crippled the system for the past five years. The Commission wants to cut 70% of free allocations, and distribute those that remain according to the carbon-leakage potential of the respective sectors. Other suggested changes aim to foster innovation and the use of low-carbon technologies and help create new job opportunities.

To help the EU meet its commitment to reduce its emissions by at least 40% by 2030, compared to 1990 levels, it is expected that the overall number of emission allowances (or "carbon credits") will decline at an annual rate of 2.2% from 2021 onward, compared to 1.74% currently. The European Parliament approved a proposal for a "linear reduction factor" to this effect in February 2017, with a view to increasing the rate of reduction to 2.4% per year by 2024. This is equivalent to an additional drop in emissions in the sectors covered by the EU ETS of around 556 million tons over the decade, the same as the annual emissions of the United Kingdom (whose own future in the ETS is one of the many uncertainties that must be resolved during the "Brexit" negotiations). These changes will bring the EU climate policy in line with the aims of the Paris Agreement.

Members of the European Parliament also voted to double the capacity of the MSR to absorb the excess of credits on the market. This would allow 800 million allowances to be removed from the MSR as of January 2021. The Parliament also proposes the establishment of three further funds to be financed by auctioning ETS allowances: a modernization fund to support the upgrade of energy systems in lower-income Member States; an innovation fund to provide financial support for renewable-energy and low-carbon innovation projects;[4] and a "just transition fund," pooling auction revenues to promote skill formation and reallocation of labor affected by the transition of jobs in a decarbonizing economy. Following the vote in February 2017, these measures are being negotiated with the Presidency of the Council to reach an agreement on the final legislation, which will then be returned to Parliament.

Other mechanisms are also being presented as ETS reform is debated, including by business leaders concerned that the rising carbon tax will make Europe less competitive when it comes to globally traded industries. For example, Lakshmi Mittal, the chairman of steel giant ArcelorMittal, is proposing a carbon border tax to protect Europe's competitiveness against imports, and avoid a situation where "European jobs are exported and carbon is imported – with no meaningful impact on total global emissions" (Mittal 2017). This proposal is closely mirrored by the one presented to the new U.S. administration in February 2017 by a group including two former Treasury Secretaries, which incorporates a gradually increasing carbon tax and carbon border adjustments (Baker et al. 2017). These proposals add some credence to the idea that the expansion of carbon pricing could be compatible even with the recent trend toward more protectionist economic stances being taken by some governments. The first decade of the EU ETS is something of a test case in "what not to do"; the coming years promise to provide more positive inspiration for other regions planning emissions trading schemes.

Inspiration can also be found in other examples where taxes are used to raise prices and reduce demand so as to shift behavior away from "bads." During our conference session, the author highlighted as a case in point the use of consumption taxes to raise the price of tobacco products: widely viewed as the most effective approach for governments to address the tobacco epidemic. Numerous experts endorse tobacco taxation as the most cost-effective public-health intervention available, when it is part of a comprehensive set of measures to reduce smoking prevalence.[5] This is recognized in Article 6 of the WHO Framework Convention on Tobacco Control (FCTC), "Price and Tax Measures to Reduce the Demand for Tobacco." The FCTC, which has been called the world's single most important tool for saving lives, not only addresses taxation and price measures but regulates all aspects of the tobacco trade as part of the global Tobacco Free Initiative. WHO studies show that a 10% increase in the

---

4. http://www.europarl.europa.eu/news/en/news-room/20170210IPR61806/meps-back-plans-to-cut-carbon-emission-allowances-and-fund-low-carbon-innovation.
5. Such measures would include, for example: support to help smokers quit, advertising bans, help for tobacco farmers and other industry workers, and youth smoking prevention. For a detailed discussion, see Chapter 10 in this volume.

real price of cigarettes leads, on average, to a 4% reduction in tobacco consumption, simultaneously increasing government revenues and reducing health costs (WHO 2015).

The parallels with carbon pricing are clear, and the lessons learned over many decades of tobacco taxation and regulation are instructive. This includes the experience of facing objections from tobacco manufacturers, whose arguments have subsequently inspired the fossil fuel industry. Favorite tobacco-industry arguments against higher tobacco taxes involved ostensible threats to jobs, costs to the poor and vulnerable, and risks of illicit trade, contraband, and counterfeiting (with the fossil-fuel industry equivalent being "carbon leakage"). Over the years, these arguments have been debunked by overwhelming evidence of the massive health benefits and fiscal gains brought about by tobacco taxes. Evidence has likewise shown that tobacco-industry spokespersons exaggerated the threat of illicit trade in tobacco products (smuggling and counterfeiting) following tax hikes. Higher tobacco taxes have proven to have little impact on either jobs or economies, as smokers have redirected their consumer spending to other – less damaging and more productive – sectors (Savedoff and Alwang 2015).

Other struggles faced by tobacco taxation are also comparable to those confronting carbon pricing, most significantly the fact that – like carbon prices – tobacco taxes in most countries are still too low to slow the epidemic of smoking-related diseases. Only 8% of the world's population lives in a country where tobacco taxes are high enough to affect consumption (WHO 2013), and most of these are in Europe (Savedoff and Alwang 2015). As with air pollution, developing countries have the most to gain and are beginning to realize the benefits of raising tobacco taxes. Also, while governments collect some USD 145 billion in tobacco excise tax revenue, just USD 1 billion is spent on tobacco control. Carbon pricing initiatives should take note and design schemes that integrate different measures to speed up the low-carbon transition with support for the development, implementation, and scaling up of innovations and shifts to alternative technologies.

§9.05 FRAMEWORK CONVENTION FOR CARBON CONTROL (FCCC)

The Paris Agreement is a major milestone and source of hope, but the commitments within it should be seen as the beginning of the search for global solutions to climate change, not the endpoint. Ambitions must be raised and action must accelerate, if the world is to meet the 2°C target, and move closer to the 1.5°C target that states have recognized.

Carbon pricing is a proven, powerful, and cost-effective tool for unlocking that extra ambition, and mobilizing the resources and ingenuity needed to both drive the transition to a low-carbon future and support the global development agenda. It can help generate the resources needed to finance low-carbon infrastructure, the implementation of the SDGs, and a wide range of other measures, while protecting developing countries from global tax base erosion.

As part of a comprehensive, coherent package of measures – including the elimination of perverse fossil-fuel subsidies, help for lower-income households, support for energy efficiency and renewable alternatives, and effective revenue spending and investment plans – a strong, predictable, and rising carbon price is an essential instrument for rapidly reducing emissions and catalyzing the historic transformation needed to prevent catastrophic climate change.

Concrete progress since the Paris summit is highly encouraging, but the years that follow the immediate aftermath of an international agreement can be a dangerous time; when attention shifts away, governments and businesses can grow complacent or even roll back on commitments. Both the public and the international community must remain vigilant to avoid this fate. The repeal of the Australian carbon tax is a warning that a short-term change in government can have long-term implications for a nation's climate action.

Lessons learned from the experience of existing carbon tax and ETS initiatives in advanced economies should prevent developing nations from repeating the mistakes of the past. Namely, the gift to industry of too many free rights can lead to a collapse of the market, while poor controls can open loopholes for fraud, as witnessed by the struggles of the EU ETS.

The role of the World Bank, IMF, and OECD, including through their joint Carbon Pricing Leadership Coalition, will be vital in promoting the ongoing expansion and improvement of carbon pricing initiatives, and providing guidelines to ensure that schemes are well structured and effective. It is promising that a growing number of developing states are joining the Coalition. The success of pilot and planned carbon pricing initiatives in South Africa, Ethiopia, and Cote d'Ivoire could inspire similar schemes in the global South, helping to raise fiscal revenues needed to meet development goals and to reduce the terrible scourge of air pollution. The Coalition aims to hold country-level dialogues in 15 countries by the end of 2017, and 30 countries by 2020, with a view to catalyze successful carbon pricing programs. This will help complement existing World Bank initiatives, including the Pilot Auction Facility and Transformation Carbon Asset Facility, which will also be scaled up.

The Carbon Pricing Leadership Coalition is calling on the international community to deliver on a goal to double the percentage of global emissions covered by carbon pricing initiatives to 25% by 2020, and then double it again to 50% within a decade. It is crucial that these carbon prices are high enough to effectively change behavior and shift investment decisions toward low-carbon alternatives.

The other goal is to enhance international cooperation by facilitating the alignment and eventual convergence of domestic carbon pricing programs, as is already being done by Quebec and California. The experience of negotiating the Paris Agreement and UNFCCC's requirement of a global consensus make it clear that imposing a global carbon price from the top down is not currently feasible. But, as the numbers of states adopting carbon pricing grows, more opportunities to link and harmonize markets and create regional ETSs – that can be designed to suit the economic reality and given priorities of the specific region – will emerge.

Regional carbon markets can inspire countries to make stronger commitments, build political and financial confidence, and unleash potential for more ambitious climate action. The World Bank recently calculated that greater cooperation through carbon trading could reduce the cost of climate-change mitigation by 32% by 2030, and by 50% by 2050 (World Bank 2016). The same report indicated that, by 2050, some of the poorer regions of the world may be able to generate financial flows equal to 2%-5% of GDP from selling carbon credits. The more states cooperate, the larger the savings and the greater the potential to raise emission reduction ambitions.

Looking forward, the author suggests the creation of a Framework Convention on Carbon Control to address the taxation and regulation of carbon emissions as a powerful platform for action for the UNFCCC, warranted by the scale and urgency of the climate crisis. Like the Framework Convention for Tobacco Control, it would provide a toolbox of measures adaptable to the specific circumstances of a given country, while encouraging harmonization that, over time, could lead to regional-scale implementation, and eventually to the introduction of a global carbon price (possibly setting different levies to reflect countries' development status) as a central component of a global Carbon Free Initiative.

The momentum generated by the Paris Agreement and Agenda 2030, coupled with relatively low energy prices and the strong support of the private sector, creates an ideal opportunity to use effective carbon pricing to correct the disastrous market failure driving climate change, close the emissions and investment gaps, and set the world on a sustainable development path.

REFERENCES

Baker, James A., Martin Feldstein, Ted Halstead, N. Gregory Mankiw, Henry M. Paulson, Jr., George P. Shultz, Thomas Stephenson, and Rob Walton. 2017. "The Conservative Case for Carbon Dividends." Climate Leadership Council, February 2017.

Coady, David, Ian Parry, Louis Sears, and Baoping Shang. 2015. "How Large Are Global Energy Subsidies?" IMF Working Paper. Washington, DC: IMF.

Global Commission on the Economy and Climate. 2015. "Technical Note: Estimates of Emissions Reduction Potential for the 2015 Report." Global Commission on the Economy and Climate.

Global Commission on the Economy and Climate. 2016. *The New Climate Economy: The Sustainable Infrastructure Imperative*. Global Commission on the Economy and Climate.

Global Justice Now. 2015. Table Comparing Government Revenues as per the CIA World Factbook 2015 and Corporate Turnover Based on Fortune Global 500.

Marcu, Andrei. 2016. "Carbon Market Provisions in the Paris Agreement (Article 6)." Centre for European Policy Studies Special Report No. 128 (January 2016). Centre for European Policy Studies.

Meltzer, Joshua P. 2016. *Financing Low Carbon, Climate Resilient Infrastructure: The Role of Climate Finance and Green Financial Systems*. Washington, DC: Brookings Institution.

Mercator Research Institute on Global Commons and Climate Change, for the Global Economic Symposium. 2016. "Carbon Pricing for Climate Change Mitigation and Financing the SDGs." Global Economic Symposium.

Mittal, Lakshmi. 2017. "A Carbon Border Tax Is the Best Answer on Climate Change." *Financial Times* (12 February 2017).

Murray, B., and N. Rivers. 2015. "British Columbia's Revenue Neutral Carbon Tax: A Review of the Latest 'Grand Experiment' in Environmental Policy." NI WP 15-04. Durham, NC: Duke University.

OECD (Organization for Economic Co-operation and Development). 2016. *Effective Carbon Rates – Pricing CO_2 through Taxes and Emissions Trading Systems*. Paris: OECD.

Parry, Ian, Chandara Veung, and Dirk Heine. 2014. "How Much Carbon Pricing is in Countries' Own Interests? The Critical Role of Co-Benefits." IMF Working Paper WP/14/174. Washington, DC: IMF.

Pradiptyo, Rimawan, et al. 2016. "Financing Development with Fossil Fuel Subsidies: The Reallocation of Indonesia's Gasoline and Diesel Subsidies in 2015." Global Subsidies Initiative (GSI) of the International Institute for Sustainable Development (IISD) (May 2016).

Savatic, Filip. 2016. "Fossil Fuel Subsidy Reform: Lessons from the Indonesian Case." IDDRI Study No. 06/16 (October 2016).

Savedoff, William, and Albert Alwang. 2015. "The Single Best Health Policy in the World: Tobacco Taxes." CGD Policy Paper 062. Washington, DC: Center for Global Development.

Stern, Nicholas. 2015. "Understanding Climate Finance for the Paris Summit in December 2015 in the Context of Financing for Sustainable Development for the Addis Ababa Conference in July 2015." Policy Paper for ESRC Centre for Climate Change Economics and Policy (March 2015).

UNEP (United Nations Environment Programme). 2016. *The Emissions Gap Report, 2016*. Nairobi: UNEP.

WHO (World Health Organization). 2015. *WHO Report on the Global Tobacco Epidemic: Raising Taxes on Tobacco*. Geneva: WHO.

World Bank. 2016. *State and Trends of Carbon Pricing 2016*. Washington, DC: The World Bank.

CHAPTER 10
Expanding the Global Tax Base: Taxing to Promote Public Goods – Tobacco Taxes

Patricio V. Marquez

§10.01 BACKGROUND AND OBJECTIVES

This chapter examines country experiences and results achieved with tobacco taxation.[1] Tobacco taxes are a policy measure with the capacity to promote several key public goods at once: reducing behaviors that are harmful for health; preventing illness, disability, and premature mortality due to tobacco-related diseases; reducing countries' health care expenditures; and at the same time increasing fiscal revenues. As such, strengthened tobacco taxation is an option that may interest all countries seeking to emerge from the "tax wars" with improved health and wellbeing for their populations.

Rather than creating a broad summary of the session that might have lost its richness and the distinctive voices of the expert participants, we have chosen to present an edited transcript that closely follows the structure and dynamics of the actual session. This record captures the words and perspectives of our speakers: both in their many areas of consensus and on those points where expert views may differ – and thus where new questions and new knowledge are emerging.

This gives the chapter a different structure from that of most other essays in the present volume. We believe this approach best mediates the distinctive scientific and policy debates that inform the current tobacco taxation agenda.

---
1. This chapter was prepared by Patricio V. Marquez, Lead Public Health Specialist, Health, Nutrition and Population Global Practice, and Co-coordinator of the Global Tobacco Control Program, World Bank Group, who organized and moderated the panel session.

§10.02 MAKING THE PUBLIC-HEALTH CASE FOR TOBACCO TAXATION

The scientific evidence accumulated over the last five decades is clear and irrefutable: tobacco use kills. Tobacco taxation, along with measures to reduce the social acceptability of smoking, is one of the most cost-effective public health measures to prevent people, particularly youth, from becoming addicted to a product that causes ill health, premature mortality, and disability, as well as high direct and indirect costs for families, communities, and society at large.

Tobacco use, and its negative health, social, and economic impact, is a global problem. It is estimated that 1.1 billion people smoke globally. According to the 2015 World Health Organization (WHO) Report on the Global Tobacco Epidemic, in 2013, 21% of adults globally were current smokers – 950 million men and 177 million women.

Tobacco use is a leading global disease risk factor and underlying cause of ill health, preventable death, and disability. It is estimated to kill more than five million people each year across the globe. If current trends persist, tobacco will kill more than eight million people worldwide each year by 2030, with 80% of these premature deaths taking place in the developing world.

The 2015 WHO report on tobacco taxation raises a troubling question for policymakers across the world: If, as shown by scientific evidence, tobacco is a leading global disease risk factor, why then are so few governments levying appropriate levels of tax on cigarettes and other tobacco products to raise prices and reduce consumption?

The importance of this question is accentuated by the widely accepted fact that raising taxes on tobacco products is one of the most cost-effective measures to reduce consumption of products that kill. Besides the potential health benefits of tobacco taxation, this policy measure could help broaden the tax base of countries and generate additional revenue to finance priority investments and programs that benefit the entire population.

Thus, price and tax measures on tobacco can offer, not only effective means to reduce tobacco consumption and health care costs, but a revenue stream for development financing. This was explicitly recognized in the "Financing for Development Action Agenda" approved by Heads of State and Government at the Third International Conference on Financing for Development, held in Addis Ababa, Ethiopia, in mid-July 2015. The principle was subsequently endorsed at the United Nations General Assembly (UNGA), in September 2015, as part of the Sustainable Development Goals (SDGs) to be achieved by 2030.

Despite these strong foundations in international accords, findings in the WHO report show that only 33 countries currently impose taxes that constitute more than 75% of the retail price of a pack of cigarettes – the taxation level recommended to have an impact on consumption. Most countries that do tax tobacco products have extremely low tax rates. And some countries do not have a special tax on tobacco products at all.

Given this situation, what can be done to make the case and encourage governments to look at accumulated evidence worldwide, not simply the tobacco industry's arguments, and to use tax policies to increase the retail price of tobacco products as one of the best available public-health policy measures?

If we do not want to be passive spectators to the unhindered growth of this threat to global health, then political will at the highest levels of government needs to be galvanized, coupled with sustained support from civil society and international organizations. This is required not only to shine a light upon this deadly but entirely preventable health risk but more importantly, to promote effective and sustained action to deal with it.

For precisely these reasons, the World Bank Group's Global Tobacco Control Program supports governments to look at accumulated country evidence and use tax measures to increase the retail price of tobacco products.

Some important lessons from international experience about how to effectively implement tobacco tax policy to achieve public-health objectives can be adopted and adapted in policy dialogue and operational support to countries. Such lessons include (IMF 2016; Sunley 2009; WHO 2015; World Bank 1999):

– Negative externalities from smoking – harm suffered, in some form, by non-smokers – have traditionally been the primary economic argument for taxing tobacco products more heavily than the generality of goods. Such externalities arise from two main sources. The first is the annoyance that smokers can cause to individuals around them, and more severely, the tobacco-related diseases among non-smokers who are forced to breathe other people's smoke (e.g., restaurant staff, children of smokers, etc.). Second, in countries where health systems are funded publicly – to any extent – it is also possible that smokers will on average consume more health care than they on average pay for (which might also be the case with private insurance); there is then a strong case to "internalize" these costs through tobacco taxes. Account also needs to be taken of "internalities": self-control problems that can provide a distinct reason (additional to external effects) for heavy taxes on smoking (Gruber and Koszegi 2001). The magnitude of externalities – and hence the appropriate corrective tax – will also be affected by non-tax tobacco policies: they tend to be reduced, for instance, by smoking bans (Christiansen and Smith 2012).
– While nearly all countries tax tobacco products, an excise tax is the most important type of tobacco tax, since it applies uniquely to tobacco products and raises prices relative to those of other goods and services.
– Simpler tobacco tax structures are more effective than complex (tiered) ones which are difficult to administer and can undermine the health and revenue impacts of tobacco excise taxes. Simpler tax structures also increase tax-administration transparency and thus reduce opportunities for corruption.
– Use of specific (a fixed monetary value per physical unit of the excised good) and uniform excise taxes enhances the impact of tobacco taxation on public health by reducing price gaps between premium and lower-priced alternatives, which limits opportunities for users to switch to less-expensive brands in response to tax increases. Taxing all tobacco products comparably reduces

incentives for substitution. The health effects of tobacco use are proportional to the quantity consumed and not to the value of the product, which tilts the balance in favor of specific excises.
- Contrary to specific excises, ad valorem excises (a percentage of the value of the excised good) are more responsive to inflation, and the multiplier effect of ad valorem taxation can help keep prices in check if the industry is concentrated. Ad valorem excises are sometimes used as a protective device, shielding low quality local cigarettes against higher quality imports by increasing the price differential (or conversely). However, ad valorem taxes are difficult to implement and weaken tax policy impact. Since they are levied as a percentage of price, companies have greater opportunities to avoid higher taxes and preserve or grow the size of their market by manufacturing and selling lower-priced brands. Companies can also establish wholesale intermediaries too artificially but legally lower the value of tobacco products at the place excise taxes are applied (port or factory). This also makes government tax revenues more dependent on industry pricing strategies and increases the uncertainty of the tobacco tax revenue stream.
- Specific excise taxes need to be adjusted for inflation to remain effective, and tax increases should reduce the affordability of tobacco products. In many countries, where incomes and purchasing power are growing rapidly, large price increases are required to offset growth in real incomes.
- Strong tax administration is critical to minimize tax avoidance and tax evasion, to ensure that tobacco tax increases lead to higher tobacco product prices and tax revenues, as well as reductions in tobacco use and its negative health consequences. One of the key challenges is to find the tax rate "sweet spot" that maximizes revenue increase and smoking decline. Tax levels set too low reduce potential revenue and are less of a deterrent to smoking.
- Regional agreements on tobacco taxation can be effective in reducing cross-border tax and price differentials and in minimizing opportunities for individual tax avoidance and larger-scale illicit trade.

There are challenges to increasing tobacco taxes, as observed in many countries. These include lobbying by vested commercial interests (e.g., tobacco growers, producers, and sellers of tobacco products), exploitation of psychological weaknesses by marketers, particularly targeting advertisement to youth, and consumers' present-bias, i.e., the inclination to use tobacco now, irrespective of the risk of developing tobacco-related diseases in the future.

The powerful impact of the multiplier effect on market structure makes a choice between ad valorem and specific taxes a central point of industry lobbying, in addition to the level of taxes. Tactics used by the tobacco industry to interfere with tobacco control efforts include: maneuvering to hijack the political and legislative process; exaggerating the economic importance of the industry; manipulating public opinion to gain the appearance of respectability; fabricating support through front groups; discrediting proven science; and intimidating governments with litigation or the threat of litigation (WHO 2015).

§10.03 A FRAMEWORK FOR DISCUSSION

George Akerlof (2001 Nobel Prize Laureate in Economics and University Professor at Georgetown University and author of *"Phishing for Phools": The Economics of Manipulation and Deception)*

The challenge posed by tobacco use globally becomes clear by understanding insights from the economics of manipulation and deception.

Ever since Adam Smith, the central teaching in economics has been that free markets provide us with material well-being, as if by an invisible hand. But this fundamental insight in economics is challenged by the fact that markets harm as well as help us. As long as there is profit to be made, sellers will systematically exploit our psychological weaknesses and our ignorance through manipulation and deception. That is, rather than being essentially benign and always creating the greater good, markets are inherently filled with trick and traps and will "phish" us as "phools" (Akerlof and Shiller 2015).

In regards to human behavior, the job of psychologists is to ferret out our psychological weaknesses or susceptibilities. In a free-market equilibrium, if we have some weaknesses, they will be exploited as long as there is a profit to be made. In free competitive markets, we are free to choose, but also "free to phish."

The four "we-could-not possibly-wants" are personal financial insecurity, financial/macroeconomic instability, ill health, and bad government. In significant ways, sellers play to our weaknesses. They are "phishing for phools." "Humans think in terms of stories, and decisions are consequently determined by the stories we tell ourselves. Advertisers use this to their advantage by 'graph[ing] their story' onto ours, and thereby influencing the decisions we make – in this case, to get us addicted to tobacco use, particularly teenagers and low-income people" (Akerlof and Shiller 2015).

This insight could also be used to promote tobacco control. An example of this is the 1964 United States (U.S.) Surgeon General's Report. The story told was that "smoking is stupid." This led to free airtime and bans on indoor smoking in the U.S.. The arsenal of effective consumer protection regulations that have contributed to reduce the social acceptability of smoking also includes advertising bans, smoke-free public spaces, and restricting sales to minors. In the U.S., as mandated by the U.S Food and Drug Administration (FDA) by the 2009 "Family Smoking Prevention and Tobacco Control Act," regulatory agencies have authority to regulate the manufacture, distribution, and marketing of tobacco products, including e-cigarettes, like any other drug.

Another recent example is Australia's 2012 legislation that was adopted to reduce the appeal of smoking by restricting the use of logos, colors, brand images, or promotional information on packaging, other than brand names and product names displayed in a standard color and small font below hard-hitting warnings depicting the negative health consequences of smoking.

In the two years following the law, tobacco consumption declined 12.8%, which some have attributed, in part, to the legislation.

Other countries are starting to follow Australia's example. Similar regulations approved in France and the United Kingdom were set to begin implementation in 2016, and they are under formal consideration in several other countries across the world. Uruguay and Thailand already mandate that at least 80% of front and back of the packaging be covered with graphic health warnings. And Mauritius leads Africa in terms of requirements for tobacco packaging and labeling.

Cigarette taxes also play an important role in tobacco control. Taxing tobacco leads to better health, increased revenues, reduction in health costs, and protection of the lives of loved ones. And, "The role of stories in all of this is that they legitimate the higher taxes and make them collectible, and as well as promote political and social acceptance of other regulatory measures to control tobacco use" (Akerlof and Shiller 2015).

Philip Cook (Professor of Public Policy and Economics at Duke University and former Director of Duke University's Sanford Institute of Public Policy and author of *"Paying the Tab": The Costs and Benefits of Tobacco and Alcohol Control*).

High excise taxes on tobacco and alcoholic beverages are not an attractive source of revenue unless they are effective in reducing use and abuse.

Why? Such taxes could be regressive by the usual standard, and the high prices that result could constitute a particular burden on the poor and often disabled heavy users.

That would be a dubious proposition if usage were completely insensitive to prices. Hence, high taxes must be justified by evidence that "they are effective in reducing abuse and improving public health."

Making that case persuasively is not easy. In the past, most experts on smoking and alcohol abuse did not believe that prices mattered, nor did the public. For alcohol abuse, for example, the dominant school of thought was that the main problem was alcoholism and that alcoholism was an addiction characterized by loss of control. It stood to reason that addicts would find a way to drink their fill, even if prices went up. A tax amounting to, say, an extra dime a drink, was not going to make any difference to people who were already suffering great personal losses for the sake of sustaining their habit. The primary effect of a high tax would be to make their difficult lives even more so. Of course, it could be argued that it is simply "fair" for the smoker or drinker to compensate the public for negative externalities of their use. But "fairness" in that regard assumes that the bad habits are a choice, freely made.

This argument has intuitive appeal but is incorrect in important ways. First, the problem of alcohol abuse is not synonymous with alcoholism. Youths and other non-alcoholic drinkers who get drunk occasionally can do a lot of damage, as reflected in statistics on highway safety, injuries, violent crime, domestic violence, and even death by alcohol poisoning or ethylic coma.

Second, even if the direct effects of prices are on the consumption habits of relatively moderate drinkers, heavy drinkers can be affected indirectly. There is good evidence that drinking occurs in a social context, and that drinkers across the spectrum influence each other. So if alcohol prices can affect the drinking patterns at the median, then the upper tail of the distribution will shift inward. That is to say, there will be a reduced prevalence of heavy drinking.

There is no need to just speculate on these matters. The so-called "laboratory of the states" in the U.S., for example, provides strong evidence. Over the past 20 years, there have been scores of cases in which states increased their alcohol excise taxes. Those cases could be seen as trials in a sort of natural experiment, with states that did not change their tax as the control group. The assessments done utilized administrative data on alcohol sales and health-related outcomes, so as not to rely on survey data – which are always suspect when it comes to drinking and smoking.

The assessments found that an increase in the state tax consistently resulted in a reduction in tax-paid sales per capita. That was a first step, but not enough, because skeptics could say that some drinkers were avoiding the higher tax by buying their booze in neighboring states. It is also possible that only the moderate drinkers were cutting back, so that the reduction had little effect on the amount of alcohol-related harm.

So, in addition to analyzing sales data, the assessment also analyzed the effect on the cirrhosis mortality rate. Cirrhosis mortality is a good indicator of the prevalence of long-term heavy drinking, and in particular alcoholism. What was found was the same pattern as for sales – cirrhosis mortality dropped when taxes went up. In other words, higher prices postponed or prevented deaths due to liver disease. That was direct evidence that the tax reduced the consumption of heavy drinkers and a clear indication that the tax was effective with one of the target populations.

In the 35 years since the initial period of study, there have been numerous studies of the effects of alcohol tax changes, for a variety of outcomes – injury mortality, violent crime, STDs, suicide, domestic violence, and so forth. The results are consistently positive. One of the recent studies found that, when the U.S. Congress doubled the federal beer tax in 1991, the result in just the first year was to save 7,000 lives.

These days, most experts are on board with the idea that higher alcohol taxes tend to reduce alcohol abuse and dependence, and the costly consequences thereof. But that conclusion remains a tough sell with the public and the politicians, especially given the alcohol industry's lobbying and disinformation campaign. And since 1991, the U.S. Congress and most of the states have little to legislate in this area, letting inflation gradually erode the value of alcohol excises. In fact, inflation has in effect repealed the 1991 legislation that doubled the federal beer tax.

Tobacco taxes have been a very different story in the U.S. in recent years. The politics changed in 1998 with the Tobacco Master Settlement Agreement (MSA), originally established between the four largest U.S. tobacco companies (Philip Morris Inc., R. J. Reynolds, Brown & Williamson, and Lorillard – the "original participating manufacturers," also referred to as the "Majors") and the attorneys general of 46 states, which settled the states' Medicaid lawsuits against the tobacco industry for recovery of their tobacco-related health-care costs. Large increases in federal and state tax rates have generated many billions in extra revenues, despite the resulting decline in smoking. It is widely acknowledged that much of that decline has been induced by the increased post-tax tobacco prices.

Interestingly, some of the best evidence that higher taxes are effective in curtailing tobacco use is similar to the evidence for alcohol abuse: it comes from the "laboratory of the states" in the U.S., and in particular from analysis of data generated by many instances in which state legislatures changed tobacco taxes. While there is no doubt that nicotine addiction plays a powerful role in smoking cigarettes, higher prices appear helpful in discouraging initiation and encouraging cessation.

Alcohol and tobacco differ in one important respect, namely the public health goal. For tobacco, the best answer is abstention – there is no safe level of smoking. But for drinking, it is moderation, where some scientists actually believe, as many people do, that a drink or two a day is good for health. As a result, one objection to the alcohol excise tax is that, even if it is an effective public health measure, it is poorly focused, in effect punishing all drinkers regardless of whether their drinking is problematic.

But in fact, the alcohol tax is surprisingly well focused on negative externalities of drinking. Consider a proposed increase of 10 cents per drink, which would amount to an annual payment of USD 60 per capita on average. But that average conceals a huge range. One-third of adults in the U.S. abstain, and they would obviously pay nothing if the tax were increased. Most drinkers do not drink much, and for them, the tax would be just a few extra dollars per year. The bulk of the extra revenue would come from the top 15% of the drinkers (who average eight or nine drinks per day); they consume 75% of all the alcohol and hence would pay 75% of new tax. That is also the group that accounts for most of the alcohol-related damage. Hence the claim that it is well targeted.

If the extra revenue were returned directly to the public as a sort of uniform dividend, most adults would receive more than they paid in. And most everyone would benefit from reduced drinking and abuse, starting with the financial benefit of reduced insurance rates and a reduced threat of violent crime.

In conclusion, the case for higher excise taxes begins with the evidence that they are effective in controlling excess use. While experts are now in agreement that alcohol and tobacco excises are powerful public-health instruments, we are a long way from persuading the public of that truth, especially for alcohol. While we all know much of the context on the rationale for taxing tobacco and alcohol, we also know that the key to change is action at the country level.

Jason Furman (Chairman of the United States President's Council of Economic Advisers – *Six lessons from the U.S. Experience with Tobacco Taxes*)

When people think about what the Obama Administration did to improve public health, they often think immediately of the Affordable Care Act (ACA), and appropriately so. The ACA is undoubtedly the single most important health-related legislation of not just the Obama Administration, but of recent decades. But the Obama Administration also took many other steps that have improved Americans' health. The legislation that President Obama signed in his first month in office in 2009, which raised the Federal cigarette tax from USD 0.39 per pack to approximately USD 1.01 per pack, was his most important public-health legislation.

Plausible estimates suggest that this increase in cigarette taxes will reduce the number of premature deaths due to smoking by between 15,000 and 70,000 for two young population cohorts (12-17 and 18-25). The health benefits will be progressively distributed, representing a far larger fraction of income for lower-income families, and even more so when counting the benefits of the expansion of children's health insurance coverage that the increase funded, as discussed below.

It is important to understand that these tax measures complement a range of other steps to reduce the threat to public health posed by tobacco products. In 2009, President Obama signed legislation providing the FDA with authority to regulate tobacco products, and requiring FDA approval of certain new tobacco products, building on a series of steps that began with the U.S. Surgeon General's 1964 report on the harms of tobacco.

The ACA requires health insurance to cover tobacco counseling and interventions without cost sharing and requires that Medicaid programs cover cessation services for pregnant women. With funding from the ACA's Prevention Fund, the U.S. Centers for Disease Control and Prevention (CDC) launched an aggressive, graphic media campaign highlighting the health and physical impacts of smoking called Tips from Former Smokers. In May 2016, the FDA finalized a rule extending its regulatory authority to all tobacco products, including e-cigarettes, cigars, hookah tobacco, and pipe tobacco.

Externalities, Internalities, and Addictive Goods

Before diving into the estimates, it is useful to briefly discuss the underlying theory and motivation, because it affects not only the assessment of past policies but also the analysis and motivation for future ones. Tobacco imposes a number of costs on society that can be understood through the traditional economic concept of "externalities," including the negative health and amenity effects of second-hand smoke, the large costs to children and society more broadly of low birthweight, which is more likely to affect babies whose mothers smoke during pregnancy, and the additional health costs borne by all of us to help care for smokers.

But smoking has its largest effects on smokers themselves. Each pack of cigarettes consumed will ultimately impose a cost of about USD 25 to USD 50 on a typical smoker, in terms of shorter life expectancy and other negative health effects. A "rational" person should have an additional pack of cigarettes, if the benefit to him or her exceeds at least USD 25 plus the relatively modest cost of producing the pack of cigarettes itself.

In most cases it could be assumed that government policy should address externalities, but that rational consumers would fully take into account all of the internal costs and come to the optimal decision with no further need for public policy intervention. However, in the case of tobacco use, there are a number of reasons to believe this simplistic analysis is incorrect. First, and perhaps most important, is what economists call the present-bias problem. Across a wide range of domains, we have evidence that people overweigh the present at the expense of the future. In the case of tobacco use, which has large costs that appear many years in the future, this leads to smoking at rates above the socially optimal.

The highly addictive nature of tobacco greatly exacerbates this problem, since, once people have started smoking, it is difficult to stop, even if they decide they want to. Evidence suggests that overly optimistic assessments of one's ability to quit also play a role in smoking initiation. In surveys, far more teenagers who smoke report that they will quit than those who ultimately do. Teenagers may excessively discount the future health costs, assuming that they will be able to quit smoking when, in reality, quitting is much more difficult than they think.

When individuals do not take into account costs they impose on themselves for whatever reason, economists refer to it as an "internality." Finally, although we have made major strides in increasing public awareness of the health risks of smoking, traditional informational shortcomings may also play a role in smoking initiation.

Lesson #1: Smoking Plays a Major Role Not Just in Mortality, but in the Inequality of Mortality

There is a substantial concern in the U.S. and around the world about growing inequality. Recently a number of scholars have advanced the stark and troubling thesis that the U.S. is witnessing a dramatic increase not just in income inequality but also in life expectancy inequality (Chetty et al. 2016, National Academies 2015). The truth is a little more complicated than that, however, and smoking plays an important role in the story.

First, the broader public-health story. Age-adjusted death rates in the U.S. have fallen sharply since the 1950s, with particularly notable declines in death rates from heart disease and stroke, among others, as shown in Figure 10.1 (CDC 2016). Decreasing death rates have led to a substantial increase in period life expectancies at birth, from 68.2 years in 1950 to 78.8 years in 2013. But, while all-cause death rates were falling rapidly, death rates for lung cancer were rising rapidly, tripling from 1950 to 1990. Since 1990, however, death rates for lung cancer have dropped by nearly one-third. This result partly reflects the success of the sustained campaign to combat smoking waged in the U.S. over the past half century, a phenomenal public health achievement.

The data on mortality inequality tells a more nuanced tale. Troublingly, for those who have reached middle age, the gap in life expectancy between higher-income individuals and lower-income individuals has grown substantially. At the same time, mortality rates early in life are actually falling more quickly in low-income areas than in high-income areas (Currie and Schwandt 2016).

Chapter 10: Expanding the Global Tax Base §10.03

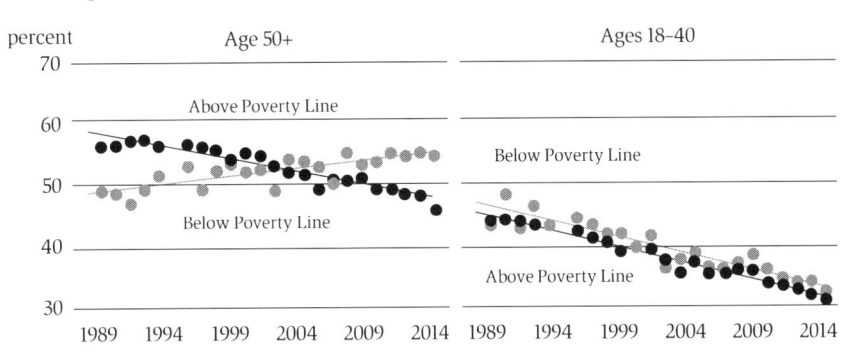

Figure 10.1   Percent That Ever Smoked by Poverty Status, U.S., 1991-2014

Source: NHIS and CEA calculations following Currie and Schwandt (2016).

Differing trends in smoking rates by income are likely one important factor driving differences in the evolution of mortality rates for the young and old. The share of the population 50 and older below the poverty line that has ever smoked has grown over the last 25 years, while the share of the population 50 and older above the poverty line that has ever smoked has decreased. In contrast, smoking rates for the population ages 18-40 have declined substantially, regardless of poverty status, and smoking rates for people living in poverty are only slightly higher than for those not living in poverty.

Lesson #2: Price Plays an Important Role in Smoking

From 1954 to 1983, inflation-adjusted cigarette prices were essentially flat, coinciding with an increase in per capita cigarette consumption. Since 1983, cigarette prices have increased rapidly and, in parallel, consumption has plummeted (Figure 10.2). Of course, these changes were driven by a variety of factors in addition to price, including public education campaigns, access to approved cessation tools, and other factors, many of which have been the subject of extensive research.

Research into the relationship between cigarette prices and smoking typically estimates elasticities of demand: the percentage decrease in cigarette demand that would result from a 1% increase in price. However, due to the addictive nature of tobacco products, we are concerned with more than the simple quantity of cigarettes consumed. For example, some research examines the impact of prices on smoking initiation, and other studies look at the impact of price on quit attempts or the fraction of the population that smokes.

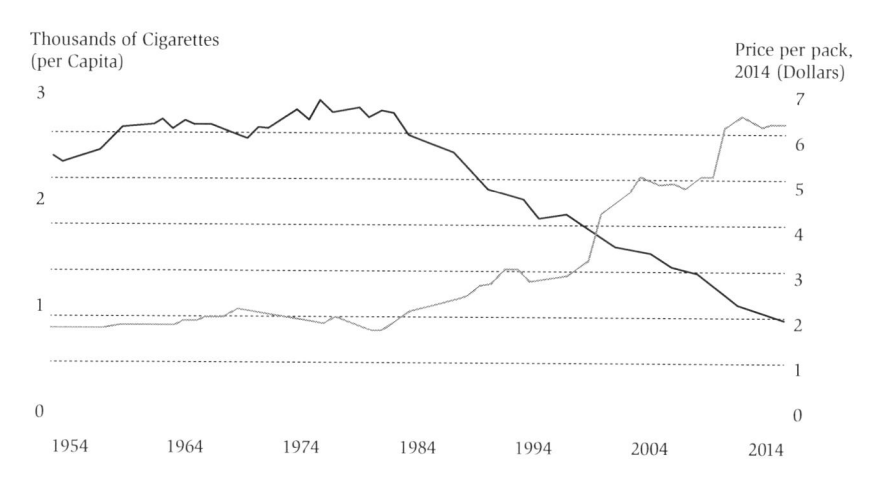

Figure 10.2   U.S. Cigarette Prices and Consumption, 1954-2014

Source: Orzechowski and Walker (2015): Bureau of Labor Statistics: CEA Calculations.

Meta-analyses of the relationship between tobacco prices and use suggest that the overall elasticity of demand for adults lies between 0.3 and 0.7 (Chaloupka and Warner 2000, CBO 2012, Gallet and List 2003, IARC 2011): that is to say that a 10% increase in cigarette prices will lead to a 3% to 7% decline in consumption. These meta-analyses find that about half of this reduction comes from existing users smoking less (the intensive margin) and about half comes from a decline in the number of smokers (the extensive margin).

Though subject to some debate, a number of studies suggest the relevant elasticities for youths and young adults are higher than those for adults, which is to say that youths and young adults respond relatively more to prices.

Lesson #3: Cigarette Taxes Play an Important Role in Cigarette Prices

U.S. cigarette taxes fell sharply in inflation-adjusted terms through the 1970s and early 1980s, as inflation eroded their value (Figure 10.3). Federal cigarette taxes were increased in 1983 but remained well below their inflation-adjusted value from decades before. However, around 2000, cigarette taxes took on an increased role as part of tobacco and health policy, and tax rates increased sharply in the first decade of this century, driving the substantial increase in cigarette prices since then. In addition, the MSA reached in 1998 between the attorneys general of 46 states and the District of Columbia and the four largest tobacco companies included substantial annual payments to the Government that function as a further tax on tobacco.

Chapter 10: Expanding the Global Tax Base   §10.03

Figure 10.3   Average U.S. Cigarette Taxes and Prices, U.S., 1954-2014

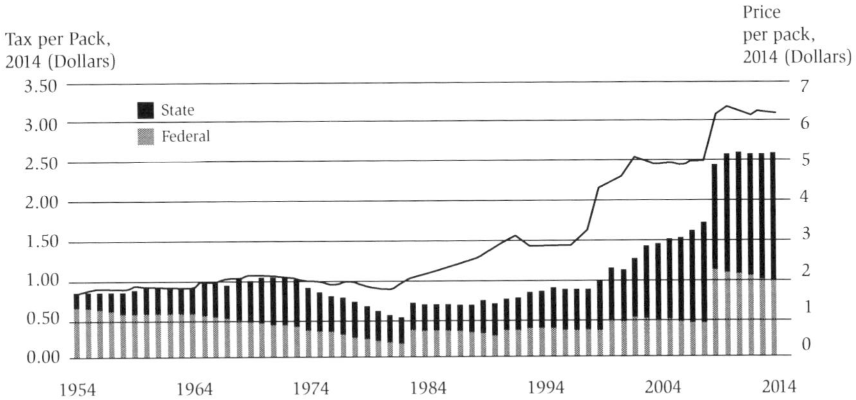

Source: Orzechowski and Walker (2015): Bureau of Labor Statistics: CEA calculations.

Lesson #4: Cigarette Taxes Have Large Aggregate Benefits for Public Health

By increasing cigarette prices, cigarette taxes substantially reduce smoking rates and generate large improvements in public health. This finding is borne out both by the body of existing research on the topic and the experience of the 2009 tobacco tax increase, which is discussed in some detail below.

Two studies that examine the impact of the most recent increase in Federal tobacco taxes, in 2009, find resulting reductions in smoking among youths. The more recent study (van Hasselt et al. 2015) concluded that smoking initiation for youths age 12-17 fell more than 15%, and initiation for young adults' 18-25 fell by 8% (Figure 10.4). Past-month use likewise fell by about 15% for youths 12-17 and by about 5% for young adults 18-25. While all of these results are economically significant, the estimated effect on smoking initiation for young adults 18-25 is not statistically significant. The other study (Huang and Chaloupka 2012) found similar decreases, concluding that the percentage of 8th-, 10th-, and 12th-grade students who smoked in the past month fell by between 10% and 13%.

The findings from these recent studies are broadly consistent with the results from the earlier literature. Combining the estimates from these two studies, an analysis of cigarette taxes and smoking by the U.S. Congressional Budget Office (CBO 2012), and estimates from a study of youth smoking by Carpenter and Cook (2008), the evidence suggests that the 2009 Federal cigarette tax increase could plausibly have reduced the number of smokers in a cohort of 18 year-olds by between 45,000 and 220,000 people, roughly 3% to 15%.

We can also apply estimates of the health impacts of smoking, the frequency and success of quit attempts, and so forth, to the estimates presented above on the impact of the cigarette tax increase on smoking rates to obtain an estimate of the health benefits associated with the tax increase. For these calculations, we can adopt an assumption that roughly one-third of young smokers die prematurely due to smoking (U.S. Surgeon General 2014). Based on these assumptions, the 2009 cigarette tax increase plausibly reduced the number of premature deaths due to smoking in each cohort (12-17 and 18-25) by between 15,000 and 70,000.

Figure 10.4   Changes in Smoking Behavior Due to 2009 Tax Increase in the U.S.

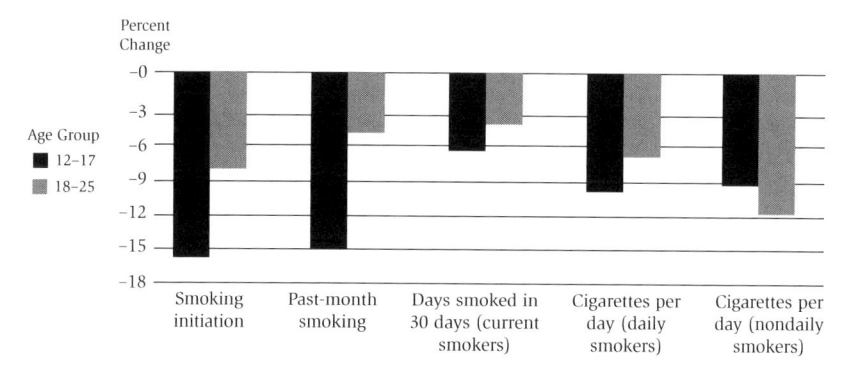

Source: van Hasselt et al. (2015).

We are unlikely to have reached the optimal level of tobacco taxation, especially when the average combined Federal and State tax is about USD 2.50 per pack, and estimates of the harm associated with smoking a pack of cigarettes range from about USD 25 to USD 50 or more per pack (although consumers take some of the costs of this harm into account in making their decisions). To this end, President Obama proposed to further raise the Federal cigarette tax from USD 1.01 to USD 1.95 per pack and to index it to inflation going forward (along with proposing to harmonize tax rates on different tobacco products). This increase in tobacco taxes is part of an effort to fund high-quality early education for all Americans, a policy that itself would have enormous economic benefits (CEA 2016). The proposal would reduce the number of premature deaths due to smoking in a youth cohort by between about 10,000 and 50,000, based on assumptions similar to those used to analyze the 2009 increase.

Lesson #5: Tobacco Taxes Disproportionately Benefit Lower-Income Households

Tobacco taxes are sometimes criticized for being regressive, but this criticism is backward. The health benefits of tobacco taxes far exceed the increase in tax liability, and they accrue disproportionately to lower-income households. Moreover, it is important to also evaluate what the additional revenue raised by the tobacco tax may be used for. The most recent increases in U.S. tobacco taxes, enacted in 1997 and 2009, were used to create and expand a very progressive children's health insurance program. The Obama Administration's proposal to further increase tobacco taxes would finance a highly progressive, high-quality early education proposal.

Chapter 10: Expanding the Global Tax Base §10.03

Welfare and Distributional Impact of the 2009 Tobacco Tax Increase

Figure 10.5 provides an illustrative estimate of the distributional impacts of the 2009 tobacco tax increase based on a plausible set of assumptions. However, we would not place too much weight on any one number; the point here is to illustrate why applying standard distributional analysis to tobacco tax changes can go so badly awry.

The illustrative distribution is computed by allocating the burden of tobacco taxes according to the distribution of tobacco taxes reported in Rosenberg (2015), allocating USD 37.5 billion in health benefits proportional to the tax burden, allocating a USD 9.4 billion utility offset proportional to the health benefits (and thus also proportional to the tax burden), and allocating Children's Health Insurance Program (CHIP) benefits equal in value to the tax increase, proportional to the distribution of children with CHIP coverage in a March population survey (CPS).

In particular, the blue bars in Figure 10.5 portray the traditional finding that tobacco tax increases, by themselves, are regressive – leading to the largest percentage reductions in pre-tax incomes for the lowest-income households. But the picture changes markedly when we count the benefits of reduced mortality and morbidity as shown in the second set of estimates in orange. These benefits are strongly progressive, for two reasons. First, smoking is more prevalent with lower incomes, so the reductions in smoking are larger for those groups (not considering the fact that they may also be more sensitive to price increases, a factor that is not included here). Second, these estimates assume the dollar value of the health benefit does not vary with income and thus is proportionately more important to lower-income households, although other assumptions on this question are also possible.

Figure 10.5 Illustrative Distribution of the 2009 Tobacco Tax Increase in the U.S.

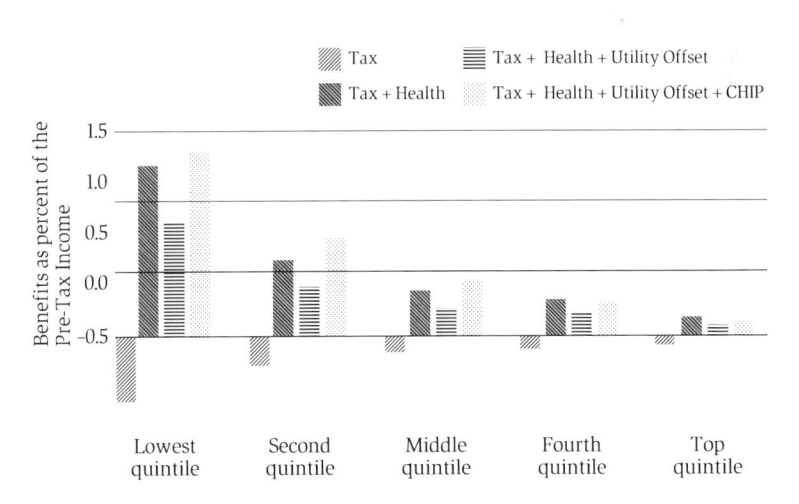

Note: Lower estimate for van Hasselt et al. (2015) is based on results for 18-25 year-olds; higher estimate is based on results for 12-17 year-olds.

Source: Huang and Chaloupka (2012); van Hasselt et al. (2015); CBO (2012); Carpenter and Cook (2008); CEA calculations.

The third set of estimates in grey takes into account a "utility offset" reflecting the fact that people who stop smoking may lose some of the utility they would otherwise have derived from smoking. If people were fully rational, this utility offset would roughly match the internal health costs, but, as discussed above, this is not the case with tobacco, so these estimates assume an illustrative 25% offset. The 25% offset, reflecting the high end of estimates in a recent analysis conducted by the U.S. Department of Health and Human Services (HHS 2015), is merely illustrative and arguably very high for a good with addictive properties. Moreover, there are good arguments that in the case of people dissuaded from taking up smoking in the first place, this offset could be much smaller and possibly zero. The point is to show that, even with this large offset, the tobacco tax increase is still highly progressive, albeit slightly less so.

Finally, the last set of estimates incorporates not just the direct effects of the tax, but also the use of the revenue it generates – in this case expanding health insurance coverage for low- and moderate-income children. Accounting for this coverage expansion adds to the progressivity of the overall legislative package.

The bottom line is that these estimates are positive for all groups and large on average for low-income households.

Lesson #6: It is Really Important to Tax Similar Tobacco Products at Similar Rates

One often-overlooked aspect of tobacco taxation is the importance of harmonizing the tax rate on different tobacco products. Currently, there is a wide disparity in tax rates in the U.S. between tobacco products (Figure 10.6). For example, pipe tobacco is taxed at a rate of less than USD 3 per pound while roll-your-own tobacco is taxed at a rate of nearly USD 25 per pound. These disparities can lead to substitution between tobacco products and can mitigate the positive health effects of tobacco tax increases.

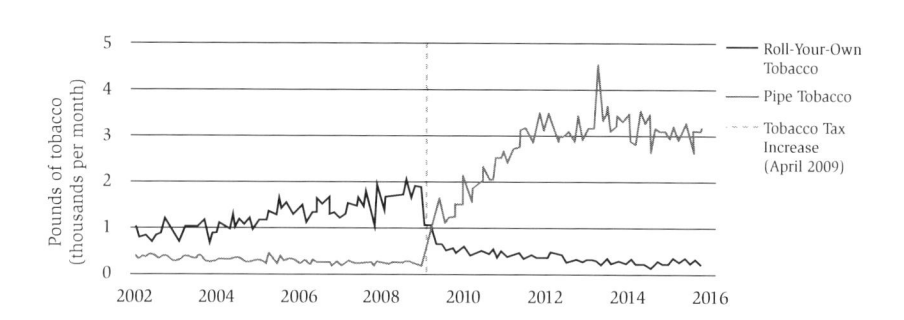

Figure 10.6 Sales of Roll-Your-Own and Pipe Tobacco, U.S, 2002-2016

Source: Department of the Treasury, Alcohol and Tobacco Tax and Trade Bureau.

The problem is that if you raise the tax on one product without raising it on another, consumers can substitute to the cheaper product, potentially undoing some of the public health benefit the tax was intended to encourage. This is not just a theoretical possibility but visible in the data. For example, consider the patterns in the sale of roll-your-own and pipe tobacco and in small and large cigars following the enactment of the 2009 tobacco tax increase. Prior to the law's enactment, the tax rates on roll-your-own tobacco and pipe tobacco were the same. After the law's enactment, the tax rate on roll-your-own tobacco was over USD 20 per pound higher than the tax on pipe tobacco. And, as you can see in the figure, sales of roll-your-own tobacco plummeted after the law, and sales of pipe tobacco increased by a factor of 10. Similarly, as the law disadvantaged modestly priced small cigars relative to modestly priced large cigars, sales of small cigars plummeted and sales of large cigars rose. In fact, many manufacturers of small cigars slightly increased the weight of their product to classify it as a large cigar (GAO 2012).

In the extreme case where different tobacco products are perfect substitutes, a tax increase on one product alone would have no impact on overall consumption and resultant health harms. In reality, of course, substitution is imperfect but still larger than one might expect. When President Obama's proposal was being developed to increase and harmonize taxes on tobacco, economists in the Treasury Department estimated that the reduction in tobacco consumption under a harmonization proposal would be nearly two and a half times the size it would be under an increase in the cigarette tax alone that raises comparable revenue. This implies additional health benefits of more than USD 100 billion over 10 years. This is not just a technical detail.

China's 2015 Tobacco Tax Adjustment and Initial Impact

Rose Zheng (Economics and Tax Professor, School of International Trade and Economics (SITE), University of International Business and Economics (UIBE), Beijing, China, and Director of China's WHO Tobacco Control Collaboration Center)

China is the leading producer and consumer of tobacco in the world, with 44% of the world's cigarettes consumed in China. About 300 million people in China smoke, some 30% of the country's total population, with a 53% prevalence of tobacco smoking among men aged 15-69, among the highest in the world.

Tobacco use is one of the top three health risk factors that have contributed significantly to the rapid growth of non-communicable diseases (NCDs) in China. Smoking is a major killer. Approximately 1 million deaths every year are caused by tobacco, despite improved access to medical care, thanks to the expansion in recent years of national health insurance coverage.

In the face of this dire reality, what to do? Wait to treat people when they develop lung cancer and other tobacco-related diseases or adopt measures to prevent the onset of disease in the first place? Governments have an obligation and the means to protect their population's wellbeing by adopting effective fiscal and regulatory measures, in addition to providing medical care to those persons who fall ill. In that sense, 2015 may prove to be a landmark year for tobacco control in China, as the Government adopted a national tax reform on cigarettes as well as a ban on smoking in public places in Beijing and Shanghai – a ban that is proposed to be expanded across the country.

Initial assessments done by a team from WHO's Collaborating Center for Tobacco and Economics at Beijing's UIBE show that the 2015 tobacco tax reform is proving to be a win-win for both fiscal and public health in China. That is, it is contributing to:

- Reducing cigarette consumption.
- Shaping cigarette market share.
- Influencing tobacco industry profit margin and hence influencing the industry's production and marketing strategy.
- Increasing government revenue.
- Changing smokers' behavior, including quitting and switching up/down.

2015 Tobacco Tax Reform

- Exercise tax rate at the wholesale segment was increased from 5% to 11%
- An additional specific tax of RMB 0.1 (USD 0.015) per pack (with 20 sticks) was introduced at the wholesale level.

The 2015 cigarette exercise tax adjustment		
	Before May 10, 2015	**After** May 10, 2015
At Producer price level		
Specific exercise tax (per pack)	RMB 0.06	RMB 0.06
Ad valorem tax		
> =7RMB	56%	56%
<7 RMB	36%	36%
At Wholesale price level		
Specific exercise tax (per pack)	0	RMB 0.10
Ad valorem tax	5%	11%

STMA (State Tobacco Monopoly Administration) price announcement responding to tax adjustment:

- Wholesale price has increased 6%.
- STMA provincial branches can set up cigarette retail price in the province based on local –market under STMA retail price guidance and at the same time need to meet the required principle that the retailer's profit margin shouldn't be lower than 10%.
- Both new cigarette tax and pricing policy took effective from May 10, 2015.

On May 10, 2015, 10 years after the ratification, the Chinese Ministry of Finance officially raised the tax on cigarettes, and China's State Tobacco Monopoly Administration (STMA) passed the tax on to the retail price of cigarettes.

Using a tobacco tax as an instrument for tobacco control is a significant step for the Chinese government. To understand the significance of the 2015 tobacco tax policy adjustment, it is useful to understand the role of China's tobacco industry, the cigarette pricing mechanism, and the tobacco tax structure in the Chinese economy (Hu, Zhang, and Zheng 2016). The Chinese tobacco industry is a government-owned national monopoly, the STMA. In 2013, STMA produced more than 2.0 trillion cigarettes, which contributed 816 billion RMB (USD 130 billion), or about 6.3% of China's central government tax revenue. Owing to the importance of the tobacco economy in China, STMA has the advantage of being able to work with the central and local governments. STMA's goal is to promote the industry, even though the harmful health effects of smoking are now well known in China.

STMA is responsible for the centralized management of cigarette factories, cigarette companies and retailers, and it determines the cigarette prices. Cigarette factories decide the cigarette producer prices, cigarette companies decide the cigarette wholesale prices (the producer prices and wholesale prices need to be reported and to be approved by the State Administration of Taxation), and cigarette retailers decide the retail price of cigarettes by adding a regulated market profit margin set by STMA to the wholesale price.

The Chinese government collects five different taxes from the tobacco industry: tobacco leaf tax, value-added tax (VAT), excise tax and urban construction/ educational supplemental tax. The VAT is not tobacco-specific, but has a uniform rate (17%) across all products. Within these five types of taxes, only the excise tax directly influences the magnitude of the retail price of cigarettes.

Initial Evidence of the Impact of the 2015 Tobacco Tax Increase

– *Impact on price and market structure.* The weighted average wholesale price increased by 8.9%, from RMB 10.27 per pack in 2014 to RMB 11.18 per pack in 2015. The average retail price increased by 10.29%, from RMB 11.61 per pack to RMB 12.81 per pack. However, from a global perspective, the weighted average cigarette price in China is still relatively cheap: less than USD 2 per pack on average. Also, as the low-end price categories increased more than middle and premium price categories of cigarettes, the price gaps between tiers have been reduced. This encourages smokers up-shifting from the low-end categories (Class V and Class IV) to the middle and upper price categories (Class III and Class II).

Impact on Prices								
Wholesale Price (RMB/pack)	Class	Class I (Premium)	Class I (Average)	Class II	Class III	Class IV	Class V	Total in average
	2014	36.00	20.60	11.60	8.30	4.50	2.25	10.27
	2015	38.16	21.84	21.84	12.30	4.77	2.39	11.18
	Δ	2.16	1.24	0.70	0.50	0.27	0.14	0.92
	Δ%	6.00%	6.00%	6.00%	6.00%	6.00%	6.00%	8.9%
Retail Price (RMB/pack)	2014	43.00	23.00	13.00	9.50	5.00	2.50	11.61
	2015	45.00	25.00	14.00	10.00	5.50	3.00	12.81 ($2)
	Δ	2.00	2.00	1.00	0.50	0.50	0.50	1.19
	Δ%	4.65%	8.70%	7.69%	5.26%	0.00%	20.00%	10.3%

- *Impact on tax incidence.* The sales-weighted tax share as a percentage of retail price increased from 52% in 2014 to 56% in 2015, which is still lower than WHO recommended standard of 75%. The sales-weighted average excise tax as a percentage of retail price increased by 4%, from 31% in 2014 to 35% in 2015.

Tax as % of Retail Price								
Total tax as % of retail price	Class	Class I (Premium)	Class I (Average)	Class II	Class III	Class IV	Class V	Total in average
	2014	52%	55.40%	58.50%	44.82%	47.23%	53.72%	52%
	2015	55%	58.84%	61.73%	50.37%	52.22%	55.98%	56%
	Δ	3%	3.44%	3.23%	5.55%	4.99%	2.25%	4%
Total excise as % of retail price	2014	36%	38.86%	40.66%	27.47%	28.91%	33.37%	35%
	2015	39%	42%	45%	33%	34%	36%	39%
	Δ	3%	3.48%	4.07%	5.61%	5.19%	2.95%	4%

- *Impact on consumption.* For the first time since 2001, as confirmed by the STMA, the volume of cigarette sales decreased by 2.36% in 2015 compared to 2014. After the 2015 tax adjustment, sales continued to decrease by 4.61% over May 2015-April 2016, compared with May 2014-April 2015, and by 5.36% between October 2015-September 2016, compared with October 2014-September 2015.
- *Impact on government tax revenue.* The Chinese government profits financially from the manufacture and sale of tobacco, as well as from tobacco taxes collected by the government. According to STMA data, the tobacco industry in

China contributed RMB 840.4 billion (about USD 129.29 billion) in tax revenue from tobacco products in 2015, an increase of 9% over the 2014 level. As a state-owned enterprise, it also contributed an additional 190.97 billion RMB (USD 29.38 billion) profit to the central government, plus RMB 63.6 billion (USD 9.79 billion) enterprise income tax to the central government. The 2015 tax increase, which was applied at the wholesale level rather than at the retail level, generated an additional RMB 57.8 billion (USD 8.89 billion) in excise tax at the wholesale level.

- *Impact on public health.* A preliminary estimation suggests that within 12 months following the 2015 tax increase, the total number of smokers would decrease by about 5 million (Figure 10.7).

§10.03   Patricio V. Marquez

Figure 10.7   Impact on Consumption and Market Structure

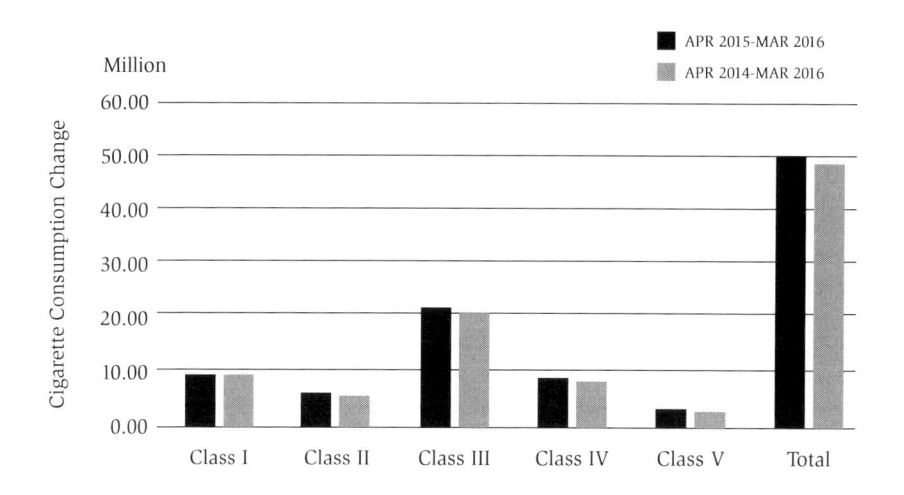

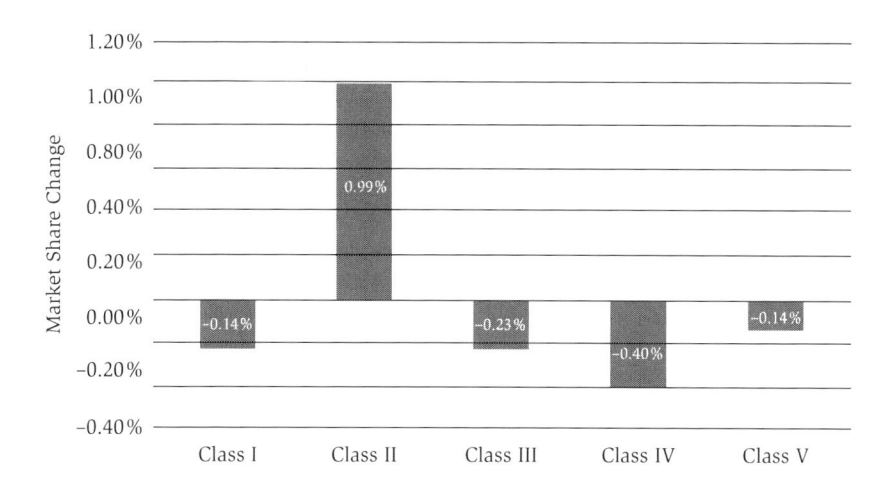

Chapter 10: Expanding the Global Tax Base §10.03

	Impact on Government Tax Revenue									
	Tobacco Tax & Profit	Tobacco Tax	Tobacco Industry Profit	Tax & Profit Contribution to Central Govt	Profit Corporate Before Income Tax		SOE Profit Contribution Rate	SOE Profit Contribution	Add'l Contribution	Add'l Excise Contribution
	Billion USD	Billion USD	Billion USD	Billion USD	Billion USD	Billion USD	%	Billion USD	Billion USD	Billion USD
2014	161.81	118.43	43.38	140.16	33.83	8.46	25%	6.34	6.92	
2015	175.94	129.29	46.65	168.46	39.14	9.79	25%	7.34	13.15	8.89
Δ		9%	8%	21%						

165

While the impact of the 2015 tobacco tax increase is generating measurable benefits, the price of cigarettes in China continues to be low and increasingly affordable for a population that enjoys rapid wage increases. Indeed, the tobacco tax rate in China is still relatively low compared to the WHO-recommended benchmark, which is 75% of the retail price – the taxation level recommended to have an impact on consumption. It is also below the rates in OECD countries such as Australia (63%), Canada (65%), New Zealand (73%), Germany (75%), France (80%), and in neighboring countries such as Thailand (66%) and the Philippines (64%).

Cigarette prices in China have also not increased much during the past decade. According to the China National Statistical Yearbook, from 2000 to 2012 the price index of cigarettes rose by just 4% (year 2000 = 100, 2012 = 103.9). In contrast, food prices doubled (2000 = 100, 2012 = 195.1), the alcohol price index increased by 40% (2000 = 100, 2012 = 140.90), and the price of tea and soft drinks went up by 15% (2000 = 100, 2012 = 115.5). Therefore, the rate of increase of cigarette prices in China is far behind that of many food products (Hu, Zhang, and Zheng 2016).

Tobacco taxes must be increased regularly in order to reduce tobacco use. Otherwise, if incomes rise more quickly than inflation, the relative cost of tobacco products can actually decrease over time. This has been the case in China over the last decade, as the economy has grown, incomes have increased, and tobacco products have become more affordable. China saw rapid economic growth between 2000 and 2012, with an annual rate of GDP growth of more than 9%. During this period, the affordability index of cigarette consumption in China increased from 1.00 in 2000 to 1.69 in 2012, an almost 70% increase in purchasing power. As a result, cigarettes in China are now about 70% more affordable than they were in the year 2000.

If the ultimate goal is to help smokers quit and prevent the next generation from getting addicted to smoking cigarettes, then additional tobacco tax policy reforms are needed in China, especially for re-orienting the excise tax structure towards specific excise taxes at the retail level in the medium term and towards a uniform tax system at the retail level in the long term. This is because a simple and unified excise tax system that taxes all cigarettes at the same level is more appropriate for reducing smoking, while at the same time leading to a more effective tax administration and higher tax revenues. Additional tax increases adjusted for inflation and growing per capita incomes are required to reduce affordability over time, and hence consumption, tobacco-related diseases, and the risk of ill health, premature mortality, and disability. Also, the differential mixture of both ad valorem and specific excises provides incentives for price manipulations to the extent that manufacturers can alter their pricing or production behavior to avoid higher tax liabilities.

If carried out, as estimated in a recent study, a 50% increase in tobacco price through excise tax would lead over 10 years to 5.3 million years of life gained, and reduce expenditures on tobacco-related disease treatment by USD 2.4 billion (Verguet et al. 2015).

Looking into the future, as evidenced in a 2011 World Bank study, "Toward a Healthy and Harmonious Life in China: Stemming the Rising Tide of Non-Communicable Diseases," with stronger tobacco control measures including steeper

Chapter 10: Expanding the Global Tax Base   §10.03

tobacco tax increases, the rapid rise in China's NCDs can be halted, resulting in major gains for people's health and the country's social and economic development.

Philippines' "Sin Tax Reform Law"

Jeremias Paul (former Under Secretary of Finance in the Philippines, and currently Coordinator of the Tobacco Taxation Unit at WHO)

The Philippines is among the top smoking countries in Southeast Asia, and tobacco taxes and prices are among the lowest in the world. A strong tobacco lobby hindered previous tobacco excise tax reform efforts. While President Aquino had promised "no new taxes" during his campaign for office, the Philippines had ratified the WHO Framework Convention on Tobacco Control (FCTC) in 2005, and the government faced a one-year deadline for compliance with a WTO decision on distilled spirits. The rationale put forward by the Aquino Administration to enact the "sin tax" reform was to help finance the expansion of universal health care, address public health issues relating to alcohol and tobacco consumption, and simplify the existing excise tax system on alcohol and tobacco products. The goals also included fixing long-standing, structural fiscal weaknesses, for example by removing the price/brand classification freeze; leveling the playing field; reducing the number of tax tiers; and making the tax system more buoyant by indexing tax rates to inflation (Figure 10.8).

The adoption by Congress in December 2012 of the "Republic Act 10351 on Restructuring the Excise Tax on Alcohol and Tobacco Products (RA 10351)" was a landmark legislative action enacted under the Aquino Administration (it passed the Senate by only one vote). This law can be seen as a fundamentally good governance measure with positive impacts on both fiscal and public health.

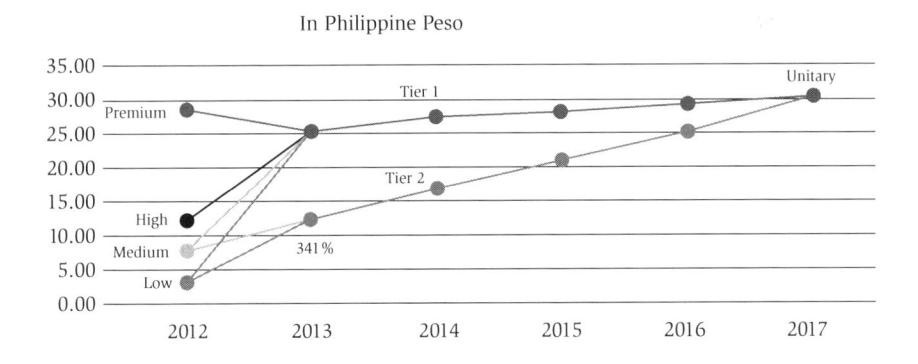

Figure 10.8   Philippine Tobacco Tax Reform Path at a Glance

In Philippine Peso

```
35.00 ─────────────────────────────────────────────── Unitary
                          Tier 1
30.00 ──── Premium ●
25.00
20.00                Tier 2
15.00     High ●
10.00   Medium ●       341%
 5.00     Low ●
 0.00
       2012    2013    2014    2015    2016    2017
```

Key Features
- Removal of price classification freeze/tax advantages of legacy brands.
- Unitary tax structure 2017.
- Tax rates indexed to inflation starting 2017.

167

§10.03   Patricio V. Marquez

- Health impact/WHO FCTC compliance a major consideration in rate setting.
- Bulk of incremental revenues earmarked for UHC
- Safety nets for tobacco farmers /others.

In Billion Pesos	2013	2014	2015	2016	2017
Projected Incremental Revenue (Tobacco)	23.4	29.6	33.5	37.1	40.9
Projected Incremental Revenue (Alcohol)	10.6	13.3	17.1	19.8	23.3
Projected Incremental Revenue (Total)	34.0	42.9	50.6	56.9	64.2
Estimated Earmark for Health as of 2012	30.5	38.4	45.6	51.3	58.0

Some of the key claims raised by the opponents of the "sin tax" law in regards to raising tobacco taxes were that the measure would reduce, not increase, revenues, adversely affect tobacco farmers, increase smuggling and illicit trade, negatively impact the poor, increase unemployment, and destroy the local tobacco industry.

As shown in Figures 10.9 and 10.10, the early implementation of the "sin tax" law over 2013-2016, however, the actual incremental revenues have been higher than projected, reversing the declining trend of tobacco and alcohol excise contributions to GDP.

Figure 10.9   Win for Revenues: Actual Incremental Revenues Higher Than Projected Versus Actual Incremental Revenue from RA 10351

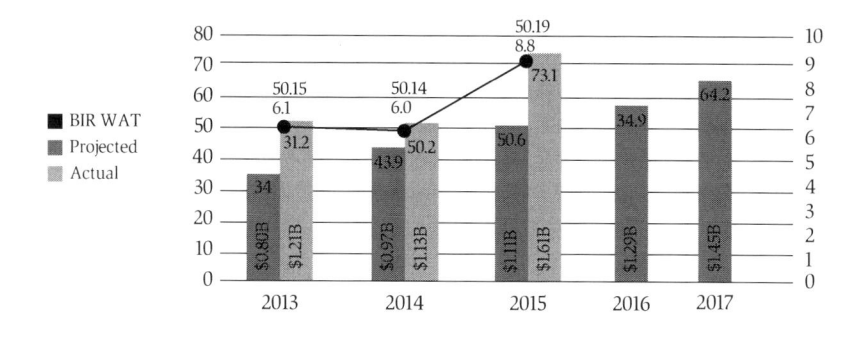

Chapter 10: Expanding the Global Tax Base §10.03

Figure 10.10 Win for Revenues: Sin Tax Law Reversed the Declining Trend of Tobacco and Alcohol Excise Collections to GDP | Tobacco & Alcohol Excise Collection

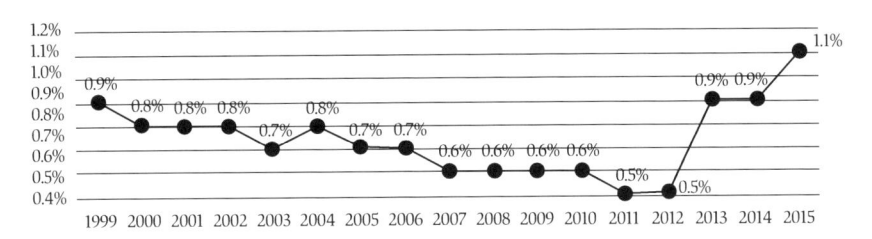

The contribution of excise tax revenues from tobacco increased from 0.3% to 0.8% of GDP during 2013-2016 (Figure 10.11). Apart from tax administration measures, this was the only tax policy measure adopted during the Aquino Administration.

Figure 10.11 Win for Revenues: Tobacco Taxes Accounted for Bulk of Collections with Share of Tobacco Excise Tax Collections to GDP Highest in 2015

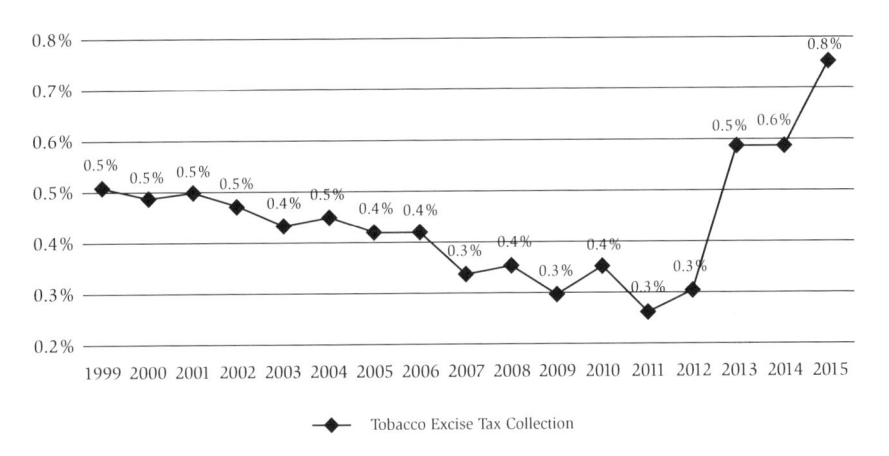

Along with other factors, like low inflation, high international reserves, declining debt to GDP ratios, and good governance, the "sin tax" law also made it possible to achieve Philippine's first investment grade rating (Table 10.1). The rating agencies informed the Ministry of Finance that they were just waiting for implementation of the measure, as approved by Congress 2012.

Table 10.1 Win for the Economy: Adoption of Sin Tax Law Contributed to Philippines' First Investment Grade Rating

MOODY'S	Investment Grade Baa3 Positive (Oct. 3, 2013); Upgraded to Baa2 Stable (Dec. 11, 2014)
FITCH RATINGS	Investment Grade BBB- Stable (March 27, 2013); Affirmation (March 25, 2014); Upgraded to BBB- Positive (Sept. 24,2015)
STANDARD & POOR'S	Investment Grade BBB-/Stable (May 2, 2013) Upgraded to BBB /Stable (May 8, 2014) Affirmation (April 24. 2015)
JAPAN CREDIT RATING AGENCY (JCRA)	Investment Grade BBB/Stable (May 7, 2013); Affirmation (May 30.2014); Upgraded to BBB+/Stable (July 6, 2015)
RATINGS INVESTMENT (R&I) INFORMATION, INC.	Investment Grade BBB/Stable (July 9, 2014); Affirmation (July 20, 2015)

For public health, the Philippines' health budget is now almost triple 2012 levels (Figure 10.12). As mandated by the "sin tax" law, the incremental revenues from the tax collection were earmarked for health following regular budgetary processes. Section 8 (C) of the Republic Act 10351 states that after deducting the allocations under Republic Act Nos. 7171 and 8240 (allocations to tobacco farmers), 80% of the revenue collected should be allocated to the National Health Insurance Program and 20% to the Ministry of Health's health facilities enhancement program. The tax revenue collected from the application of the "sin tax" law increased the number of people with free health insurance – from 5.2 million poor primary members in 2012 to 15.4 million in 2015 (Figure 10.13).

Figure 10.12 Win for Public Health: Health Budget Almost Triple 2012 Levels DOH Budget (In B PhP)

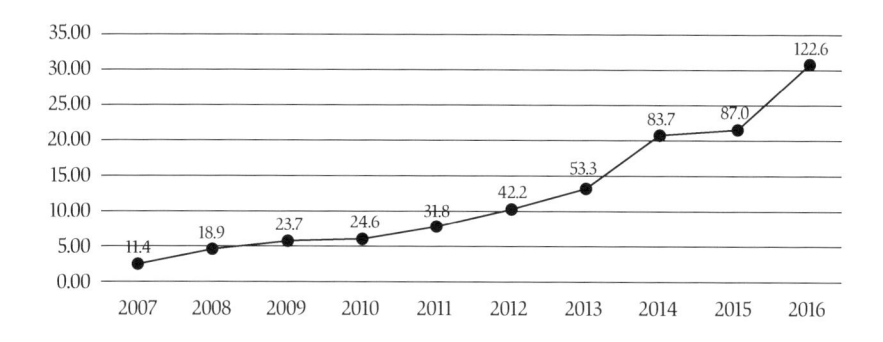

Chapter 10: Expanding the Global Tax Base   §10.03

Figure 10.13   Win for the Poor: National Governmental Allocation for Health Insurance Premiums for the Poor

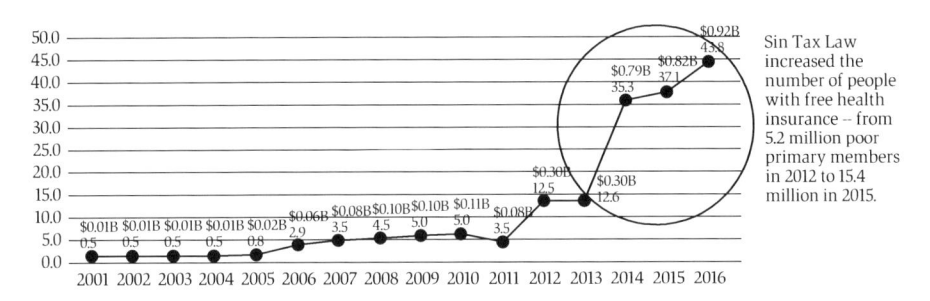

[Chart showing values from 2001-2016: $0.01B (0.5) for 2001-2004, $0.02B (0.8) 2005, $0.06B (2.9) 2006, $0.08B (3.5) 2007, $0.10B (4.5) 2008, $0.10B (5.0) 2009, $0.11B (5.0) 2010, $0.08B (3.5) 2011, $0.30B (12.5) 2012, $0.30B (12.6) 2013, $0.79B (35.3) 2014, $0.82B (37.1) 2015, $0.92B (43.8) 2016. Note: Sin Tax Law increased the number of people with free health insurance – from 5.2 million poor primary members in 2012 to 15.4 million in 2015.]

Additionally, smoking prevalence has declined among the young and poor. Results of the Smoking Prevalence Study done by Dans et al., based on National Nutrition Health Survey 2013 and 2015 data, showed that:

- Prevalence of smoking among adult Filipinos went down from 31.0% in 2008 to 25.4% in 2013, and then to 23.3% in 2015.
- There are about 4.0 million fewer smokers in the country because of the application of the "sin tax" law. The drop is partly from people who stopped smoking, but mostly from people who have avoided starting to smoke.
- At least 70,000 deaths have been averted since 2013.

The experience in the Philippines shows that raising tobacco taxes is an easy way to raise domestic revenues for health while reducing health risks associated with tobacco-related diseases. Framing the "sin tax" law as a health measure allowed the Philippines to raise tobacco taxes substantially more than would otherwise have been possible, if the law was framed as a revenue measure. Political support at the highest level was critical for ensuring the approval of the law in Congress. The collaboration established between the ministries of finance, health, and other sectors was important, as government agencies need to collaborate and adopt a systems perspective and whole of government/society approach. It is also important to be vigilant and systematically monitor progress and outcomes.

Uruguay's Experience – Fernando Serra *(Director of the Tax Advisory Unit, Ministry of Economy and Finance of Uruguay)*

Uruguay became a Party to the WHO FCTC on September 9, 2004, and has adopted some of the most comprehensive tobacco control laws in the world, including Latin America's first ban on smoking in enclosed public places in 2006, the world's largest pictorial warnings on 80% of the front and back of the pack in 2009, and the first-ever ban on differentiated branding (i.e., applying the same brand to a family of tobacco products) in February 2009. Additionally, Uruguay has legislation to counter illegal trade in tobacco products, where contraband is viewed as a customs infringement dealt with in civil and criminal law. Uruguay ratified the FCTC's Protocol on Illicit Trade on Tobacco in 2014.

Uruguay has also imposed several tax increases on tobacco products since 2005, with tax increases adopted in 2007 and 2010, including excise taxes (*impuestos especificos internos* or IMESI) and VAT, as well as increases in the *"precios fictos"* (*"precios fictos"* are ex-factory and/or wholesale prices of cigarettes multiplied by a government-determined coefficient). Table 10.2 summarizes Uruguay's recent series of tobacco tax hikes.

Table 10.2 Tobacco Tax Increases, 2007-2016[*]

Period	Measure	Excise Tax / Retail Price	VAT/ Retail Price	COFIS / Retail Price	Total Tax Burden
Until July 2007	Tax Exempt	62%	0%	3%	64%
After July 2007	22% VAT adopted	48%	18%	0%	66%
After June 2009	Increase in the base price, for taxing tobacco	47%	18%	0%	65%
After February 2010	Increase in the base price, for taxing tobacco	54%	18%	0%	72%
After December 2014	Increase in the base price, for taxing tobacco	48%	18%	0%	66%
After June 2015	Increase in the base price, for taxing tobacco	48%	18%	0%	66%
After January 2016	Increase in the base price, for taxing tobacco	47%	18%	0%	66%

[*]Pack of 20 cigarettes.

Chapter 10: Expanding the Global Tax Base   §10.03

In 2016, IMESI and VAT taxes accounted for 66% of the retail price for the most popular cigarette brand. The increase in tobacco taxes has resulted in higher prices and tax revenue collected, in spite of the lower volume of sales. The public health impact has been significant, as well: prevalence among the adult population dropped from 33.5% in 2005 to 22% in 2016, and among youth from in 22.8% 2005 to 8.2% in 2016. In addition, over the 2005-2016 period, air contamination in public spaces due to smoking was reduced by 90%.

Results

Beginning in July 2007, a VAT of 22% was imposed on cigarettes, on top of the IMESI excise tax. In subsequent years, the base price for taxing cigarettes and other tobacco products was increased.

As shown in Figure 10.14, the tax policy measures adopted over the 2007-2016 period have led to significant tax revenue collected from excise taxes + VAT in real terms.

Figure 10.14   Impact on the Tax Revenue Collected (IMESI Excise Tax and VAT) (Sales and Tax Revenue Collected, by Year, Base Year December 1999 = 100)

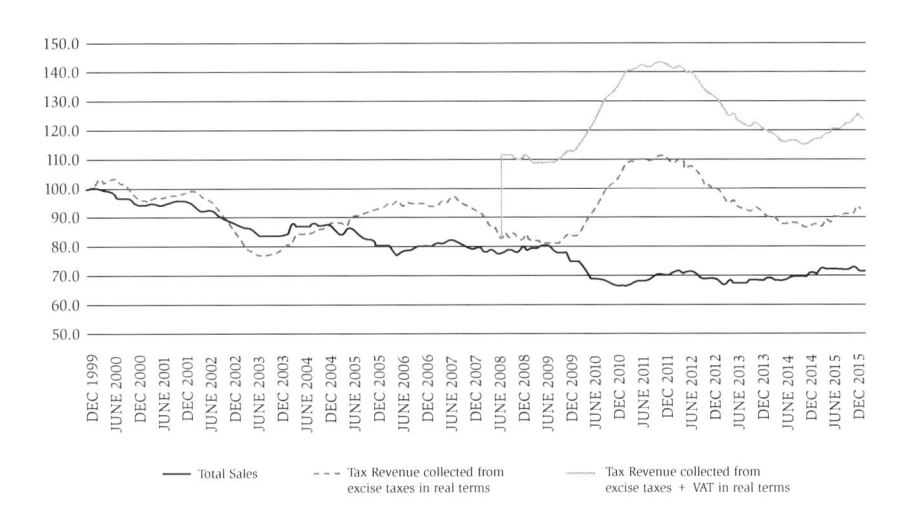

Litigation Experience with the Tobacco Industry

Uruguay, a small country in South America, offers a good example of how a government that is committed to protecting the health and well-being of its people was able to withstand, for more than six years, the pressure of litigation from a giant multinational tobacco company, whose annual revenues of more than USD 80 billion exceed the country's gross domestic product of close to USD 50 billion. As discussed in detail below, Philip Morris started legal proceedings against the Government of Uruguay in February 2010, claiming that the comprehensive tobacco control measures adopted by the Government since 2003 violated obligations under international trade and investment arrangements.

At its core, the lawsuit opposed provisions in two tobacco control measures adopted by the Government of Uruguay for protecting public health from the adverse effects of tobacco promotion. Specifically, these measures: (a) targeted "false" marketing claims that certain brand variants are safer than others, even after misleading descriptors such as "light," "mild," "ultra-light" were banned, and (b) sought to increase consumer awareness of the health risks of tobacco consumption and encourage people, particularly youth, to quit or not to take up smoking.

Ordinance 514, issued by Uruguay's Ministry of Public Health in 2008, requires each cigarette brand to have a "single presentation" and prohibits different packaging or "variants" for cigarettes sold under a given brand. Presidential Decree 287 of 2009 mandates an increase in the size of prescribed health warnings on the surface of the front and back of cigarette packages, increasing the surface area of these warnings from 50% to 80%, leaving only 20% of the cigarette pack for trademarks, logos, and other information. The application of these provisions forced Philip Morris to withdraw most of its brands (such as Marlboro Red, Marlboro Gold, or Marlboro Green) from retail stores in Uruguay.

On July 8, 2016, the International Center of Settlement of Investment Disputes (ICSID), an independent arm of the World Bank Group, dismissed the Philip Morris lawsuit in its entirety and ruled that Uruguay should be awarded compensation for all the expenses and costs associated with defending against the tobacco company's claims. In essence, the ruling accepted the claim made by the Government of Uruguay that its anti-tobacco measures were "about protection of public health, not interference with foreign investment."

As Uruguay's President, Dr. Tabaré Vázquez, an oncologist, stated in a televised address to the country after the ruling, the ICSID award reinforces the principle that: "It is not acceptable to prioritize commercial considerations over the fundamental right to health and life." Indeed, as observed by former New York City Mayor Michael Bloomberg, an international public-health champion, who provided financial support to help Uruguay deal with the litigation: "No country should ever be intimidated by the threat of a tobacco company lawsuit, and this case will help embolden more nations to take actions that will save lives." Now, countries across the world have an important legal precedent to follow in adopting tobacco control policies for the benefit of their populations.

§10.04 CONCLUSIONS

If development is lifting up lives, and new and innovative approaches for funding development are seen as "game changers," then it could be argued that the development community needs to redouble its commitment to advocate with national governments and society at large for raising taxes on tobacco products. As shown by the different country experiences presented here, taxing tobacco is one of the most cost-effective measures to reduce consumption of products that kill prematurely, make people ill with numerous tobacco-related diseases (e.g., cancer, heart disease, respiratory illnesses), and cost health systems enormous amounts of money for treating often preventable diseases.

In addition, hiking tobacco taxes can help expand a country's tax base to fund vital investments and essential public services. Such investments can benefit the entire population and help build countries' human capital base. For example, funds derived from tobacco taxation can be used to finance the progressive realization of universal health coverage, including scale-up of mental health services, as well as education for all and early childhood development initiatives.

The experiences of the U.S., China, Philippines, and Uruguay offer lessons that are applicable to a broad range of countries in both the developed and developing world. Indeed, for a number of years now, the World Bank, WHO, and others have promoted the use of tobacco taxes as the most effective means of reducing smoking prevalence on the global level. If anything, taxation as a tool to cut the prevalence of smoking may be even more effective in developing countries going forward.

While estimates of price elasticities of demand for cigarettes across countries vary from study to study, research in low- and middle-income countries has generally (though not always) found that demand for tobacco is even more price-responsive in these settings than in high-income countries (Chaloupka et al. 2000; WHO 2010). A broad range of studies of population subgroups within low- and middle-income countries (e.g., Sayginsoy, Yurelki, and de Beyer 2002; van Walbeek 2002) have also found that price-responsiveness is negatively correlated with income, as in developed countries.

And, just as in the U.S., non-harmonization of taxes across different tobacco products has been shown to lead to substitution of less-taxed products for highly taxed products in developing countries (*see*, e.g., Laxminarayan and Deolalikar 2004 for evidence from Vietnam), blunting the effectiveness of taxation as a means to reduce the overall prevalence of tobacco use.

In advancing the tobacco taxation agenda, countries need to be vigilant. The tobacco industry strongly opposes tobacco control and devotes substantial resources and effort to resisting control policies, as Uruguay's protracted legal struggles show. The industry systematically employs a wide range of tactics to interfere with the implementation of the FCTC by States Parties, and to undermine any significant tobacco control measure that may be taken by non-Parties (WHO 2015). Thus, countries setting out to reinforce their tobacco taxes must be prepared for a fight. But the fight can lead to a decisive victory for countries, as the Uruguayan experience also confirms.

To sum up, in many countries, raising tobacco taxes can offer a "win-win": higher revenue and better health outcomes. A recent (2016) IMF report argues: "Countries' circumstances and governments' weighting of revenue, health, and other objectives vary, and hence so too will the desirable level of tobacco tax rates. In many cases, however, current tax rates are evidently far below what is feasible in terms of revenue potential. Thus, tax increases could serve revenue purposes as well as health and other objectives. Of course, countries putting more weight on health objectives could raise taxes even further than the revenue-maximizing point, in which case lower tax revenue would be an implicit and accepted consequence of a higher tax level."

Developing countries may face unique challenges in governance and the efficacy of taxation. This may complicate the use of tobacco taxes as a public-health measure in some settings. But, to the extent that research findings hold true broadly, lessons from the U.S., China, Philippines, and Uruguay remind us why it is so important to overcome these challenges rather than use them as an excuse for inaction. Tobacco taxation can contribute to the achievement of WHO's goal to reduce tobacco consumption globally by 25% by 2025, as well as to the Sustainable Development Goal target to reduce premature deaths from noncommunicable diseases by a third by 2030 (Lancet 2017). This provides additional arguments for priority deployment of robust tobacco taxes in countries at all income levels.

REFERENCES

Akerlof, G.A. 2016. "Phishing for Phools: The Economics of Manipulation and Deception, Taxing to Promote Public Goods, and Tobacco Taxes." Presentation at World Bank Conference: "Winning the Tax Wars: Global Solutions for Developing Countries," May 24, 2016. http://www.worldbank.org/en/topic/ health/brief/tobacco.

Akerlof, G.A., and R.J. Shiller. 2015. Phishing for Phools: The Economics of Manipulation and Deception. New Jersey: Princeton University Press.

Brumby, J. 2014. "The Seven Salvos of Sin (Taxes)". The World Bank Blogs, March 25, 2014. Available at: http://blogs. worldbank.org/health/seven-salvos-sin-taxes.

Carpenter, C., and P.J. Cook. 2008. "Cigarette Taxes and Youth Smoking: New Evidence from National, State, and Local Youth Risk Behavior Surveys." Journal of Health Economics 27 (2): 287-299.

Centers for Disease Control and Prevention (CDC). 2016. "Table 17. Age-Adjusted Death Rates for Selected Causes of Death, by Sex, Race, and Hispanic Origin: United States, Selected Years 1950-2014." National Center for Health Statistics.

Chaloupka, F.J., T-w Hu, K.E Warner, R. Jacobs, and A. Yurekli. 2000. "The Taxation of Tobacco Products." In Jha, Prabhat and Frank J. Chaloupa, eds. Tobacco Control in Developing Countries.

Chaloupka, F.J., and K.E. Warner. 2000. "The Economics of Smoking." Handbook of Health Economics 1B: 1539-1627.

Chetty, R., M. Stepner, S. Abraham, S. Lin, B. Scuderi, N. Turner, A. Bergeron, and D. Cutler. 2016. "The Association Between Income and Life Expectancy in the United States, 2001-2014." Journal of the American Medical Association 315 (16): 1750-1766.

Christiansen, V., and S. Smith. 2012. "Externality-Correcting Taxes and Regulation." Scandinavian Journal of Economics 114(2): 358-383.

Conference of the Parties to the WHO Framework Convention on Tobacco Control (FCTC). 2016. "Delhi Declaration." Seventh session Delhi, India, 7 12 November 2016. http://www.who.int/ fctc/cop/cop7/FCTC_COP7_29_EN.pdf?ua=1.

Chapter 10: Expanding the Global Tax Base

Congressional Budget Office (CBO). 2012. "Raising the Excise Tax on Cigarettes: Effects on Health and the Federal Budget." Report.

Cook., P.J. 2011. Paying the Tab: The Costs and Benefits of Alcohol Control. Princeton, New Jersey, USA: Princeton University Press.

Cook, P. 2016. "Paying the Tab: The Costs and Benefits of Tobacco and Alcohol Control." Presentation at World Bank Conference: "Winning the Tax Wars: Global Solutions for Developing Countries," May 24, 2016. http://www.worldbank.org/en/topic/health/brief/tobacco.

Council of Economic Advisers (CEA). 2016. "Inequality in Early Childhood and Effective Public Policy Interventions." 2016 Economic Report of the President.

Currie, J., and H. Schwandt. 2016. "Mortality Inequality: The Good News from a County-Level Approach." Journal of Economic Perspectives 30 (2): 29-52.

Department of Health and Human Services (HHS). 2015. "Valuing Utility Offsets to Regulations Affecting Addictive or Habitual Goods." Report.

Fuchs, A., and F. Meneses. 2017. "Are tobacco taxes really regressive?: Evidence from Chile." World Bank Report Number 112072. Washington, DC: World Bank Group. http://documents.worldbank.org/curated/en/389891484567069411/Are-tobacco-taxes-really-regressive-evidence-from-Chile.

Furman, J. 2016. "Policy, Politics, and the Tripling of Federal Tobacco Taxes in the United States to Deter People from Smoking, Save Lives, and Mobilize Revenue over the last 30 years. Six Lessons from the U.S. Experience with Tobacco Taxes." Presentation at World Bank Conference: "Winning the Tax Wars: Global Solutions for Developing Countries," May 24, 2016. http://www.worldbank.org/en/topic/health/brief/ tobacco.

Gallet, C., and J.A. List. 2003. "Cigarette Demand: A Meta-Analysis of Elasticities." Health Economics 12 (10): 821-835.

Government Accountability Office (GAO). 2012. "Tobacco Taxes: Large Disparities in Rates for Smoking Products Trigger Significant Market Shifts to Avoid Higher Taxes." Report No. GAO-12-475.

Gruber, J. 2008. "A Modern Economic View of Tobacco Taxation". Paris: International Union Against Tuberculosis and Lung Disease.

Gruber, J., and B. Koszegi. 2001. "Is Addiction Rational? Theory and Evidence." Quarterly Journal of Economics 116(4): 1261-1303.

Hu, T-W. (editor). 2016. Economics of Tobacco Control in China: From Policy Research to Practice. Hackensack, NJ: World Scientific Publishing.

Huang, J., and F.J. Chaloupka. 2012. "The Impact of the 2009 Federal Tobacco Excise Tax Increase on Youth Tobacco Use." NBER Working Paper No. 18026.

International Agency for Research on Cancer (IARC). 2011. "Effectiveness of Tax and Price Policies for Tobacco Control." IARC Handbooks of Cancer Prevention: Tobacco Control, Vol. 14.

International Centre for Settlement of Investment Disputes (ICSID). 2016. "ICSID's Award of the Tribunal (July 8, 2016). Philip Morris Brand Sàrl (Switzerland), Philip Morris Products S.A. (Switzerland) and Abal Hermanos S.A. (Uruguay) v. Oriental Republic of Uruguay (ICSID Case No. ARB/10/7)." English (Original);

Spanish (Original). Available at: https://icsid.worldbank.org/apps/ICSIDWEB/cases/Pages/casedetail.aspx?CaseNo = ARB/10/7&tab = DOC.

Jha, P., and F.J. Chaloupka. 1999. Curbing the Epidemic: Governments and the Economics of Tobacco Control. Washington, DC: World Bank.

Jha, P., and R. Peto. 2014. "Global Effects of Smoking, of Quitting, and of Taxing Tobacco." N Engl J Med 370: 60-68. Available at: http://www.nejm.org/doi/full/10.1056/ NEJMra1308383#t = article.

Jha, P., P.V. Marquez, and S. Dutta. 2017. "Tripling Tobacco Taxes: Key for Achieving the UN Sustainable Development Goals by 2030." The World Bank Blogs, January 24, 2017. Available at: http://blogs.worldbank.org/health/role-excise-tax-meeting-sdg.

Kaiser, K., C. Bredenkamp, and R. Iglesias. 2016. "Sin Tax Reform in the Philippines: Transforming Public Finance, Health, and Governance for More Inclusive Development. Directions in Development – Countries and Regions." Washington, DC: World Bank. Available at: https://openknowledge.worldbank.org/handle/10986/24617.

Khokhar, T. 2016. "The global state of smoking in 5 charts." The World Bank Blogs, May 31, 2016. Available at: http://blogs.worldbank.org/opendata/global-state-smoking-5-charts.

Kremer, A. 2016. "Do the Right Thing: Tax Tobacco!" The World Bank Blogs, December 13, 2016. Available at: http://blogs. worldbank.org/europeandcentralasia/do-right-thing-tax- tobacco.

Lancet. 2017. "Tobacco Elimination; Economic and Public Health Imperative." Editorial. The Lancet 389: 225. January 21, 2017.

Laxminarayan, R., and A. Deolalikar. 2004. "Tobacco Initiation, Cessation, and Change: Evidence from Vietnam." Health Economics 13 (12): 1191-1201.

Marquez, P. V. 2012. "Tobacco Kills: So What to Do in Africa?" The World Bank Blogs, May 15, 2012. Available at: http://blogs. worldbank.org/nasikiliza/tobacco-kills-so-what-to-do-in-africa.

Marquez, P.V. 2013. "Back from the Cold: Russia Confronts Tobacco." The World Bank Blogs, April 5, 2013. Available at: http://blogs.worldbank.org/health/back-from-the-cold-russia- confronts-tobacco.

Marquez, P. V. 2014. "The Tobacco Dilemma: Corporate Profits or Customers' Health?" The World Bank Blogs, March 26, 2014. Available at: http://blogs.worldbank.org/health/tobacco-dilemma-corporate-profits-or-customers-health.

Marquez, P.V. 2015. "Good News from the Global War on Tobacco Use." The World Bank Blogs, March 26, 2015. Available at: http://blogs.worldbank.org/health/good-news-global-war- tobacco-use.

Marquez, P.V. 2015. "Making the Public Health Case for Tobacco Taxation." The World Bank Blogs, July 7, 2015. Available at: http://blogs.worldbank.org/health/making-public-health-case-tobacco-taxation.

Marquez, P.V. 2015. "Running Away from 'Tobacco Road'. The World Bank Blogs, December 15, 2015. Available at: http:// blogs.worldbank.org/health/running-away-tobacco-road.

Marquez, P.V. 2015. "World No Tobacco Day 2015: On Illicit Trade and Taxes." The World Bank Blogs, May 29, 2015. Available at: http://blogs.worldbank.org/health/world-no-tobacco-day- 2015-illicit-trade-and-taxes.

Marquez, P.V. 2016. "Economic Slowdown and Financial Shocks: Can Tobacco Tax Increases Help?" The World Bank Blogs, Feb 8, 2016. Available at: http://blogs.worldbank.org/voices/economic-slowdown-and-financial-shocks-can-tobacco-tax increases-help.

Marquez, P.V. 2016. "Overview of Session." Presentation at World Bank Conference: "Winning the Tax Wars: Global Solutions for Developing Countries," May 24, 2016. http://www.worldbank. org/en/topic/health/brief/tobacco.

Marquez, P.V. 2016. "Plain Packaging & Tobacco Taxes: An Antidote for Manipulation and Deception." The World Bank Blogs, May 31, 2016. Available at: https://blogs.worldbank.org/health/plain-packaging-tobacco-taxes-antidote-manipulation-and-deception.

Marquez, P.V. 2016. "Taxing Tobacco and the New Vision for Financing Development." The World Bank Blogs, April 18, 2016. Available at: http://blogs.worldbank.org/voices/taxing-tobacco-and-new-vision-financing-development.

Marquez, P.V. 2016. "Time to Put 'Health' into Universal Health Coverage." The World Bank Blogs, January 14, 2016. Available at: http://blogs.worldbank.org/health/time-put-health- universal-health-coverage.

Marquez, P.V. and Moreno-Dodson, B. 2016. "Economic Slowdown and Financial Shocks: Can Tobacco Tax Increases Help?" The World Bank Blogs, February 8, 2016. Available at: http://blogs.worldbank.org/voices/economic-slowdown-and-financial-shocks-can-tobacco-tax-increases-help.

Marquez, P.V., and M. Walker. 2016. "Uruguay: A Giant Leap to Prevent Tobacco-Assisted Suicide." The World Bank Blogs, October 10, 2016. Available at: http://blogs.worldbank.org/health/uruguay-giant-leap-prevent-tobacco-assisted-suicide.

Marquez, P.V., and R. Zheng. 2016. "China's 2015 Tobacco Tax Adjustment: A Step in the Right Direction." The World Bank Blogs, November 9, 2016. Available at: https://blogs.worldbank.org/health/china-s-2015-tobacco-tax-adjustment-step-right-direction.

Marquez, P.V., and M. Walker. 2017. "Healthy Women Are the Cornerstone of Healthy Societies." The World Bank Blogs, January 12, 2017. Available at: http://blogs.worldbank.org/ health/healthy-women-are-cornerstone-healthy-societies.

Marquez, P.V., B. Moreno-Dodson, and S. Dutta. 2017. "Recent Gains on Global Tobacco Taxation." The World Bank Blogs, March 20, 2017. Available at: http://blogs.worldbank.org/health/recent-gains-global-tobacco-taxation.

National Academies of Sciences, Engineering, and Medicine. 2015. The Growing Gap in Life Expectancy by Income: Implications for Federal Programs and Policy Responses. Washington: National Academies Press.

National Cancer Institute (NCI), in collaboration with World Health Organization (WHO). 2016. "Monograph 21: The Economics of Tobacco and Tobacco Control." Bethesda, Md.: U.S. Department of Health and Human Services, National Institutes of Health. Available at: https://cancercontrol.cancer.gov/brp/tcrb/monographs/21/docs/m21_exec_sum.pdf.

Orzechowski and Walker. 2015. The Tax Burden on Tobacco: Historical Compilation, Volume 49, 2014. Arlington, VA.

Paul, J. 2016. "The Impact of the 2013 Sin Tax Reform in the Philippines." Presentation at World Bank Conference: "Winning the Tax Wars: Global Solutions for Developing Countries," May 24, 2016. http://www.worldbank.org/en/topic/health/brief/tobacco.

Petit, P., and J. Nagy. 2016. "How to Design and Enforce Tobacco Excises?" How-to notes. Fiscal Affairs Department, International Monetary Fund, October 2016.

Philip Morris Brand Sàrl (Switzerland), Philip Morris Products S.A. (Switzerland) and Abal Hermanos S.A. (Uruguay) v. Oriental Republic of Uruguay (ICSID Case No. ARB/10/7).

Rosenberg, J. 2015. "The Distributional Burden of Federal Excise Taxes." Tax Policy Center Report.

Savedoff, W. and A. Alwang. 2015. "The Single Best Health Policy in the World: Tobacco Taxes." CGD Policy Paper 062. Washington DC: Center for Global Development. http://www.cgdev.org/publication/single-best-health-policy-world-tobacco-taxes.

Sayginsoy, O., A.A. Yurekli, and J. de Beyer. 2002. "Cigarette Demand, Taxation, and the Poor: A Case Study of Bulgaria." Health, Nutrition, and Population Discussion Paper, Economics of Tobacco Control Paper No. 4.

Schelling, T.C. 1986. "Economics and Cigarettes." Preventive Medicine 15:549-560.

Schelling, T.C. 1992. "Addictive Drugs: The Cigarette Experience." Science: 255:5043: 430+. Science in Context, link.galegroup.com/apps/doc/A11922197/SCIC?u=duke_perkins&xid=c8222b07. Accessed 18 Dec. 2016.

Serra, F. 2016. "Tobacco Taxation and International Litigation: Uruguay's Experience." Presentation at World Bank Conference: "Winning the Tax Wars: Global Solutions for Developing Countries," May 24, 2016. http://www.worldbank.org/en/topic/health/brief/tobacco.

Sunley, E. 2009. "Taxation of Cigarettes in the Bloomberg Initiative Countries: Overview of Policy Issues and Proposals for Reform." http://www.tobaccofreeunion.org/assets/Technical%20Resources/Economic%20Reports/Sunley%20White%20paper%2012%2009%2009.pdf.

U.S. Department of Health and Human Services. 1964. "Preventing Tobacco Use Among Young People: A Report of the Surgeon General." Atlanta (GA): U.S. Department of Health and Human Services, Public Health Service, Centers for Disease Control and Prevention, National Center for Chronic Disease Prevention and Health Promotion, Office on Smoking and Health, 1994. Available at: https://profiles.nlm.nih.gov/NN/B/C/F/T/_/nnbcft.pdf.

U.S. Department of Health and Human Services. 2014. "The Health Consequences of Smoking: 50 Years of Progress. A Report of the Surgeon General." Atlanta, GA: U.S. Department of Health and Human Services, Centers for Disease Control and Prevention, National Center for Chronic Disease Prevention and Health Promotion, Office on Smoking and Health, 2014. Printed with corrections, January 2014. Available at: https://www.surgeongeneral.gov/library/reports/50-years-of-progress/full-report.pdf.

U.S. National Cancer Institute and World Health Organization. 2016. "The Economics of Tobacco and Tobacco Control." National Cancer Institute Tobacco Control Monograph 21. NIH Publication No. 16-CA-8029A. Bethesda, MD: U.S. Department of Health and Human Services, National Institutes of Health, National Cancer Institute; and Geneva: World Health Organization; 2016. Available at: http://cancercontrol.cancer.gov/brp/tcrb/monographs/21/index.html.

van Hasselt, et al. 2015. "The Relation Between Tobacco Taxes and Youth and Young Adult Smoking: What Happened Following the 2009 U.S. Federal Tax Increase on Cigarettes?" Addictive Behaviors 45: 104-109.

van Walbeek, C.P. 2002. "The Distributional Impact of Tobacco Excise Increases." South African Journal of Economics 70 (3): 258-267.

Wang, S., P.V. Marquez, and J. Langenbrunner. 2011. "Toward a Healthy and Harmonious Life in China: Stemming the Rising Tide of Non-Communicable Diseases." World Bank Report Number 62318-CN. Washington, D.C.: World Bank Group.

WHO (World Health Organization). 2003. "WHO Framework Convention on Tobacco Control." http://www.who.int/fctc/en/.

WHO (World Health Organization). 2010. "WHO Technical Manual on Tobacco Tax Administration."

WHO (World Health Organization). 2015. "WHO Report on the Global Tobacco Epidemic, 2015: Raising Taxes on Tobacco." Report.

World Bank Group. Global Tobacco Control Progam website: http://www.worldbank.org/en/topic/health/brief/tobacco.

Yach, D., and H. Wipfli. 2006. "A Century of Smoke." Annals of Tropical Medicine and Parasitology 100(5-6): 465-479.

Zheng, R. 2016. "2015 Tobacco Taxation Reform in China: Results and Challenges." Presentation at World Bank Conference: "Winning the Tax Wars: Global Solutions for Developing Countries," May 24, 2016. http://www.worldbank.org/en/topic/health/brief/tobacco.

SERIES ON INTERNATIONAL TAXATION

1. Alberto Xavier, *The Taxation of Foreign Investment in Brazil*, 1980 (ISBN 90-200-0582-0).
2. Hugh J. Ault & Albert J. Rädler, *The German Corporation Tax Law with 1980 Amendments*, 1981 (ISBN 90-200-0642-8).
3. Paul R. McDaniel & Hugh J. Ault, *Introduction to United States International Taxation*, 1981 (ISBN 90-6544-004-6).
4. Albert J. Rädler, *German Transfer Pricing/Prix de Transfer en Allemagne*, 1984 (ISBN 90-6544-143-3).
5. Paul R. McDaniel & Stanley S. Surrey, *International Aspects of Tax Expenditures: A Comparative Study*, 1985 (ISBN 90-654-4163-8).
6. Kees van Raad, *Nondiscrimination in International Tax Law*, 1986 (ISBN 90-6544-266-9).
7. Sijbren Cnossen (ed.), *Tax Coordination in the European Community*, 1987 (ISBN 90-6544-272-3).
8. Ben Terra, *Sales Taxation. The Case of Value Added Tax in the European Community*, 1989 (ISBN 90-6544-381-9).
9. Rutsel S.J. Martha, *The Jurisdiction to Tax in International Law: Theory and Practice of Legislative Fiscal Jurisdiction*, 1989 (ISBN 90-654-4416-5).
10. Paul R. McDaniel & Hugh J. Ault, *Introduction to United States International Taxation* (3rd revised edition), 1989 (ISBN 90-6544-423-8).
11. Manuel Pires, *International Juridicial Double Taxation of Income*, 1989 (ISBN 90-6544-426-2).
12. A.H.M. Daniels, *Issues in International Partnership Taxation*, 1991 (ISBN 90-654-4577-3).
13. Arvid A. Skaar, *Permanent Establishment: Erosion of a Tax Treaty Principle*, 1992 (ISBN 90-6544-594-3).
14. Cyrille David & Geerten M.M. Michielse (eds), *Tax Treatment of Financial Instruments*, 1996 (ISBN 90-654-4666-4).
15. Herbert H. Alpert & Kees van Raad (eds), *Essays on International Taxation*, 1993 (ISBN 90-654-4781-4).
16. Wolfgang Gassner, Michael Lang & Eduard Lechner (eds), *Tax Treaties and EC Law*, 1997 (ISBN 90-411-0680-4).
17. Glória Teixeira, *Taxing Corporate Profits in the EU*, 1997 (ISBN 90-411-0703-7).
18. Michael Lang et al. (eds), *Multilateral Tax Treaties*, 1998 (ISBN 90-411-0704-5).
19. Stef van Weeghel, *The Improper Use of Tax Treaties*, 1998 (ISBN 90-411-0737-1).
20. Klaus Vogel (ed.), *Interpretation of Tax Law and Treaties and Transfer Pricing in Japan and Germany*, 1998 (ISBN 90-411-9655-2).
21. Bertil Wiman (ed.), *International Studies in Taxation: Law and Economics; Liber Amicorum Leif Mutén*, 1999 (ISBN 90-411-9692-7).
22. Alfonso J. Martín Jiménez, *Towards Corporate Tax Harmonization in the European Community*, 1999 (ISBN 90-411-9690-0).

23. Ramon J. Jeffery, *The Impact of State Sovereignty on Global Trade and International Taxation,* 1999 (ISBN 90-411-9703-6).
24. A.J. Easson, *Taxation of Foreign Direct Investment,* 1999 (ISBN 90-411-9741-9).
25. Marjaana Helminen, *The Dividend Concept in International Tax Law: Dividend Payments Between Corporate Entities,* 1999 (ISBN 90-411-9765-6).
26. Paul Kirchhof, Moris Lehner, Kees van Raad, Arndt Raupach & Michael-Rodi (eds), *International and Comparative Taxation: Essays in Honour of Klaus Vogel,* 2002 (ISBN 90-411-9841-5).
27. Krister Andersson, Peter Melz & Christer Silfverberg (eds), *Liber Amicorum Sven-Olof Lodin,* 2001 (ISBN 90-411-9850-4).
28. Juan Martín Jovanovich, *Customs Valuation and Transfer Pricing: Is It Possible to Harmonize Customs and Tax Rules?,* Second Edition, 2018 (ISBN 978-90-411-6134-5).
29. Stefano Simontacchi, *Taxation of Capital Gains under the OECD Model Convention: With Special Regard to Immovable Property,* 2007 (ISBN 978-90-411-2549-1).
30. Michael Lang, Josef Schuch, & Claus Staringer (eds), *Tax Treaty Law and EC Law,* 2007 (ISBN 978-90-411-2629-0).
31. Duncan Bentley, *Taxpayers' Rights: Theory Origin and Implementation,* 2007 (ISBN 978-90-411-2650-4).
32. Sergio André Rocha, *Interpretation of Double Taxation Conventions: General Theory and Brazilian Perspective,* 2008 (ISBN 978-90-411-2822-5).
33. Robert F. van Brederode, *Systems of General Sales Taxation: Theory, Policy and Practice,* 2009 (ISBN 978-90-411-2832-4).
34. John G. Head & Richard Krever (eds), *Tax Reform in the 21st Century: A Volume in Memory of Richard Musgrave,* 2009 (ISBN 978-90-411-2829-4).
35. Jens Wittendorff, *Transfer Pricing and the Arm's Length Principle in International Tax Law,* 2010 (ISBN 978-90-411-3270-3).
36. Marjaana Helminen, *The International Tax Law Concept of Dividend,* Second Edition, 2017 (ISBN 978-90-411-8394-1).
37. Robert F. van Brederode (ed.), *Immovable Property under VAT: A Comparative Global Analysis,* 2011 (ISBN 978-90-411-3126-3).
38. Dennis Weber & Stef van Weeghel, *The 2010 OECD Updates: Model Tax Convention & Transfer Pricing Guidelines - A Critical Review,* 2011 (ISBN 978-90-411-3812-5).
39. Yariv Brauner & Martin James McMahon, Jr. (eds), *The Proper Tax Base: Structural Fairness from an International and Comparative Perspective— Essays in Honour of Paul McDaniel,* 2012 (ISBN 978-90-411-3286-4).
40. Robert F. van Brederode (ed.), *Science, Technology and Taxation,* 2012 (ISBN 978-90-411-3125-6).
41. Oskar Henkow, *The VAT/GST Treatment of Public Bodies,* 2013 (ISBN 978-90-411-4663-2).
42. Jean Schaffner, *How Fixed Is a Permanent Establishment?,* 2013 (ISBN 978-90-411-4662-5).

43. Miguel Correia, *Taxation of Corporate Groups*, 2013 (ISBN 978-90-411-4841-4).
44. Veronika Daurer, *Tax Treaties and Developing Countries*, 2014 (ISBN 978-90-411-4982-4).
45. Claire Micheau, *State Aid, Subsidy and Tax Incentives under EU and WTO Law*, 2014 (ISBN 978-90-411-4555-0).
46. Robert F. van Brederode & Richard Krever (eds), *Legal Interpretation of Tax Law*, 2014 (ISBN 978-90-411-4945-9).
47. Radhakishan Rawal, *Taxation of Cross-border Services*, 2014 (ISBN 978-90-411-4947-3).
48. João Dácio Rolim, *Proportionality and Fair Taxation*, 2014 (ISBN 978-90-411-5838-3).
49. Paulo Rosenblatt, *General Anti-avoidance Rules for Major Developing Countries*, 2015 (ISBN 978-90-411-5839-0).
50. Gaspar Lopes Dias V.S., *Tax Arbitrage through Cross-Border Financial Engineering*, 2015 (ISBN 978-90-411-5875-8).
51. Geerten M.M. Michielse & Victor Thuronyi (eds), *Tax Design Issues Worldwide*, 2015 (ISBN 978-90-411-5610-5).
52. Oktavia Weidmann, *Taxation of Derivatives*, 2015 (ISBN 978-90-411-5977-9).
53. Chris Evans, Richard Krever & Peter Mellor (eds), *Tax Simplification*, 2015 (ISBN 978-90-411-5976-2).
54. Reuven Avi-Yonah & Joel Slemrod (eds), *Taxation and Migration*, 2015 (ISBN 978-90-411-6136-9).
55. Alexander Bosman, *Other Income under Tax Treaties: An Analysis of Article 21 of the OECD Model Convention*, 2015 (ISBN 978-90-411-6610-4).
56. John Abrahamson, *International Taxation of Manufacturing and Distribution*, 2016 (ISBN 978-90-411-6664-7).
57. Frederik Boulogne, *Shortcomings in the EU Merger Directive*, 2016 (ISBN 978-90-411-6713-2).
58. Angelika Meindl-Ringler, *Beneficial Ownership in International Tax Law*, 2016 (ISBN 978-90-411-6833-7).
59. Andreas Waltrich, *Cross-Border Taxation of Permanent Establishments: An International Comparison*, 2016 (ISBN 978-90-411-6832-0).
60. Sergio André Rocha & Allison Christians (eds), *Tax Sovereignty in the BEPS Era*, 2017 (ISBN 978-90-411-6707-1).
61. Peter Antony Wilson, *BRICS and International Tax Law*, 2018 (ISBN 978-90-411-9435-0).
62. Brigitte Alepin, Blanca Moreno-Dodson & Louise Otis (eds), *Winning the Tax Wars: Tax Competition and Cooperation,* 2018 (ISBN 978-90-411-9460-2).